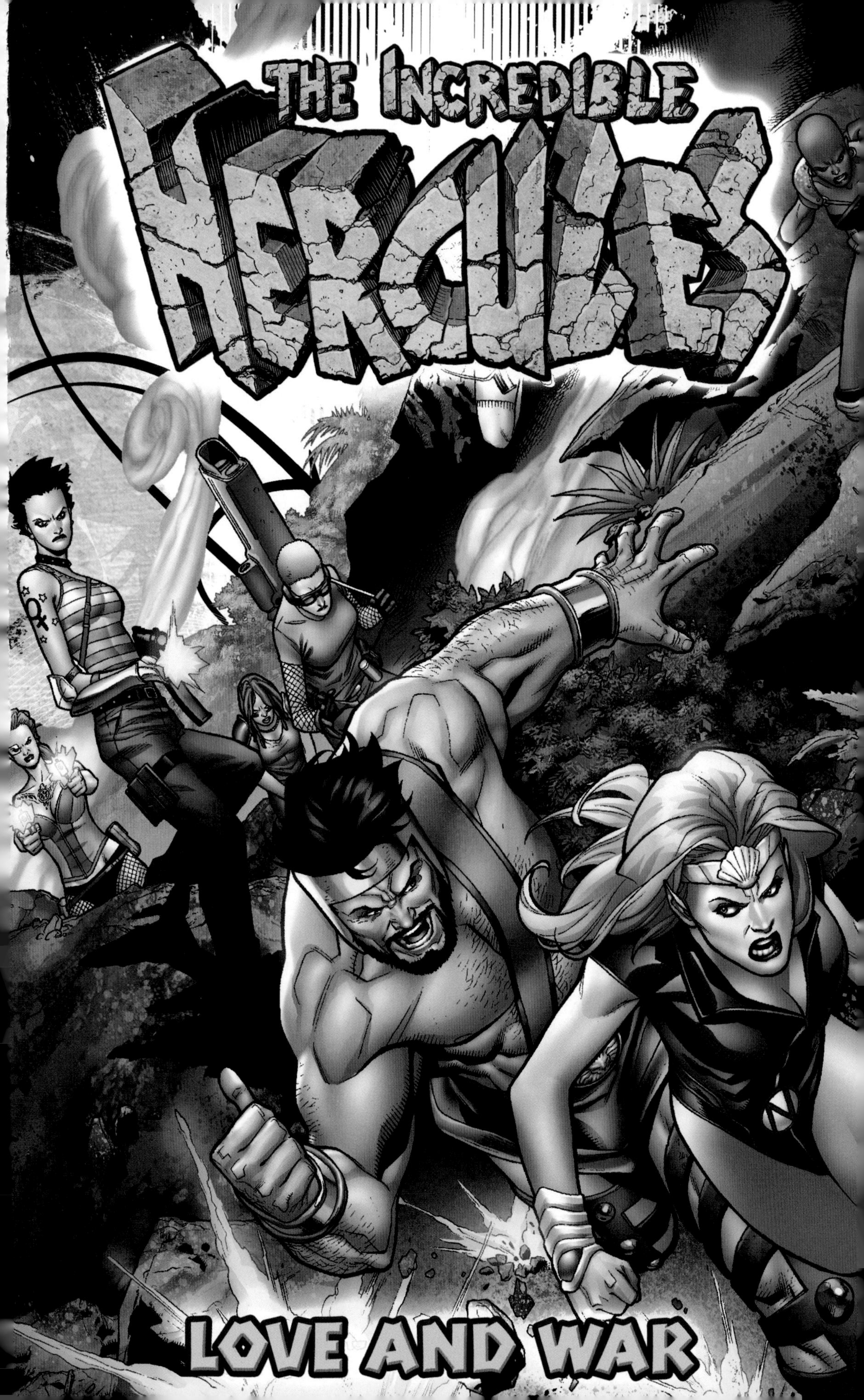
THE INCREDIBLE
HERCULES
LOVE AND WAR

THE INCREDIBLE HERCULES

Writers: **GREG PAK** & **FRED VAN LENTE**

Artists: **CLAYTON HENRY** & **SALVA ESPIN**

Colorists: **GURU EFX, RAÚL TREVIÑO** & **LEE LOUGHRIDGE**

Letterers: **VIRTUAL CALLIGRAPHY'S JOE CARAMAGNA** & **CHRIS ELIOPOULOS**

Cover Artists: **ARTHUR SUYDAM, CLAY HENRY** & **GURU EFX,**

BOB LAYTON & **GURU EFX AND ED MCGUINNESS** & **GURU EFX**

Assistant Editors: **NATHAN COSBY** & **JORDAN D. WHITE**

Editor: **MARK PANICCIA**

Collection Editor: **CORY LEVINE**

Editorial Assistant: **ALEX STARBUCK**

Assistant Editor: **JOHN DENNING**

Editors, Special Projects: **JENNIFER GRÜNWALD** & **MARK D. BEAZLEY**

Senior Editor, Special Projects: **JEFF YOUNGQUIST**

Senior Vice President of Sales: **DAVID GABRIEL**

Production: **CARRIE BEADLE**

Editor in Chief: **JOE QUESADA**

Publisher: **DAN BUCKLEY**

INCREDIBLE HERCULES: LOVE AND WAR. Contains material originally published in magazine form as INCREDIBLE HERCULES #121-125. First printing 2009. Hardcover ISBN# 978-0-7851-3334-6. Softcover ISBN# 978-0-7851-3246-2. Published by MARVEL PUBLISHING, INC., a subsidiary of MARVEL ENTERTAINMENT, INC. OFFICE OF PUBLICATION: 417 5th Avenue, New York, NY 10016. Copyright © 2008 and 2009 Marvel Characters, Inc. All rights reserved. Hardcover: $19.99 per copy in the U.S. (GST #R127032852). Softcover: $14.99 per copy in the U.S. (GST #R127032852). Canadian Agreement #40668537. All characters featured in this issue and the distinctive names and likenesses thereof, and all related indicia are trademarks of Marvel Characters, Inc. No similarity between any of the names, characters, persons, and/or institutions in this magazine with those of any living or dead person or institution is intended, and any such similarity which may exist is purely coincidental. **Printed in the U.S.A.** ALAN FINE, CEO Marvel Toys & Publishing Divisions and CMO Marvel Characters, Inc.; JIM SOKOLOWSKI, Chief Operating Officer; DAVID GABRIEL, SVP of Publishing Sales & Circulation; DAVID BOGART, SVP of Business Affairs & Talent Management; MICHAEL PASCIULLO, VP Merchandising & Communications; JIM O'KEEFE, VP of Operations & Logistics; DAN CARR, Executive Director of Publishing Technology; JUSTIN F. GABRIE, Director of Publishing & Editorial Operations; SUSAN CRESPI, Editorial Operations Manager; ALEX MORALES, Publishing Operations Manager; STAN LEE, Chairman Emeritus. For information regarding advertising in Marvel Comics or on Marvel.com, please contact Mitch Dane, Advertising Director, at mdane@marvel.com. For Marvel subscription inquiries, please call 800-217-9158.

10 9 8 7 6 5 4 3 2 1

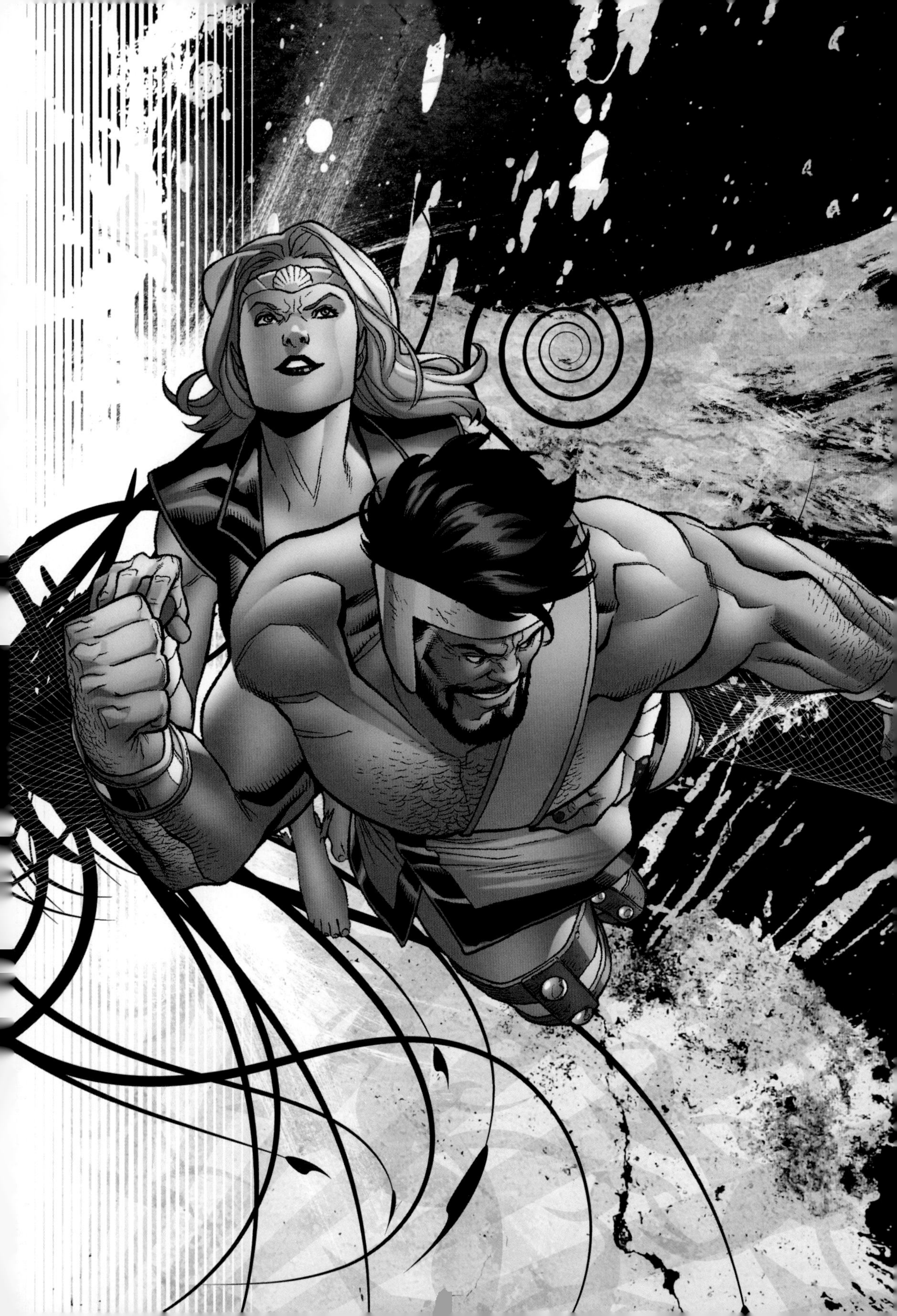

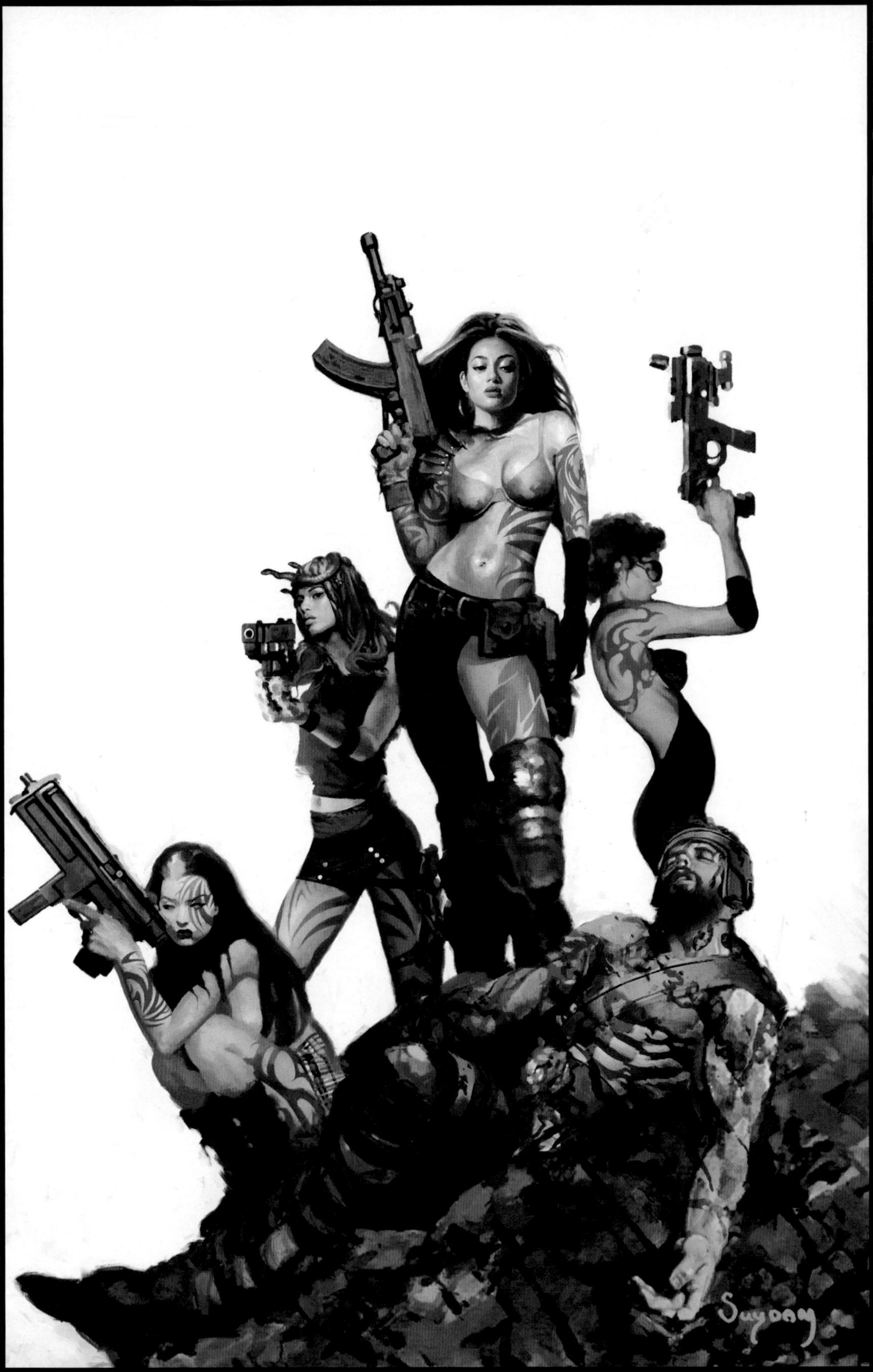
Suydam

INCREDIBLE HERCULES #121

FOREGONE IN INCREDIBLE HERCULES

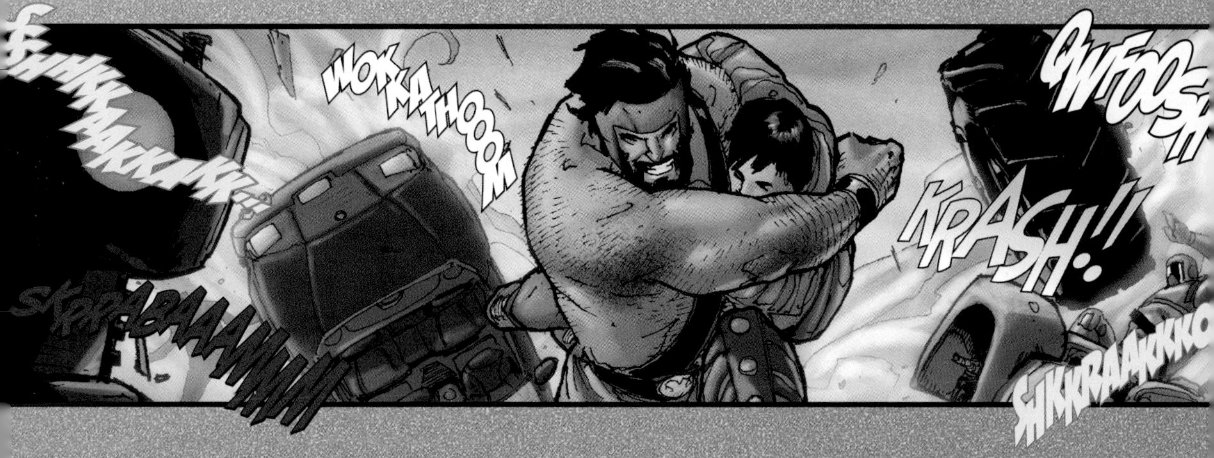
WOKKATHOOOM
KRASH!!
SKRRABAAAMMM
SHKKRAAKKKO

YON HERCULES AND CHO HAVE JOURNEYED FAR.

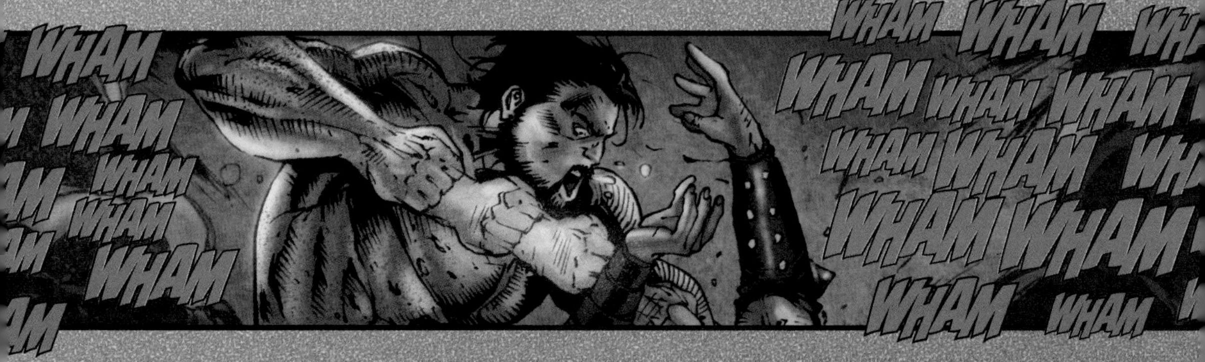
WHAM

THERE HAS BEEN MUCH BASHING THRASHING CRASHING LASHING MASHING GNASHING DASHING TRASHING GASHING AND CLASHING.

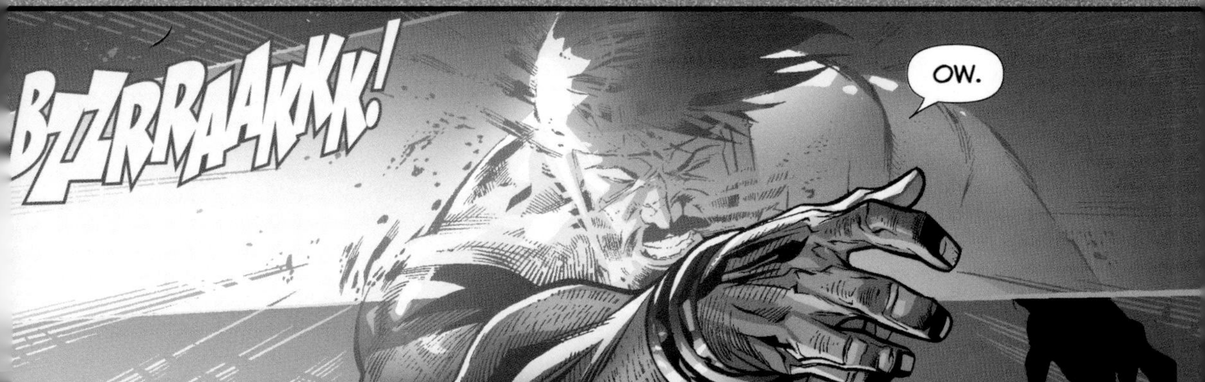
BZZRRAAKKK!
OW.

THE TIME IS RIPE FOR A CHILL-OUT, YO.
(E'EN GODS NEED A HOLIDAY)

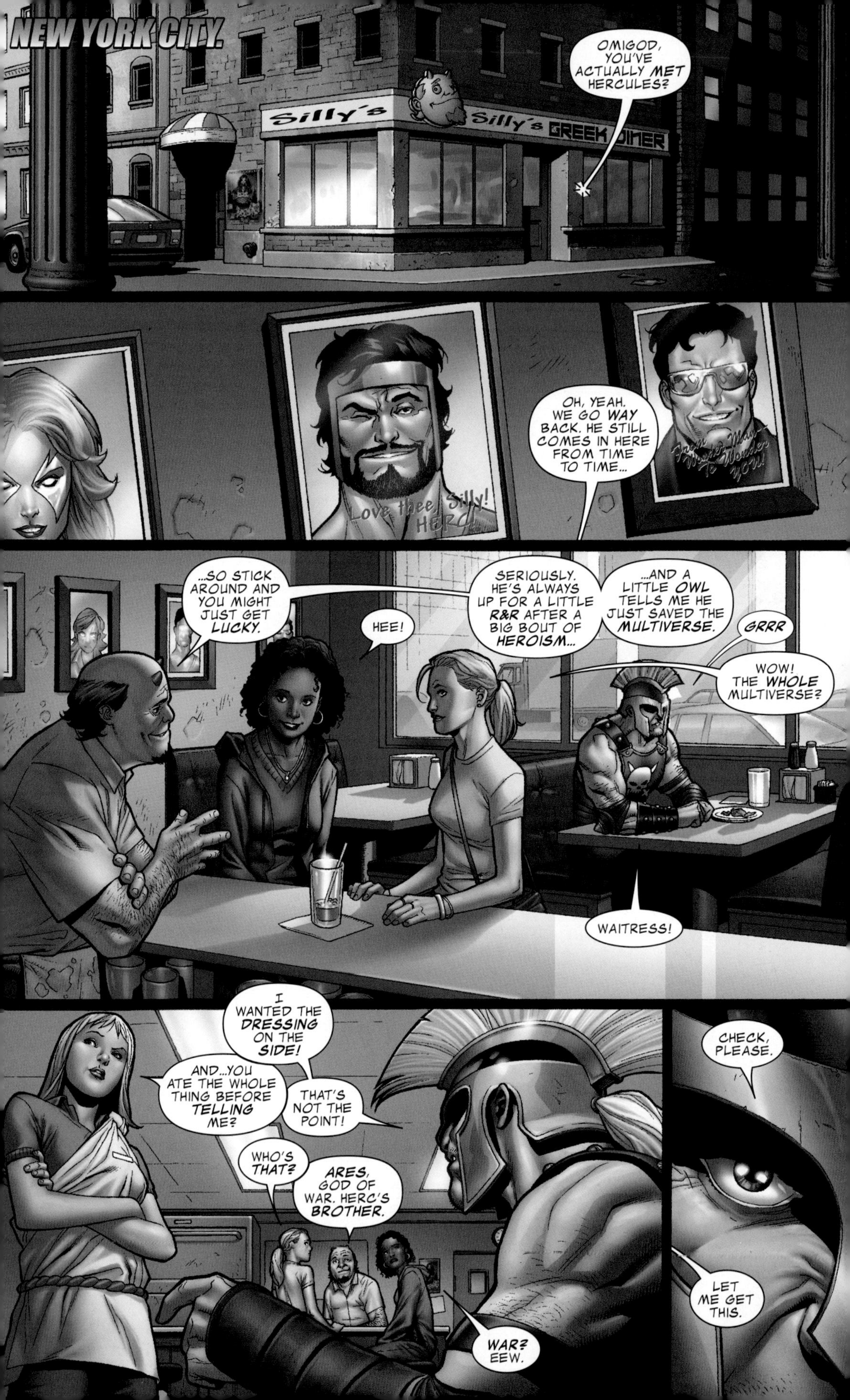
NEW YORK CITY.
Silly's
Silly's GREEK DINER
OMIGOD, YOU'VE ACTUALLY MET HERCULES?
OH, YEAH. WE GO WAY BACK. HE STILL COMES IN HERE FROM TIME TO TIME...
Love thee, Silly! HERC
From Wonder Man To Wonder YOU!
SERIOUSLY. HE'S ALWAYS UP FOR A LITTLE R&R AFTER A BIG BOUT OF HEROISM...
...SO STICK AROUND AND YOU MIGHT JUST GET LUCKY.
HEE!
...AND A LITTLE OWL TELLS ME HE JUST SAVED THE MULTIVERSE.
GRRR
WOW! THE WHOLE MULTIVERSE?
WAITRESS!
I WANTED THE DRESSING ON THE SIDE!
AND...YOU ATE THE WHOLE THING BEFORE TELLING ME?
THAT'S NOT THE POINT!
WHO'S THAT?
ARES, GOD OF WAR. HERC'S BROTHER.
WAR? EEW.
CHECK, PLEASE.
LET ME GET THIS.

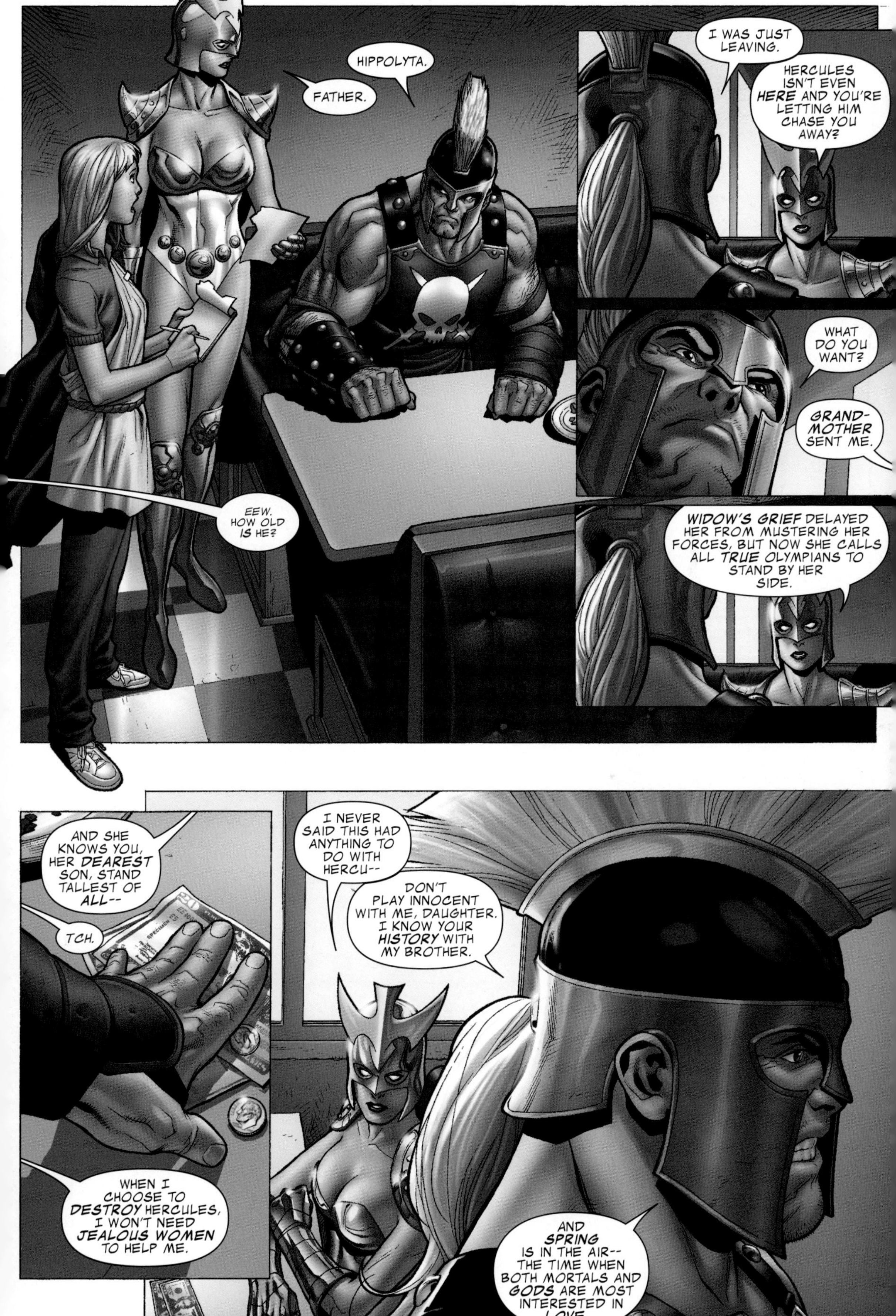

FATHER.
HIPPOLYTA.
EEW. HOW OLD IS HE?
I WAS JUST LEAVING.
HERCULES ISN'T EVEN HERE AND YOU'RE LETTING HIM CHASE YOU AWAY?
WHAT DO YOU WANT?
GRAND-MOTHER SENT ME.
WIDOW'S GRIEF DELAYED HER FROM MUSTERING HER FORCES, BUT NOW SHE CALLS ALL TRUE OLYMPIANS TO STAND BY HER SIDE.
AND SHE KNOWS YOU, HER DEAREST SON, STAND TALLEST OF ALL--
TCH.
WHEN I CHOOSE TO DESTROY HERCULES, I WON'T NEED JEALOUS WOMEN TO HELP ME.
I NEVER SAID THIS HAD ANYTHING TO DO WITH HERCU--
DON'T PLAY INNOCENT WITH ME, DAUGHTER. I KNOW YOUR HISTORY WITH MY BROTHER.
AND SPRING IS IN THE AIR-- THE TIME WHEN BOTH MORTALS AND GODS ARE MOST INTERESTED IN LOVE...

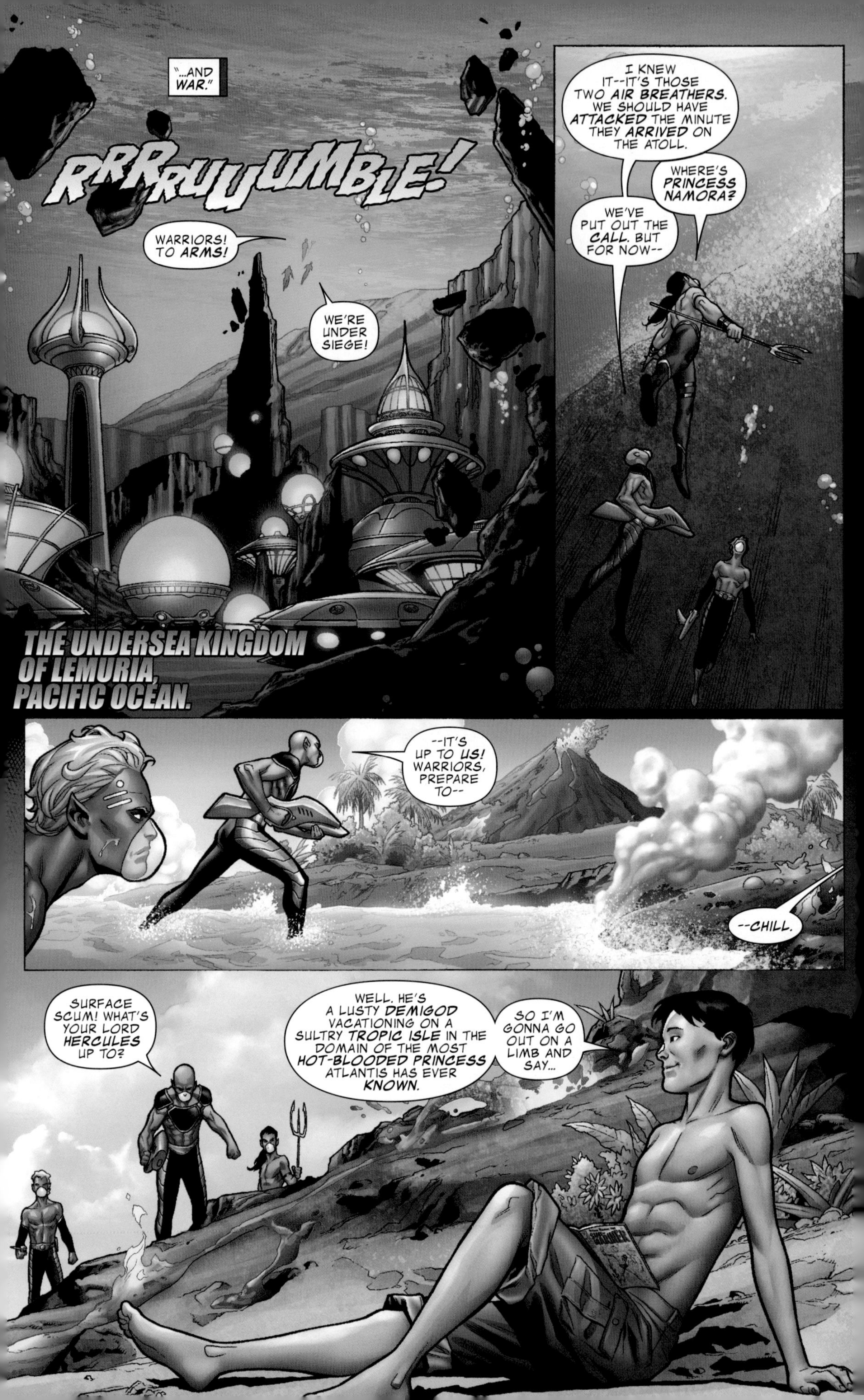

"...AND WAR."
RRRRUUUUMBLE!
WARRIORS! TO ARMS!
WE'RE UNDER SIEGE!
THE UNDERSEA KINGDOM OF LEMURIA, PACIFIC OCEAN.
I KNEW IT--IT'S THOSE TWO AIR BREATHERS. WE SHOULD HAVE ATTACKED THE MINUTE THEY ARRIVED ON THE ATOLL.
WHERE'S PRINCESS NAMORA?
WE'VE PUT OUT THE CALL. BUT FOR NOW--
--IT'S UP TO US! WARRIORS, PREPARE TO--
--CHILL.
SURFACE SCUM! WHAT'S YOUR LORD HERCULES UP TO?
WELL, HE'S A LUSTY DEMIGOD VACATIONING ON A SULTRY TROPIC ISLE IN THE DOMAIN OF THE MOST HOT-BLOODED PRINCESS ATLANTIS HAS EVER KNOWN.
SO I'M GONNA GO OUT ON A LIMB AND SAY...

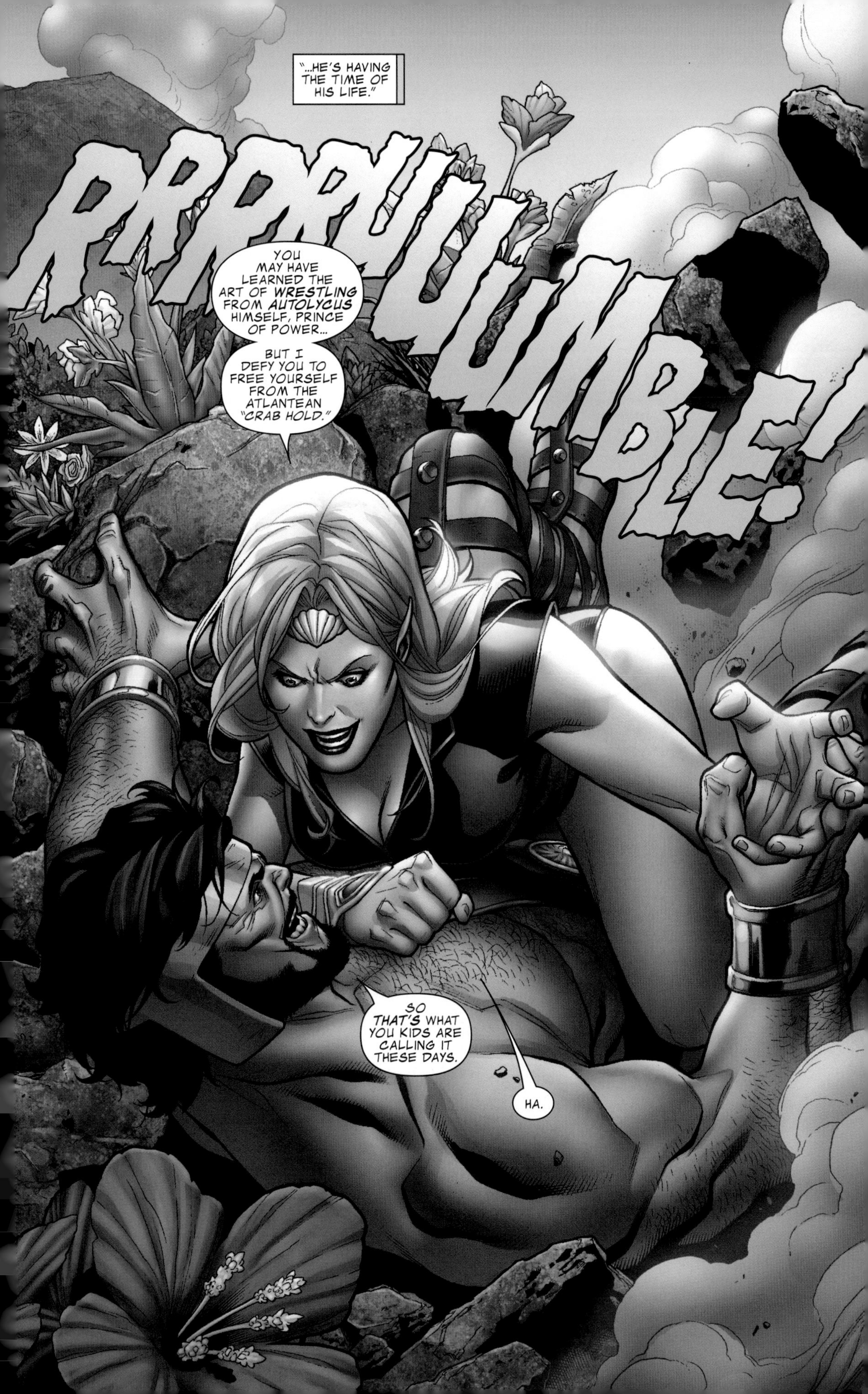
"...HE'S HAVING THE TIME OF HIS LIFE."
RRRRUUUMBLE!!
YOU MAY HAVE LEARNED THE ART OF WRESTLING FROM AUTOLYCUS HIMSELF, PRINCE OF POWER...
BUT I DEFY YOU TO FREE YOURSELF FROM THE ATLANTEAN "CRAB HOLD."
SO THAT'S WHAT YOU KIDS ARE CALLING IT THESE DAYS.
HA.

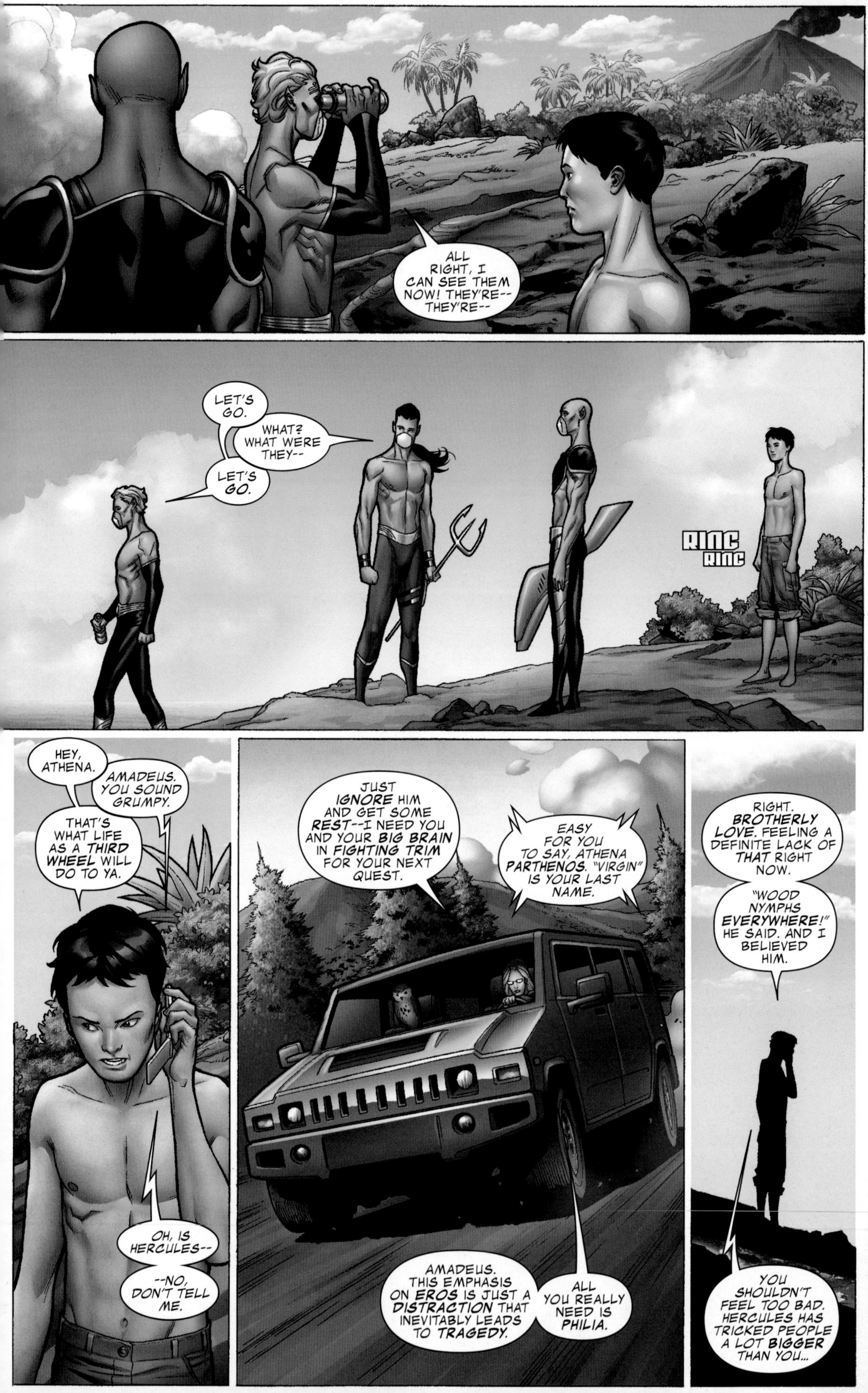
ALL RIGHT, I CAN SEE THEM NOW! THEY'RE-- THEY'RE--
LET'S GO.
WHAT? WHAT WERE THEY--
LET'S GO.
RING
RING
HEY, ATHENA.
AMADEUS. YOU SOUND GRUMPY.
THAT'S WHAT LIFE AS A THIRD WHEEL WILL DO TO YA.
OH, IS HERCULES--
--NO, DON'T TELL ME.
JUST IGNORE HIM AND GET SOME REST--I NEED YOU AND YOUR BIG BRAIN IN FIGHTING TRIM FOR YOUR NEXT QUEST.
EASY FOR YOU TO SAY, ATHENA PARTHENOS. "VIRGIN" IS YOUR LAST NAME.
AMADEUS. THIS EMPHASIS ON EROS IS JUST A DISTRACTION THAT INEVITABLY LEADS TO TRAGEDY.
ALL YOU REALLY NEED IS PHILIA.
RIGHT. BROTHERLY LOVE. FEELING A DEFINITE LACK OF THAT RIGHT NOW.
"WOOD NYMPHS EVERYWHERE!" HE SAID. AND I BELIEVED HIM.
YOU SHOULDN'T FEEL TOO BAD. HERCULES HAS TRICKED PEOPLE A LOT BIGGER THAN YOU...

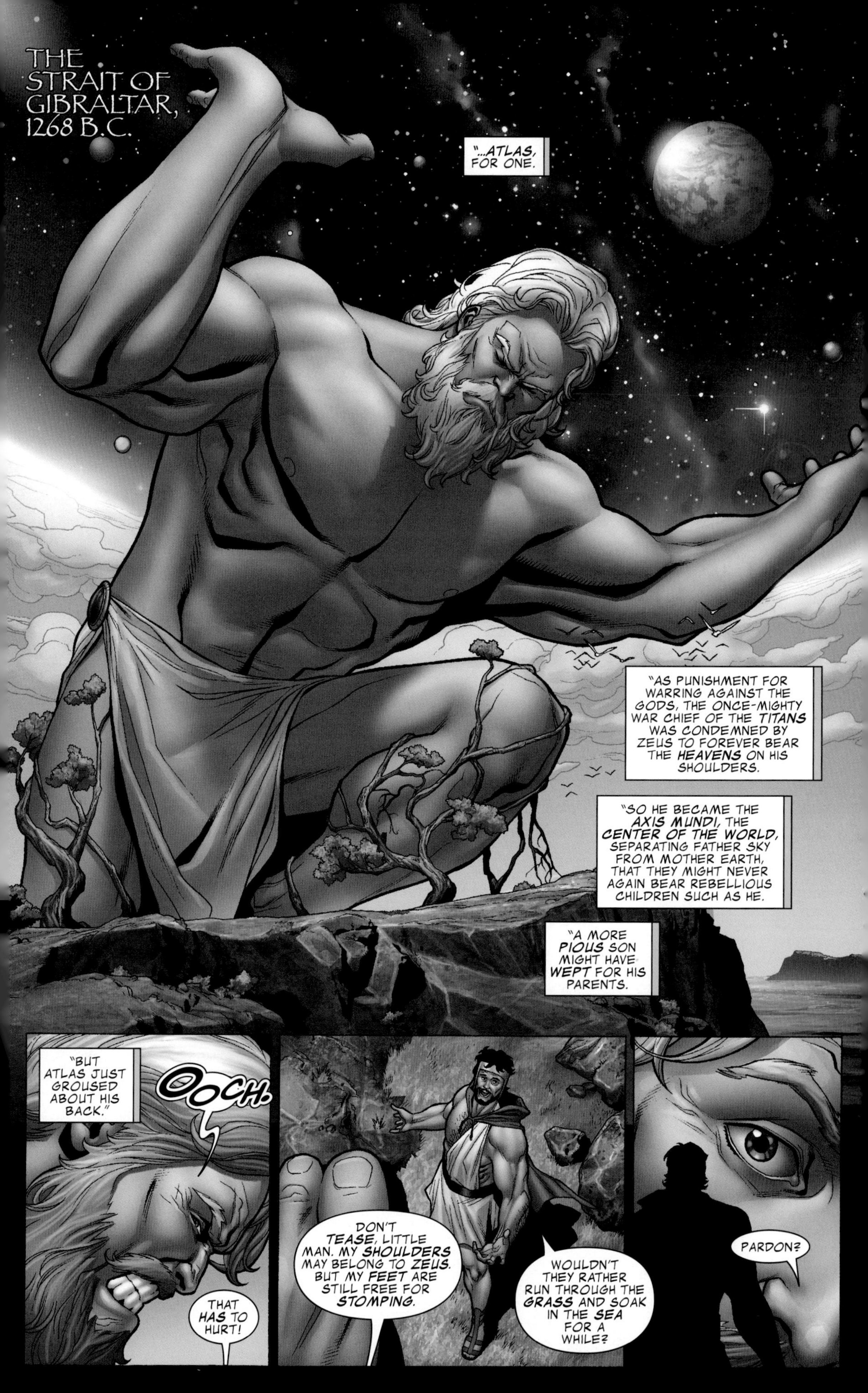
THE STRAIT OF GIBRALTAR, 1268 B.C.
"...ATLAS, FOR ONE.
"AS PUNISHMENT FOR WARRING AGAINST THE GODS, THE ONCE-MIGHTY WAR CHIEF OF THE TITANS WAS CONDEMNED BY ZEUS TO FOREVER BEAR THE HEAVENS ON HIS SHOULDERS.
"SO HE BECAME THE AXIS MUNDI, THE CENTER OF THE WORLD, SEPARATING FATHER SKY FROM MOTHER EARTH, THAT THEY MIGHT NEVER AGAIN BEAR REBELLIOUS CHILDREN SUCH AS HE.
"A MORE PIOUS SON MIGHT HAVE WEPT FOR HIS PARENTS.
"BUT ATLAS JUST GROUSED ABOUT HIS BACK."
OOCH
THAT HAS TO HURT!
DON'T TEASE, LITTLE MAN. MY SHOULDERS MAY BELONG TO ZEUS. BUT MY FEET ARE STILL FREE FOR STOMPING.
WOULDN'T THEY RATHER RUN THROUGH THE GRASS AND SOAK IN THE SEA FOR A WHILE?
PARDON?

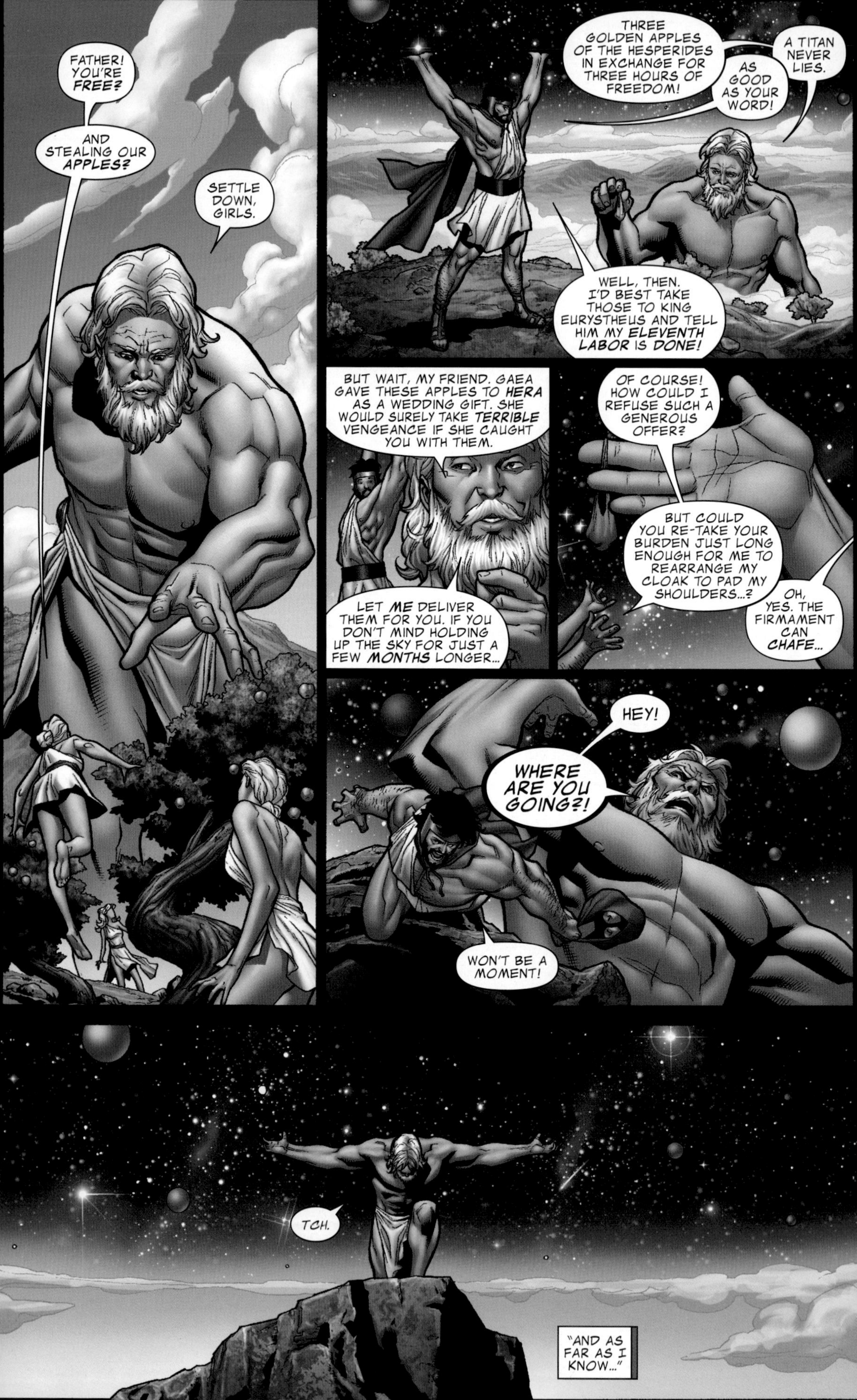
FATHER! YOU'RE FREE?
AND STEALING OUR APPLES?
SETTLE DOWN, GIRLS.
THREE GOLDEN APPLES OF THE HESPERIDES IN EXCHANGE FOR THREE HOURS OF FREEDOM!
A TITAN NEVER LIES.
AS GOOD AS YOUR WORD!
WELL, THEN. I'D BEST TAKE THOSE TO KING EURYSTHEUS AND TELL HIM MY ELEVENTH LABOR IS DONE!
BUT WAIT, MY FRIEND. GAEA GAVE THESE APPLES TO HERA AS A WEDDING GIFT. SHE WOULD SURELY TAKE TERRIBLE VENGEANCE IF SHE CAUGHT YOU WITH THEM.
LET ME DELIVER THEM FOR YOU. IF YOU DON'T MIND HOLDING UP THE SKY FOR JUST A FEW MONTHS LONGER...
OF COURSE! HOW COULD I REFUSE SUCH A GENEROUS OFFER?
BUT COULD YOU RE-TAKE YOUR BURDEN JUST LONG ENOUGH FOR ME TO REARRANGE MY CLOAK TO PAD MY SHOULDERS...?
OH, YES. THE FIRMAMENT CAN CHAFE...
HEY!
WHERE ARE YOU GOING?!
WON'T BE A MOMENT!
TCH.
"AND AS FAR AS I KNOW..."

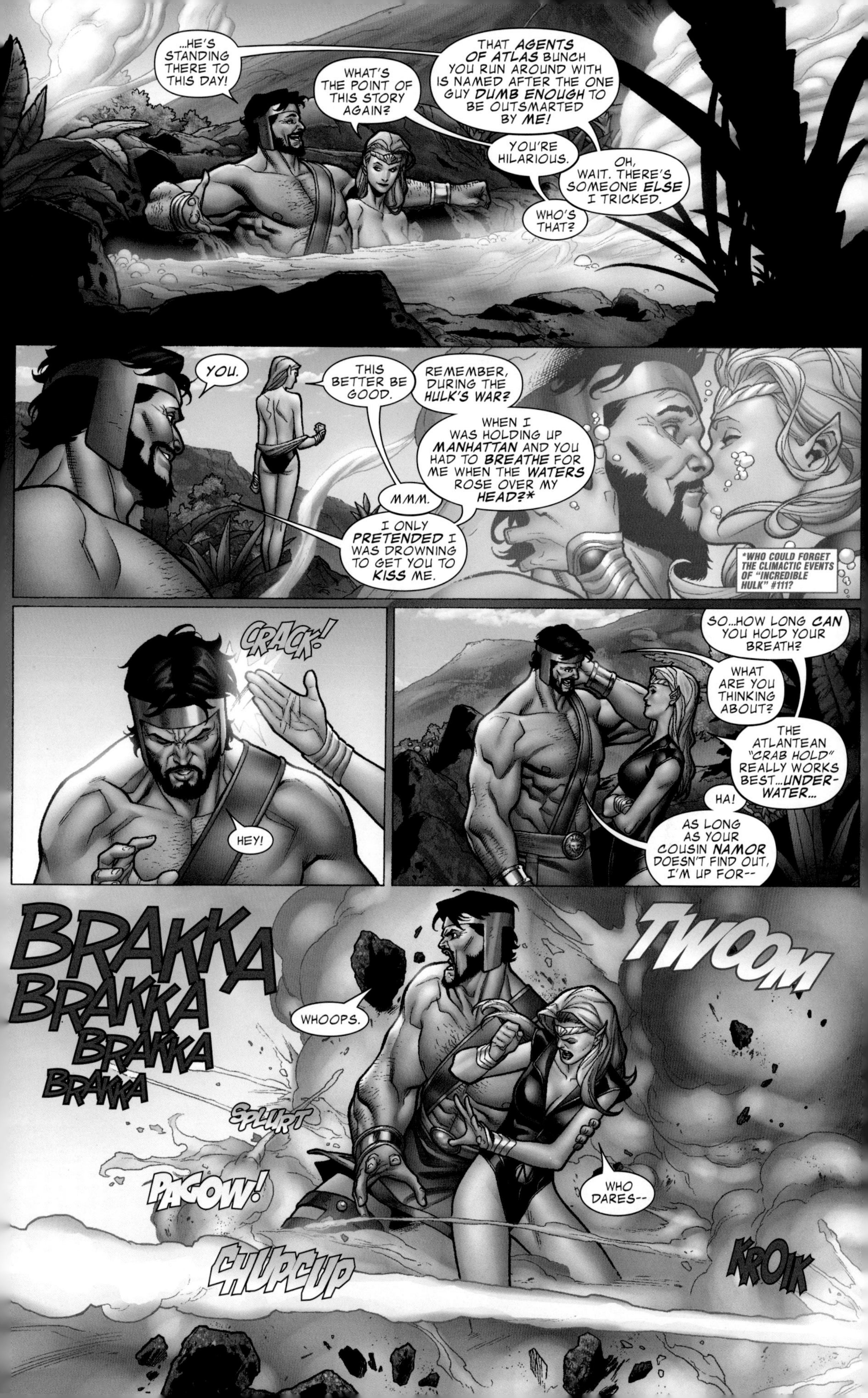
...HE'S STANDING THERE TO THIS DAY!
THAT AGENTS OF ATLAS BUNCH YOU RUN AROUND WITH IS NAMED AFTER THE ONE GUY DUMB ENOUGH TO BE OUTSMARTED BY ME!
WHAT'S THE POINT OF THIS STORY AGAIN?
YOU'RE HILARIOUS.
OH, WAIT. THERE'S SOMEONE ELSE I TRICKED.
WHO'S THAT?
YOU.
THIS BETTER BE GOOD.
REMEMBER, DURING THE HULK'S WAR?
WHEN I WAS HOLDING UP MANHATTAN AND YOU HAD TO BREATHE FOR ME WHEN THE WATERS ROSE OVER MY HEAD?*
MMM.
I ONLY PRETENDED I WAS DROWNING TO GET YOU TO KISS ME.
*WHO COULD FORGET THE CLIMACTIC EVENTS OF "INCREDIBLE HULK" #111?
CRACK!
HEY!
SO...HOW LONG CAN YOU HOLD YOUR BREATH?
WHAT ARE YOU THINKING ABOUT?
THE ATLANTEAN "CRAB HOLD" REALLY WORKS BEST...UNDER-WATER...
HA!
AS LONG AS YOUR COUSIN NAMOR DOESN'T FIND OUT, I'M UP FOR--
BRAKKA BRAKKA BRAKKA BRAKKA
TWOOM
WHOOPS.
SPLURT
PAGOW!
WHO DARES--
CHUPCUP
KROIK

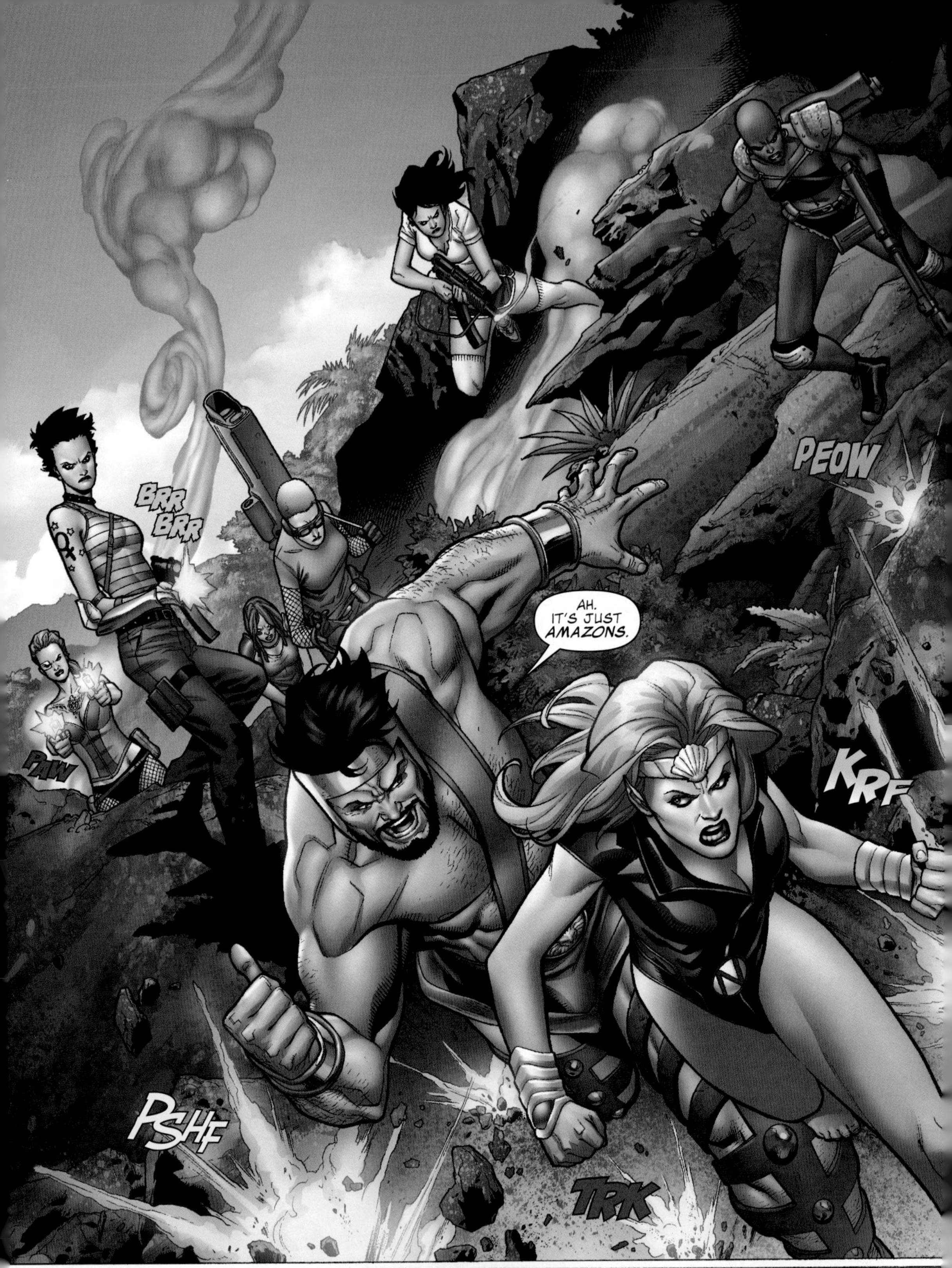
BRR BRR
PEOW
AH. IT'S JUST AMAZONS.
PAW
KRF
PSHF
TRK
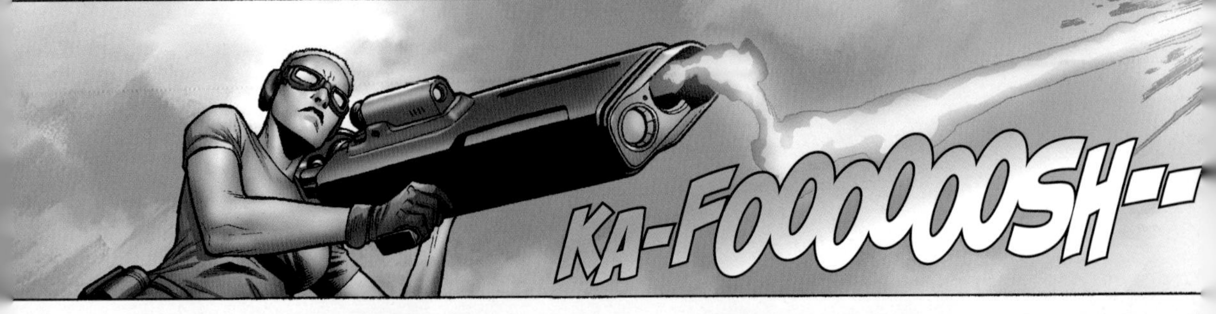
KA-FOOOOOOOSH--

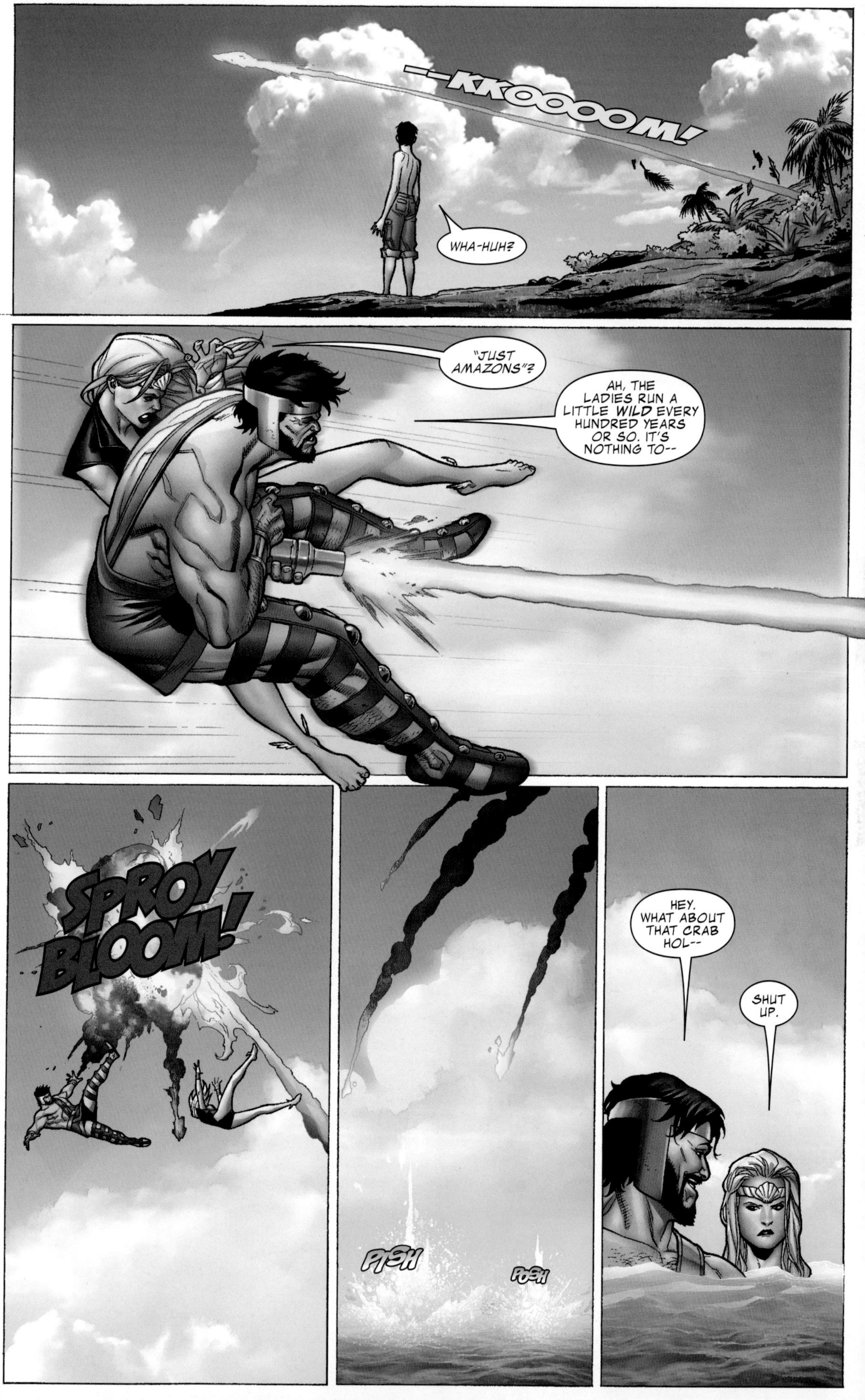
--KKOOOOM!
WHA-HUH?
"JUST AMAZONS"?
AH, THE LADIES RUN A LITTLE WILD EVERY HUNDRED YEARS OR SO. IT'S NOTHING TO--
SPROY BLOOM!
PISH
POSH
HEY. WHAT ABOUT THAT CRAB HOL--
SHUT UP.

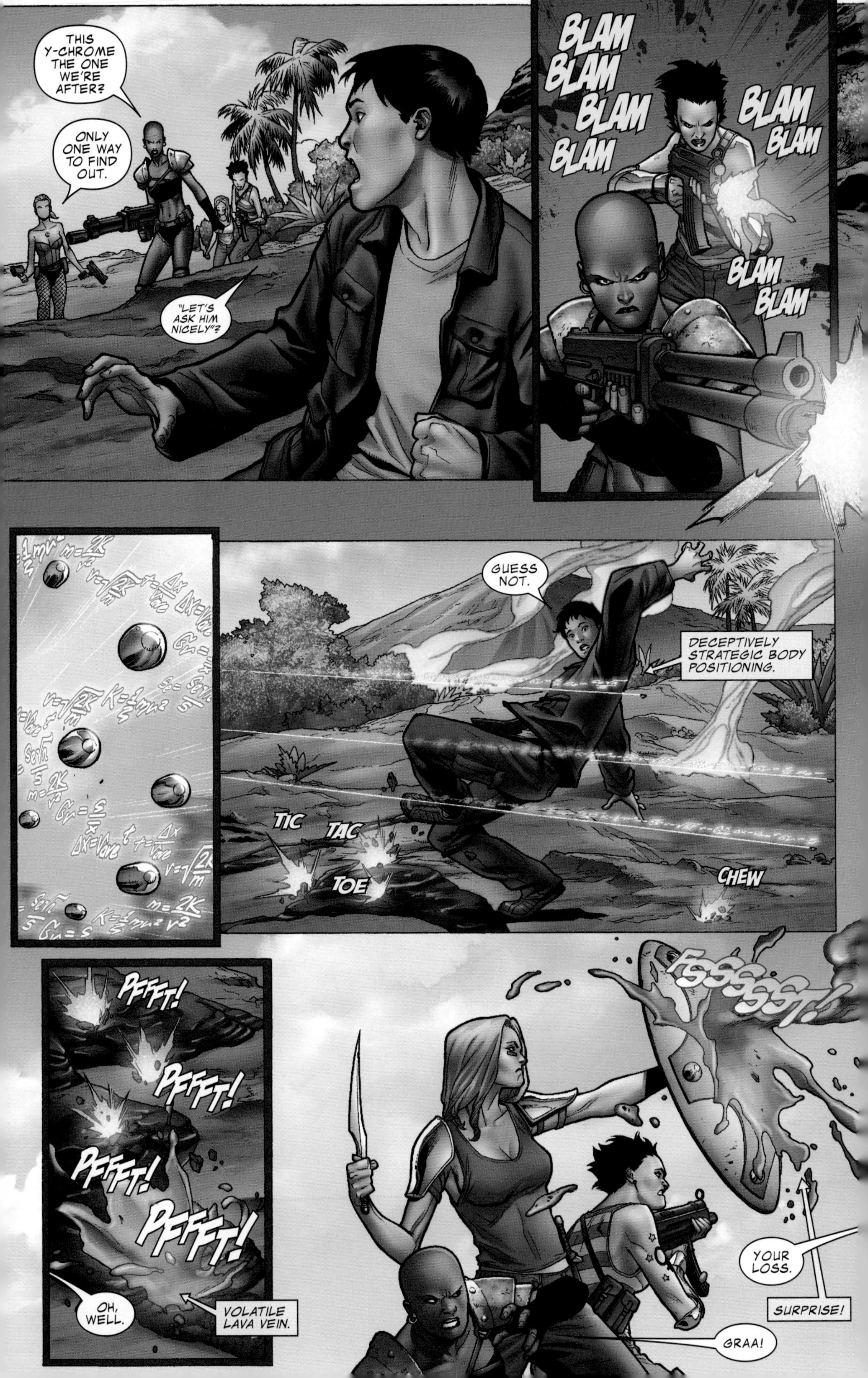
THIS Y-CHROME THE ONE WE'RE AFTER?
ONLY ONE WAY TO FIND OUT.
"LET'S ASK HIM NICELY"?
BLAM BLAM BLAM BLAM
BLAM BLAM
BLAM BLAM
GUESS NOT.
DECEPTIVELY STRATEGIC BODY POSITIONING.
TIC
TAC
TOE
CHEW
PFFFT!
PFFFT!
PFFFT!
PFFFT!
OH, WELL.
VOLATILE LAVA VEIN.
FSSSSST!
YOUR LOSS.
SURPRISE!
GRAA!

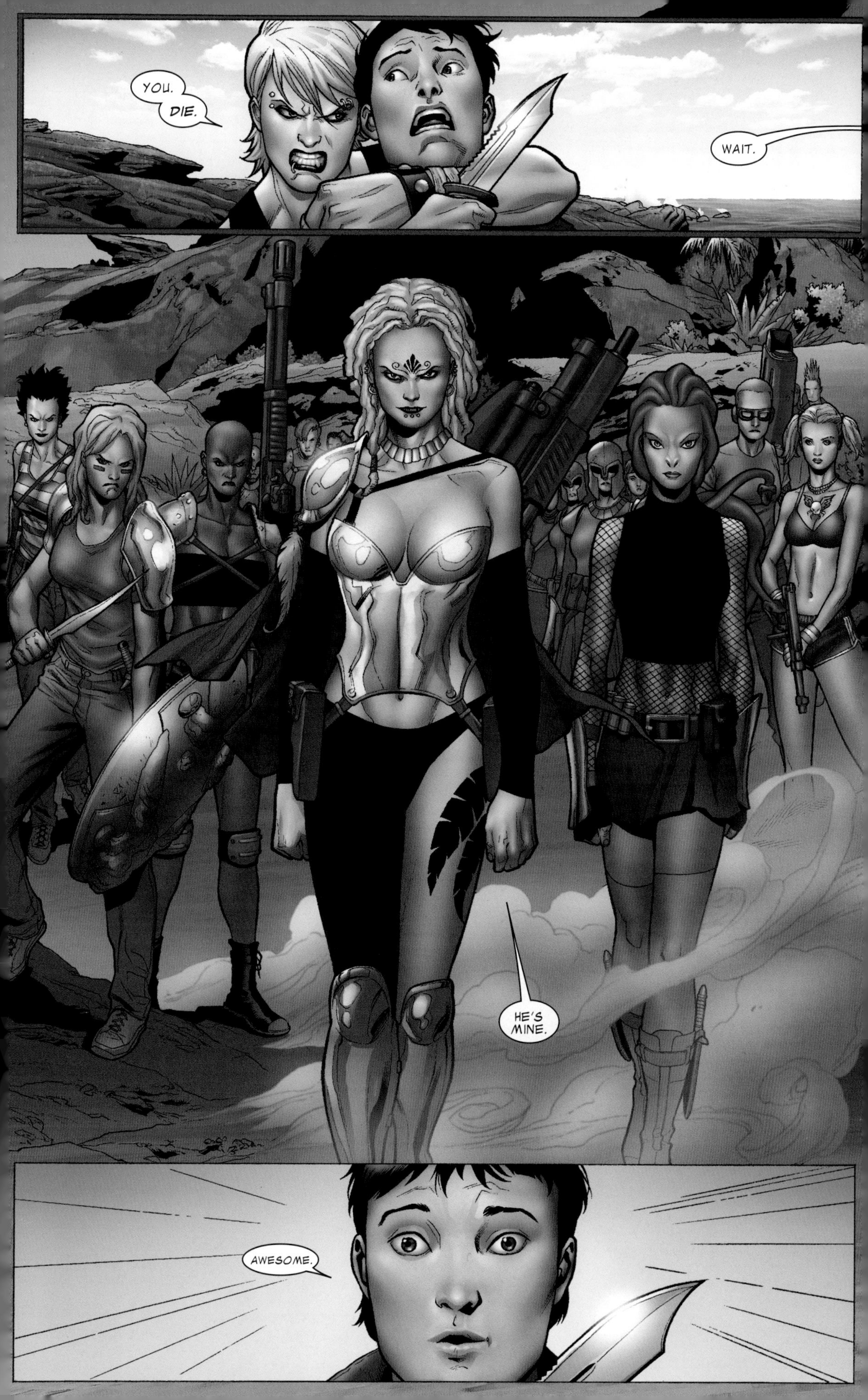
YOU. DIE.
WAIT.
HE'S MINE.
AWESOME.

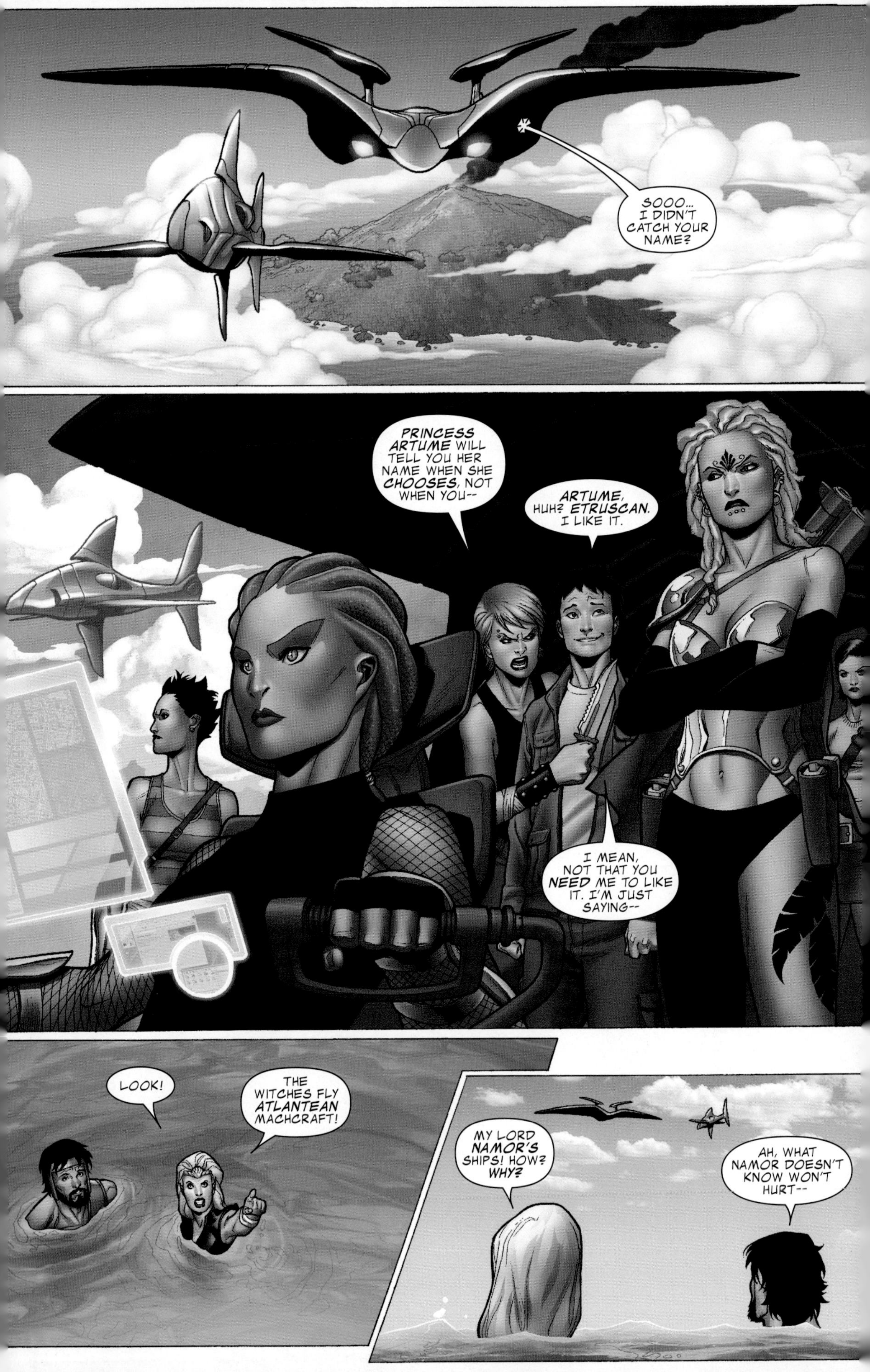
SOOO... I DIDN'T CATCH YOUR NAME?
PRINCESS ARTUME WILL TELL YOU HER NAME WHEN SHE CHOOSES, NOT WHEN YOU--
ARTUME, HUH? ETRUSCAN. I LIKE IT.
I MEAN, NOT THAT YOU NEED ME TO LIKE IT. I'M JUST SAYING--
LOOK!
THE WITCHES FLY ATLANTEAN MACHCRAFT!
MY LORD NAMOR'S SHIPS! HOW? WHY?
AH, WHAT NAMOR DOESN'T KNOW WON'T HURT--

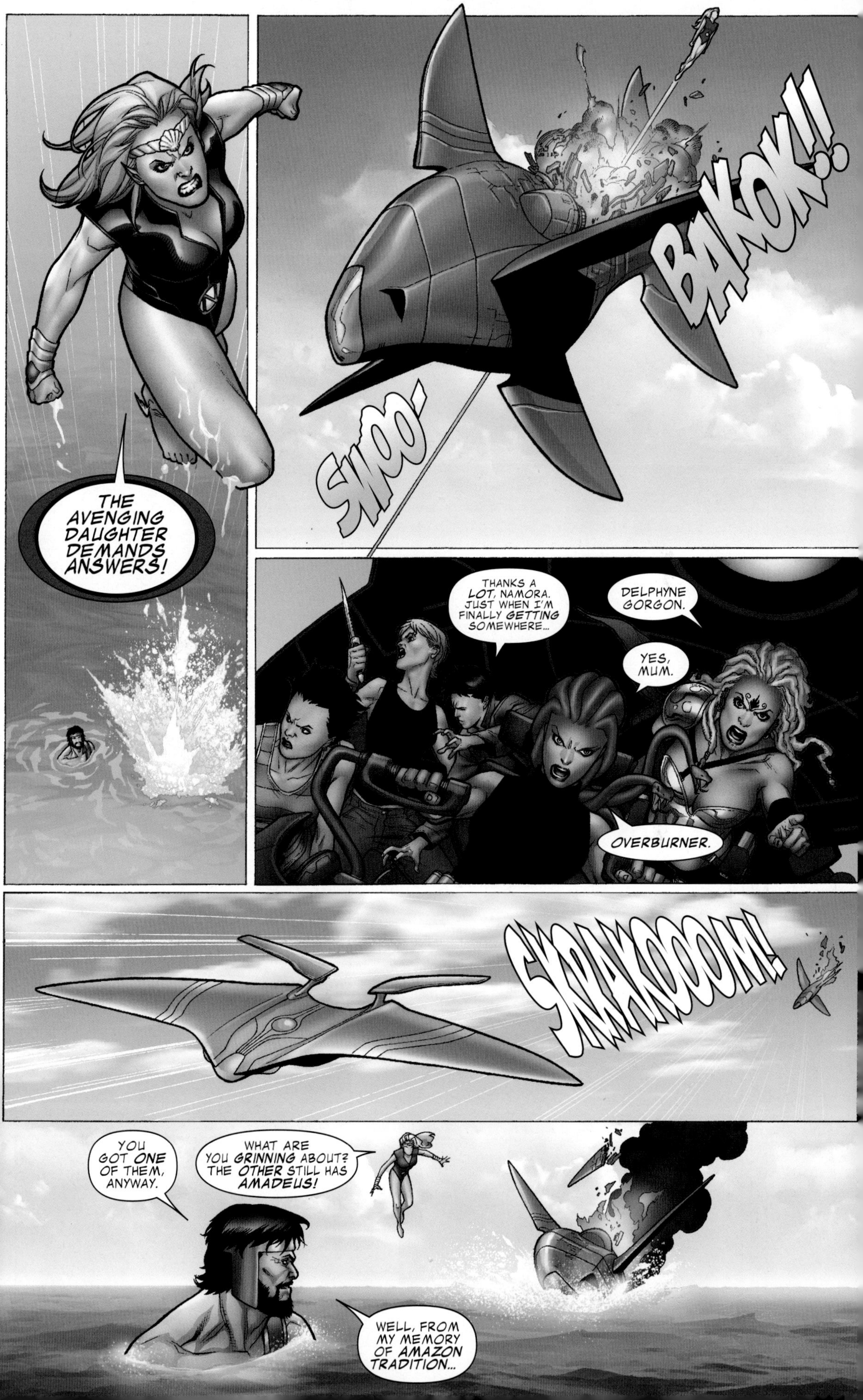

THE AVENGING DAUGHTER DEMANDS ANSWERS!
BAKOK!!
SWOO-
THANKS A LOT, NAMORA. JUST WHEN I'M FINALLY GETTING SOMEWHERE...
DELPHYNE GORGON.
YES, MUM.
OVERBURNER.
SKRAKOOOM!
YOU GOT ONE OF THEM, ANYWAY.
WHAT ARE YOU GRINNING ABOUT? THE OTHER STILL HAS AMADEUS!
WELL, FROM MY MEMORY OF AMAZON TRADITION...

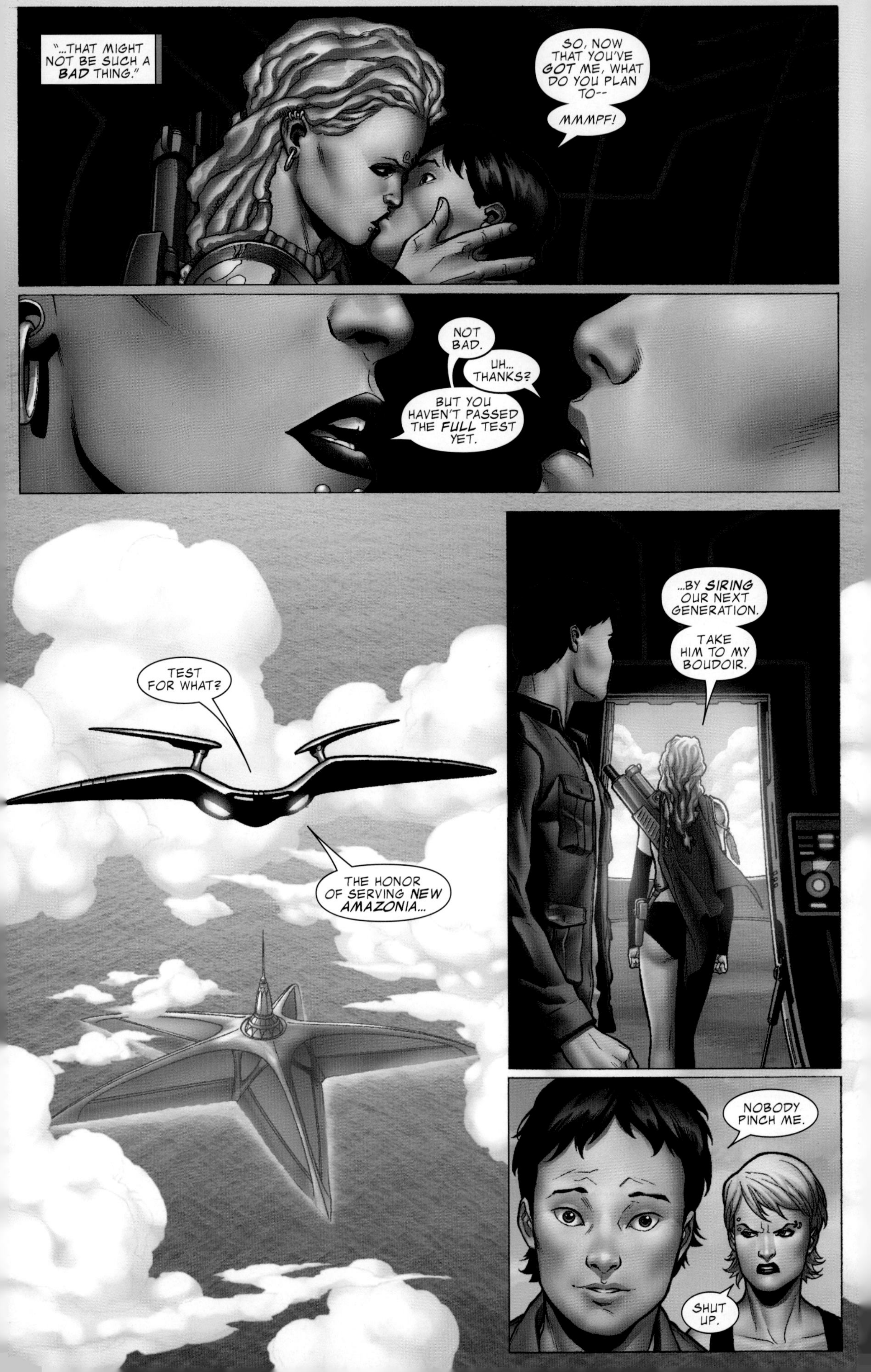
"...THAT MIGHT NOT BE SUCH A BAD THING."
SO, NOW THAT YOU'VE GOT ME, WHAT DO YOU PLAN TO--
MMMPF!
NOT BAD.
UH... THANKS?
BUT YOU HAVEN'T PASSED THE FULL TEST YET.
TEST FOR WHAT?
THE HONOR OF SERVING NEW AMAZONIA...
...BY SIRING OUR NEXT GENERATION.
TAKE HIM TO MY BOUDOIR.
NOBODY PINCH ME.
SHUT UP.

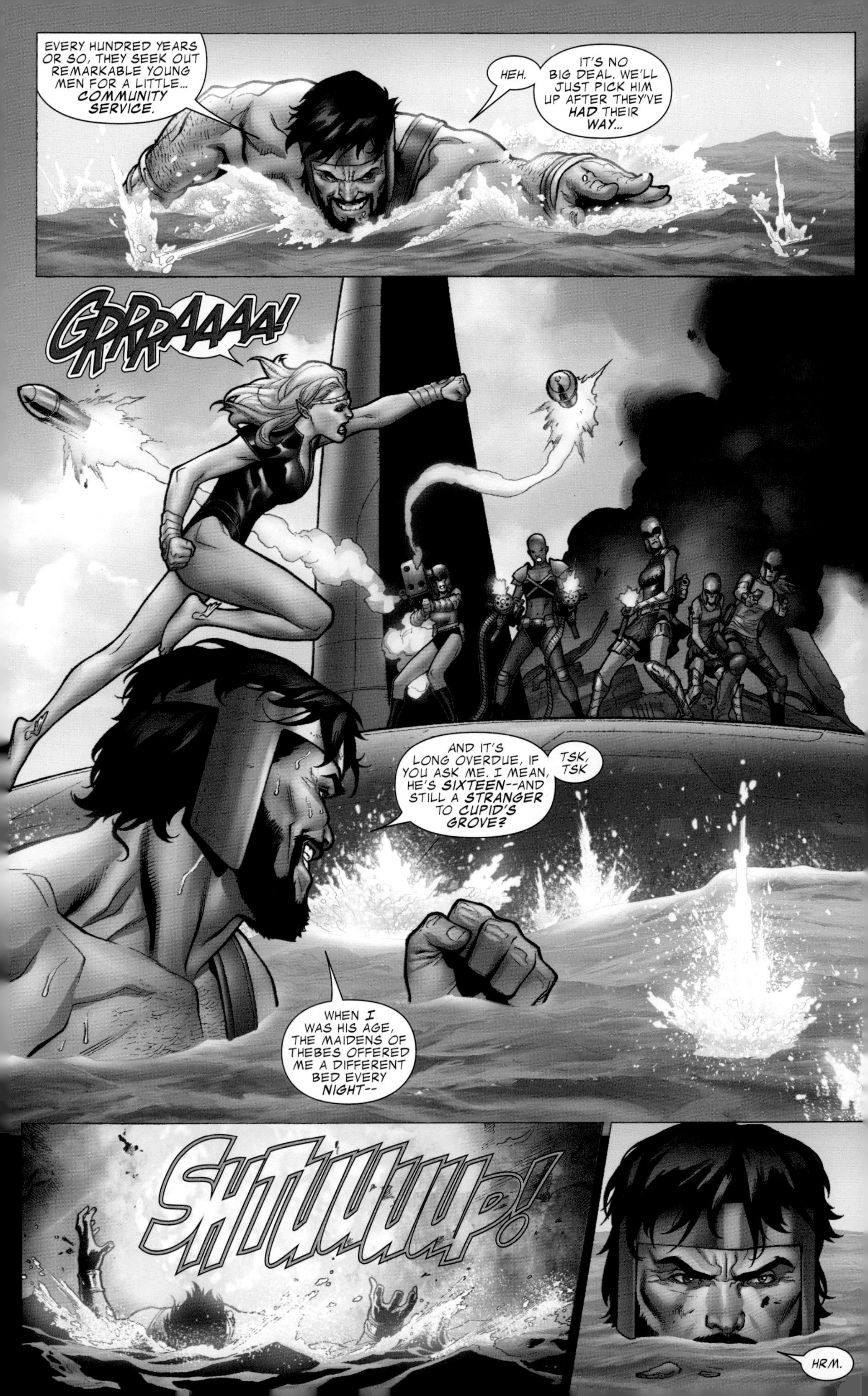
EVERY HUNDRED YEARS OR SO, THEY SEEK OUT REMARKABLE YOUNG MEN FOR A LITTLE... COMMUNITY SERVICE.
HEH.
IT'S NO BIG DEAL. WE'LL JUST PICK HIM UP AFTER THEY'VE HAD THEIR WAY...
GRRRAAAA!
AND IT'S LONG OVERDUE, IF YOU ASK ME. I MEAN, HE'S SIXTEEN--AND STILL A STRANGER TO CUPID'S GROVE?
TSK, TSK
WHEN I WAS HIS AGE, THE MAIDENS OF THEBES OFFERED ME A DIFFERENT BED EVERY NIGHT--
SHUUUUP!
HRM.

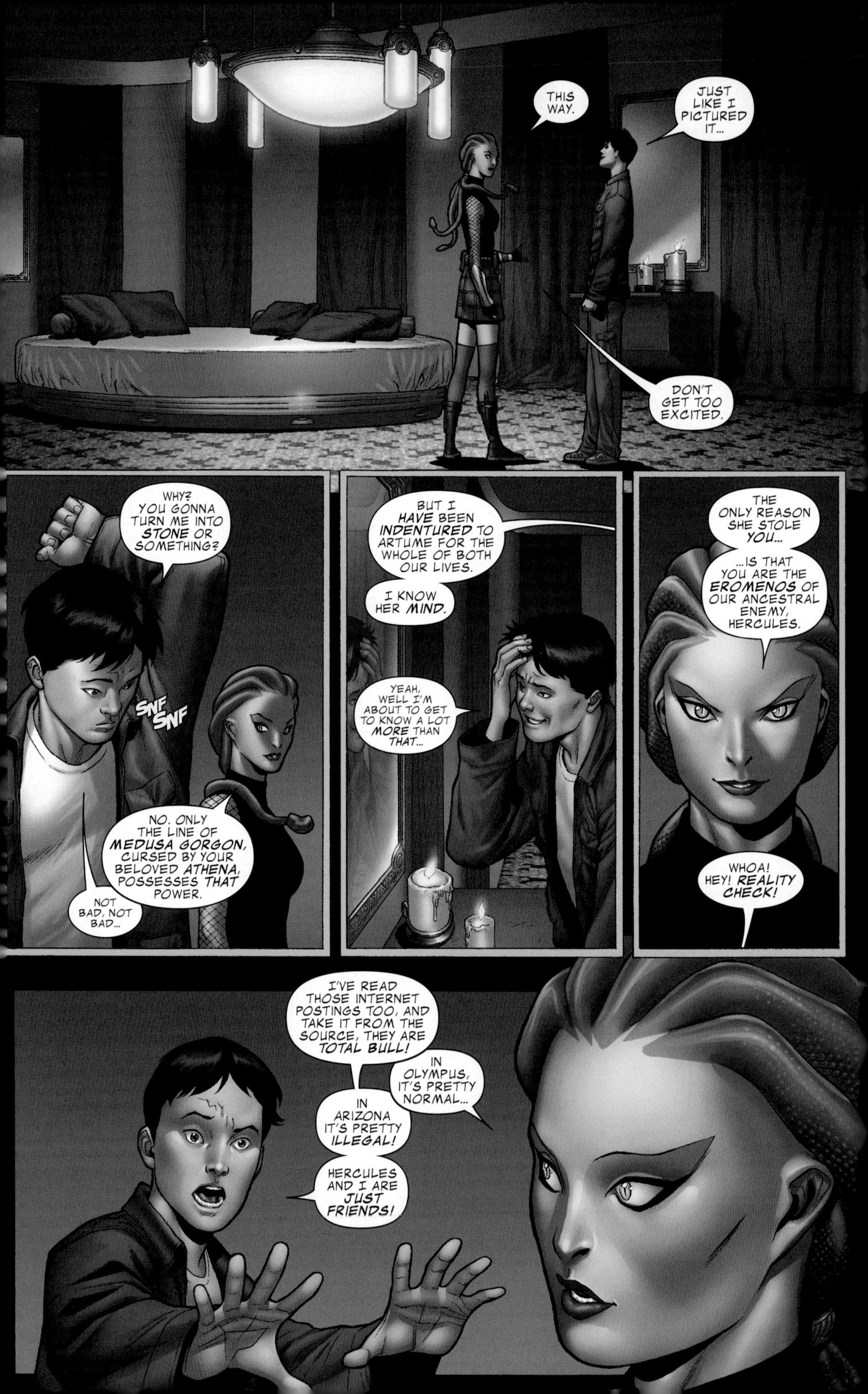
THIS WAY.
JUST LIKE I PICTURED IT...
DON'T GET TOO EXCITED.
WHY? YOU GONNA TURN ME INTO STONE OR SOMETHING?
SNF SNF
NO. ONLY THE LINE OF MEDUSA GORGON, CURSED BY YOUR BELOVED ATHENA, POSSESSES THAT POWER.
NOT BAD, NOT BAD...
BUT I HAVE BEEN INDENTURED TO ARTUME FOR THE WHOLE OF BOTH OUR LIVES.
I KNOW HER MIND.
YEAH, WELL I'M ABOUT TO GET TO KNOW A LOT MORE THAN THAT...
THE ONLY REASON SHE STOLE YOU...
...IS THAT YOU ARE THE EROMENOS OF OUR ANCESTRAL ENEMY, HERCULES.
WHOA! HEY! REALITY CHECK!
I'VE READ THOSE INTERNET POSTINGS TOO, AND TAKE IT FROM THE SOURCE, THEY ARE TOTAL BULL!
IN OLYMPUS, IT'S PRETTY NORMAL...
IN ARIZONA IT'S PRETTY ILLEGAL!
HERCULES AND I ARE JUST FRIENDS!

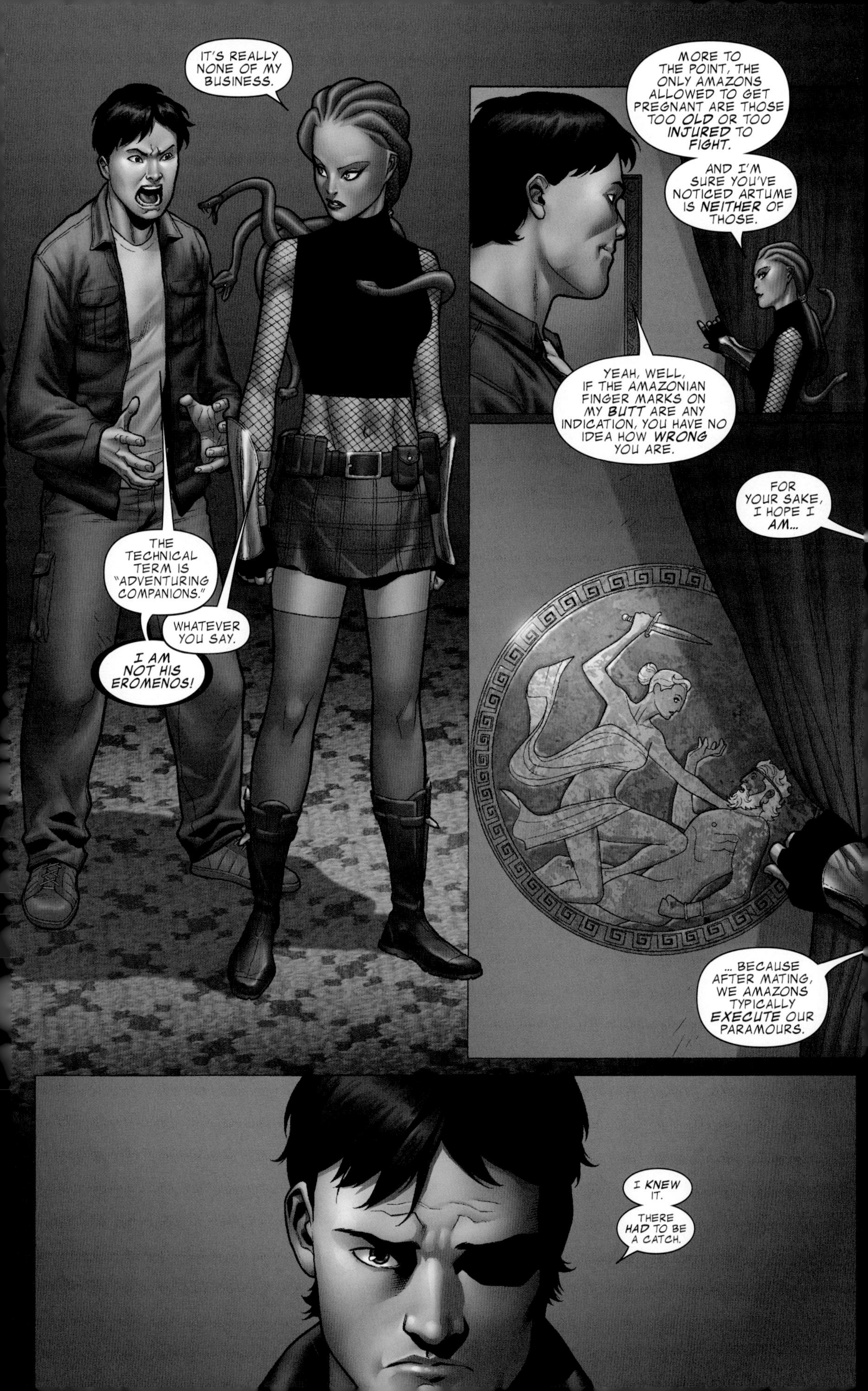
IT'S REALLY NONE OF MY BUSINESS.
THE TECHNICAL TERM IS "ADVENTURING COMPANIONS."
WHATEVER YOU SAY.
I AM NOT HIS EROMENOS!
MORE TO THE POINT, THE ONLY AMAZONS ALLOWED TO GET PREGNANT ARE THOSE TOO OLD OR TOO INJURED TO FIGHT.
AND I'M SURE YOU'VE NOTICED ARTUME IS NEITHER OF THOSE.
YEAH, WELL, IF THE AMAZONIAN FINGER MARKS ON MY BUTT ARE ANY INDICATION, YOU HAVE NO IDEA HOW WRONG YOU ARE.
FOR YOUR SAKE, I HOPE I AM...
... BECAUSE AFTER MATING, WE AMAZONS TYPICALLY EXECUTE OUR PARAMOURS.
I KNEW IT.
THERE HAD TO BE A CATCH.

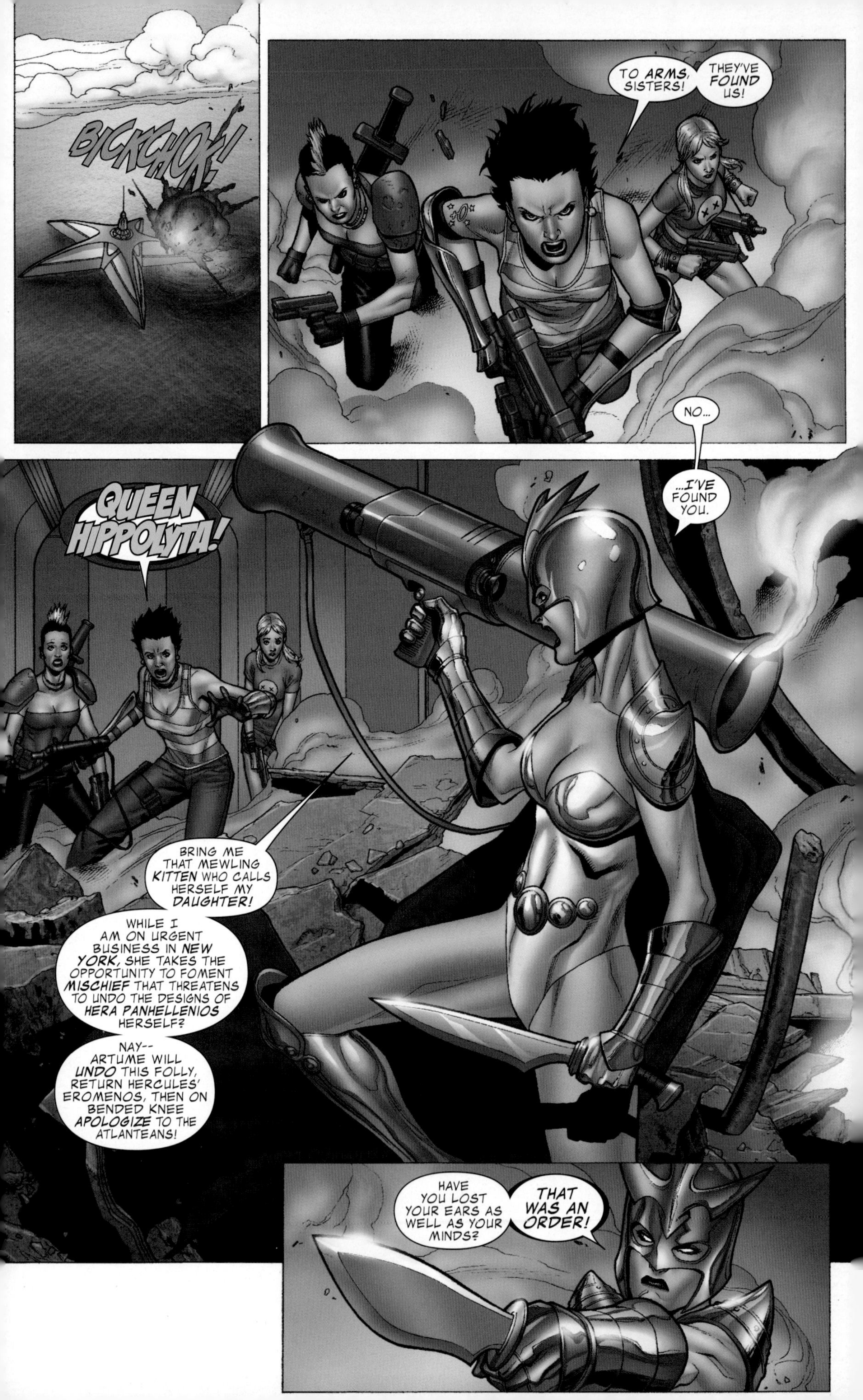
BICKCHOK!
TO ARMS, SISTERS!
THEY'VE FOUND US!
NO...
...I'VE FOUND YOU.
QUEEN HIPPOLYTA!
BRING ME THAT MEWLING KITTEN WHO CALLS HERSELF MY DAUGHTER!
WHILE I AM ON URGENT BUSINESS IN NEW YORK, SHE TAKES THE OPPORTUNITY TO FOMENT MISCHIEF THAT THREATENS TO UNDO THE DESIGNS OF HERA PANHELLENIOS HERSELF?
NAY-- ARTUME WILL UNDO THIS FOLLY, RETURN HERCULES' EROMENOS, THEN ON BENDED KNEE APOLOGIZE TO THE ATLANTEANS!
HAVE YOU LOST YOUR EARS AS WELL AS YOUR MINDS?
THAT WAS AN ORDER!

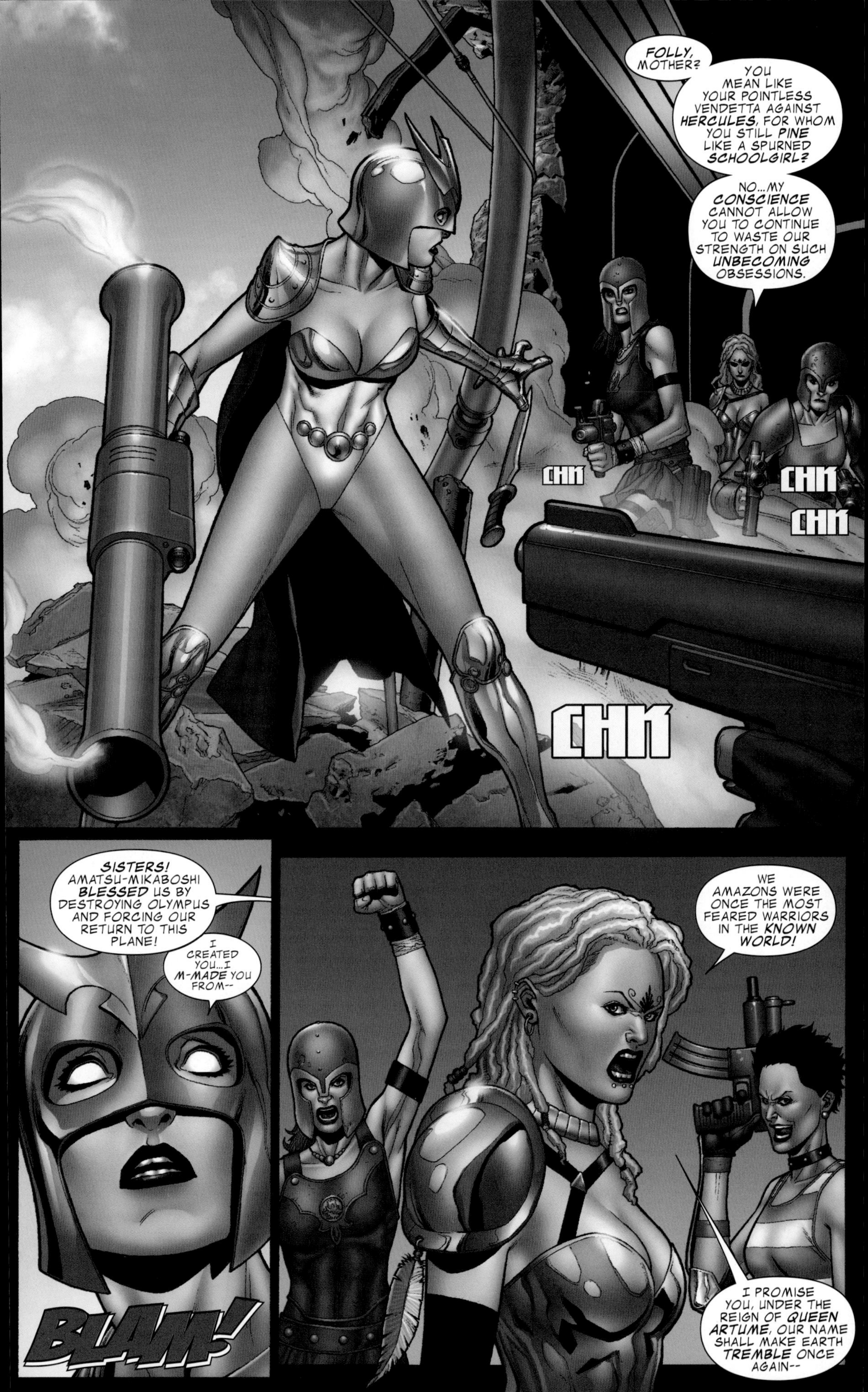

FOLLY, MOTHER?
YOU MEAN LIKE YOUR POINTLESS VENDETTA AGAINST HERCULES, FOR WHOM YOU STILL PINE LIKE A SPURNED SCHOOLGIRL?
NO...MY CONSCIENCE CANNOT ALLOW YOU TO CONTINUE TO WASTE OUR STRENGTH ON SUCH UNBECOMING OBSESSIONS.
CHK
CHK
CHK
CHK
SISTERS! AMATSU-MIKABOSHI BLESSED US BY DESTROYING OLYMPUS AND FORCING OUR RETURN TO THIS PLANE!
I CREATED YOU...I M-MADE YOU FROM--
BLAM!
WE AMAZONS WERE ONCE THE MOST FEARED WARRIORS IN THE KNOWN WORLD!
I PROMISE YOU, UNDER THE REIGN OF QUEEN ARTUME, OUR NAME SHALL MAKE EARTH TREMBLE ONCE AGAIN--

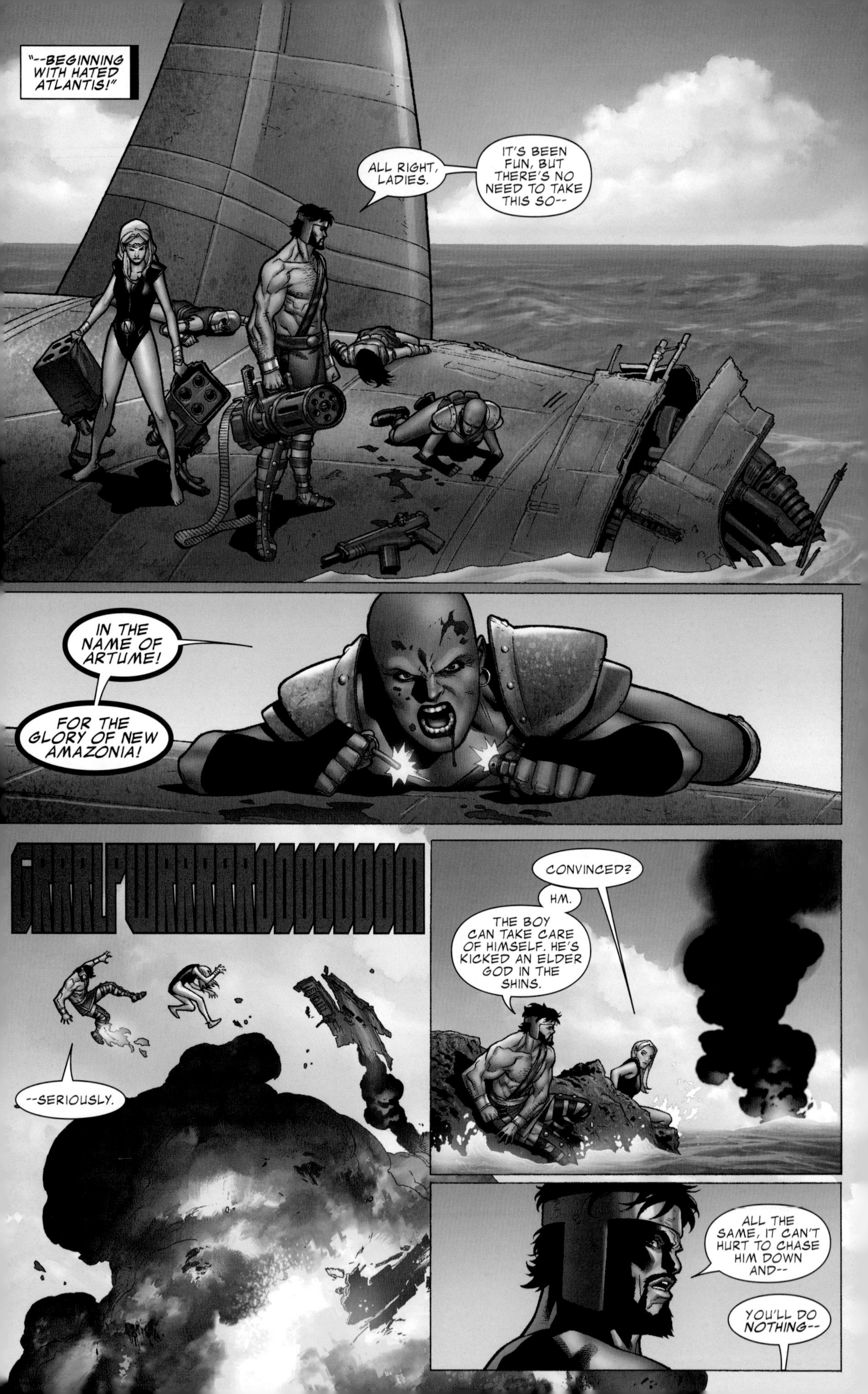
"--BEGINNING WITH HATED ATLANTIS!"
ALL RIGHT, LADIES.
IT'S BEEN FUN, BUT THERE'S NO NEED TO TAKE THIS SO--
IN THE NAME OF ARTUME!
FOR THE GLORY OF NEW AMAZONIA!
GRRRLPWRRRROOOOOOOOM
--SERIOUSLY.
CONVINCED?
HM.
THE BOY CAN TAKE CARE OF HIMSELF. HE'S KICKED AN ELDER GOD IN THE SHINS.
ALL THE SAME, IT CAN'T HURT TO CHASE HIM DOWN AND--
YOU'LL DO NOTHING--

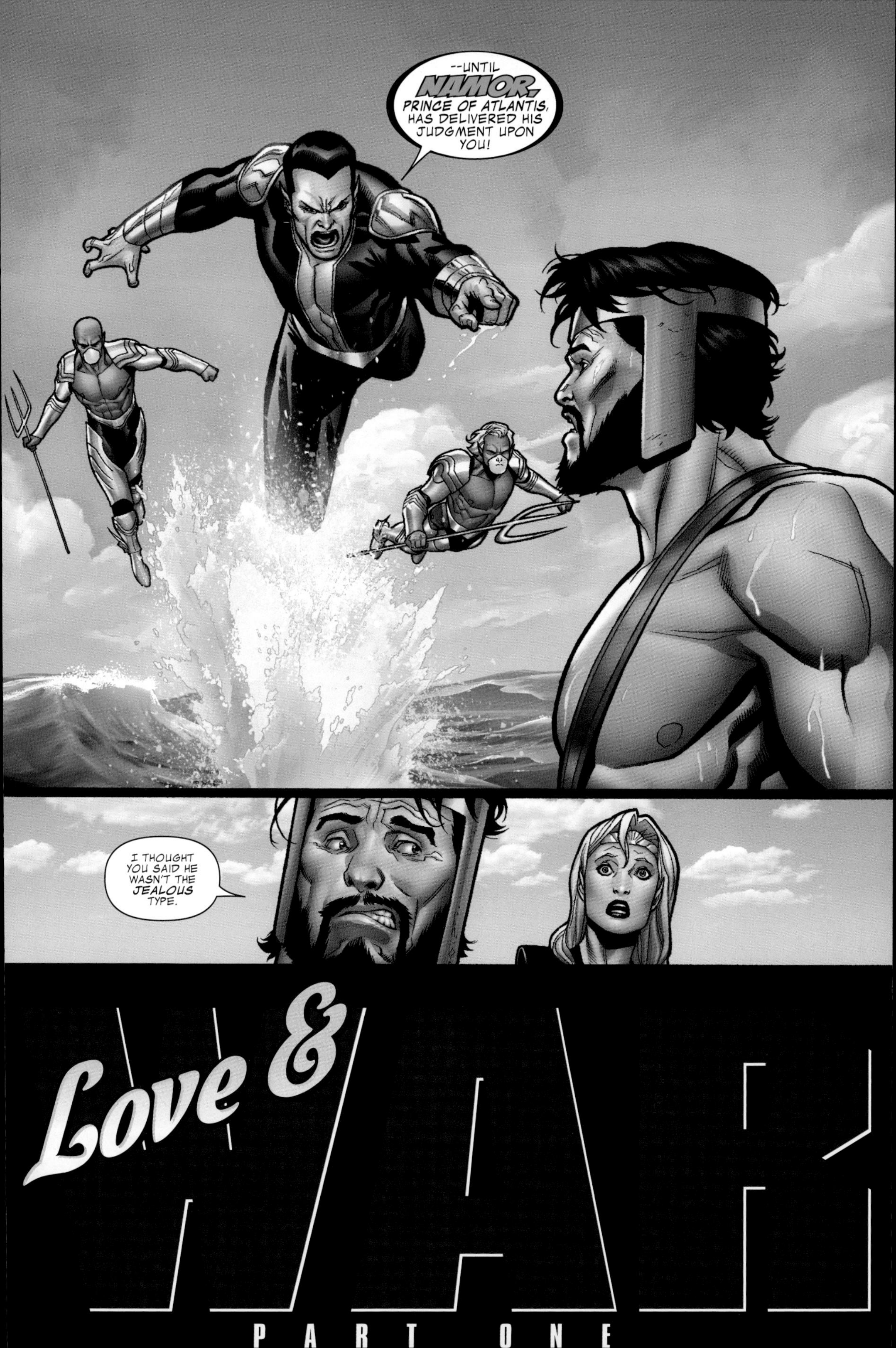
--UNTIL NAMOR, PRINCE OF ATLANTIS, HAS DELIVERED HIS JUDGMENT UPON YOU!
I THOUGHT YOU SAID HE WASN'T THE JEALOUS TYPE.
Love & WAR
PART ONE

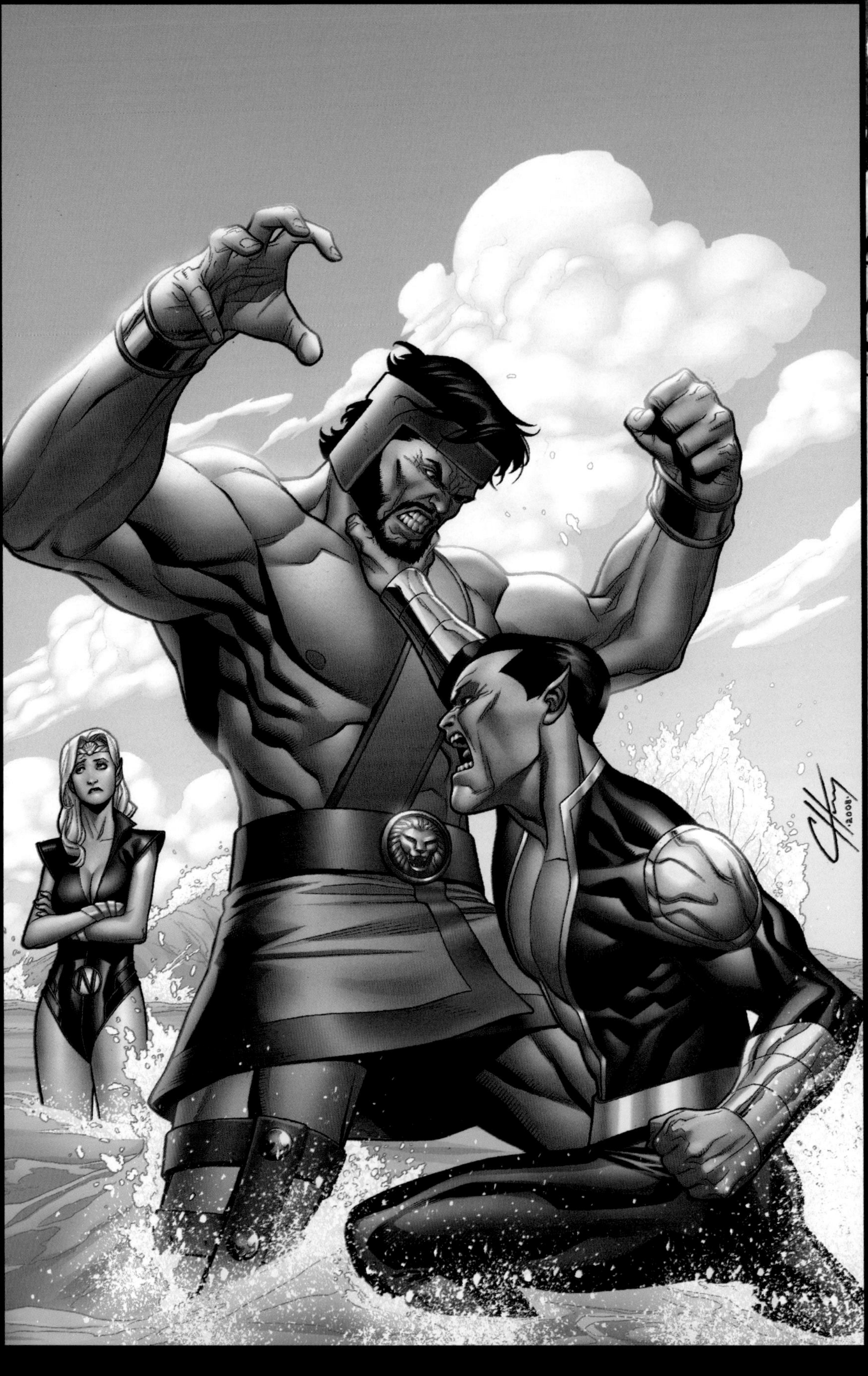

INCREDIBLE HERCULES #122

SAPPHO 31 RELOADED

By Sappho of Lesbos, liberally edited by Amadeus Cho of Arizona

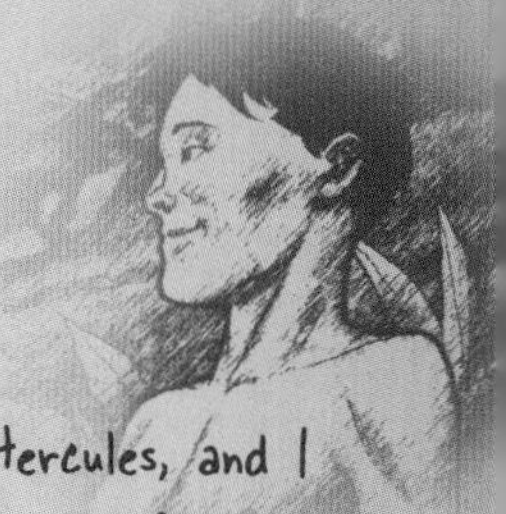

He seems to me, that man, ~~almost~~ is a god—
the man, who is face to face with you,
sitting close enough to you to hear
your sweet whispering

Yeah, his name's Hercules, and I Guarantee ya if you're female, he's just trying to get his swerve on

And your laughter, glistening, which
the heart in ~~my~~ Namora's (the SUB-MARINER'S cousin) breast beats for.
For when on you I glance, I do not,
not one sound, emit.

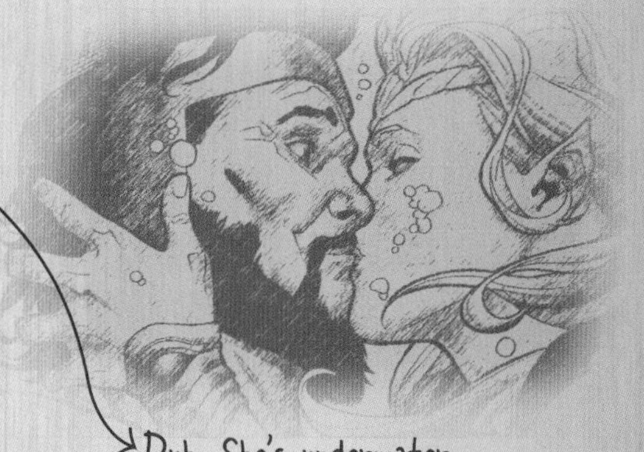

Duh, She's underwater.

But my tongue snaps, lightly
runs beneath my flesh a flame,
and from my eyes no light, and ~~rumbling~~ gunfire
comes into my ears,

cuz I've been captured by armed Amazons that want to use my body for breeding and... pleasure

And my skin grows damp, and trembling
all over racks me, and greener than the ~~grass~~ seaweed
am I, and one step short of dying
~~I seem to myself.~~

is Here, cuz SUB-MARINER just showed up to sub-marinate his @$$. . .

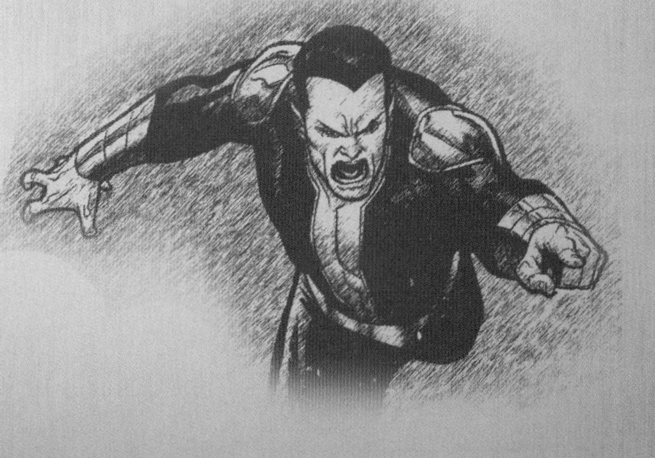

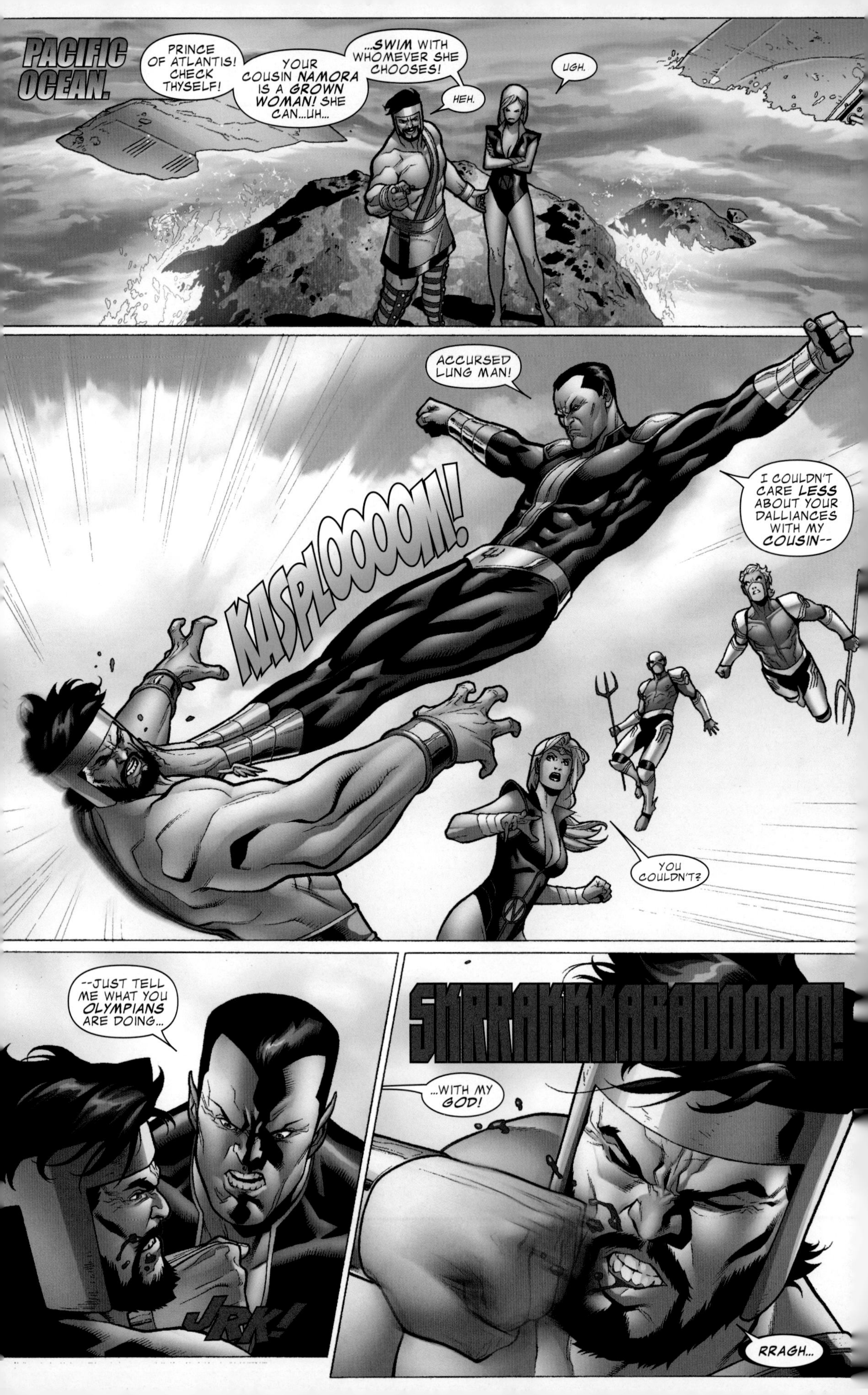
PACIFIC OCEAN.
PRINCE OF ATLANTIS! CHECK THYSELF!
YOUR COUSIN NAMORA IS A GROWN WOMAN! SHE CAN...UH...
...SWIM WITH WHOMEVER SHE CHOOSES!
HEH.
UGH.
ACCURSED LUNG MAN!
KASPLOOOOM!
I COULDN'T CARE LESS ABOUT YOUR DALLIANCES WITH MY COUSIN--
YOU COULDN'T?
--JUST TELL ME WHAT YOU OLYMPIANS ARE DOING...
JRK!
SKRRAKKKABADOOOM!
...WITH MY GOD!
RRAGH...

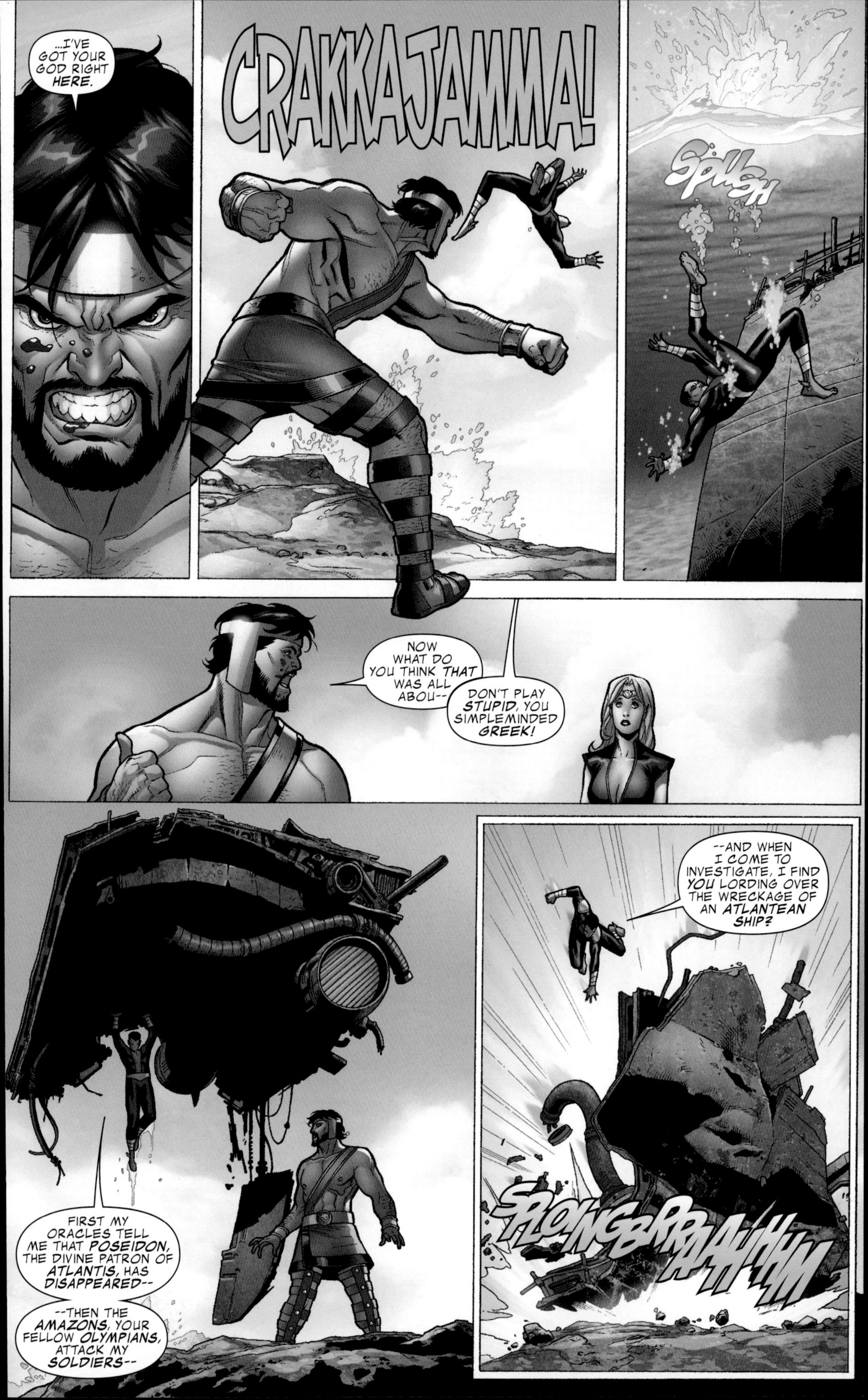

...I'VE GOT YOUR GOD RIGHT HERE.
CRAKKAJAMMA!
SPLUSH
NOW WHAT DO YOU THINK THAT WAS ALL ABOU--
DON'T PLAY STUPID, YOU SIMPLEMINDED GREEK!
FIRST MY ORACLES TELL ME THAT POSEIDON, THE DIVINE PATRON OF ATLANTIS, HAS DISAPPEARED--
--THEN THE AMAZONS, YOUR FELLOW OLYMPIANS, ATTACK MY SOLDIERS--
--AND WHEN I COME TO INVESTIGATE, I FIND YOU LORDING OVER THE WRECKAGE OF AN ATLANTEAN SHIP?
SPLOINGBRRRAAHHHM

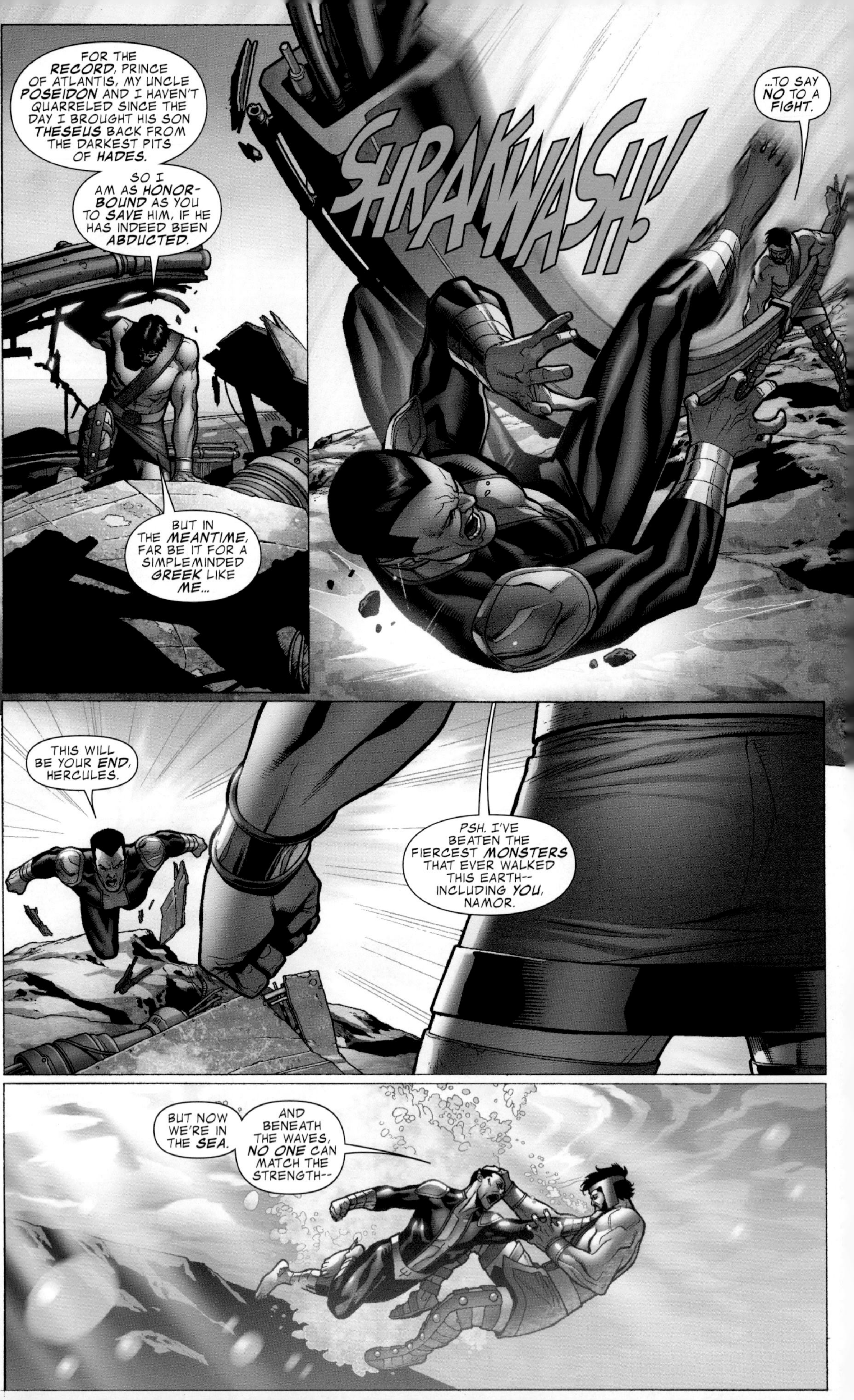

FOR THE RECORD, PRINCE OF ATLANTIS, MY UNCLE POSEIDON AND I HAVEN'T QUARRELED SINCE THE DAY I BROUGHT HIS SON THESEUS BACK FROM THE DARKEST PITS OF HADES.
SO I AM AS HONOR-BOUND AS YOU TO SAVE HIM, IF HE HAS INDEED BEEN ABDUCTED.
BUT IN THE MEANTIME, FAR BE IT FOR A SIMPLEMINDED GREEK LIKE ME...
SHRAKWASH!
...TO SAY NO TO A FIGHT.
THIS WILL BE YOUR END, HERCULES.
PSH. I'VE BEATEN THE FIERCEST MONSTERS THAT EVER WALKED THIS EARTH-- INCLUDING YOU, NAMOR.
BUT NOW WE'RE IN THE SEA.
AND BENEATH THE WAVES, NO ONE CAN MATCH THE STRENGTH--

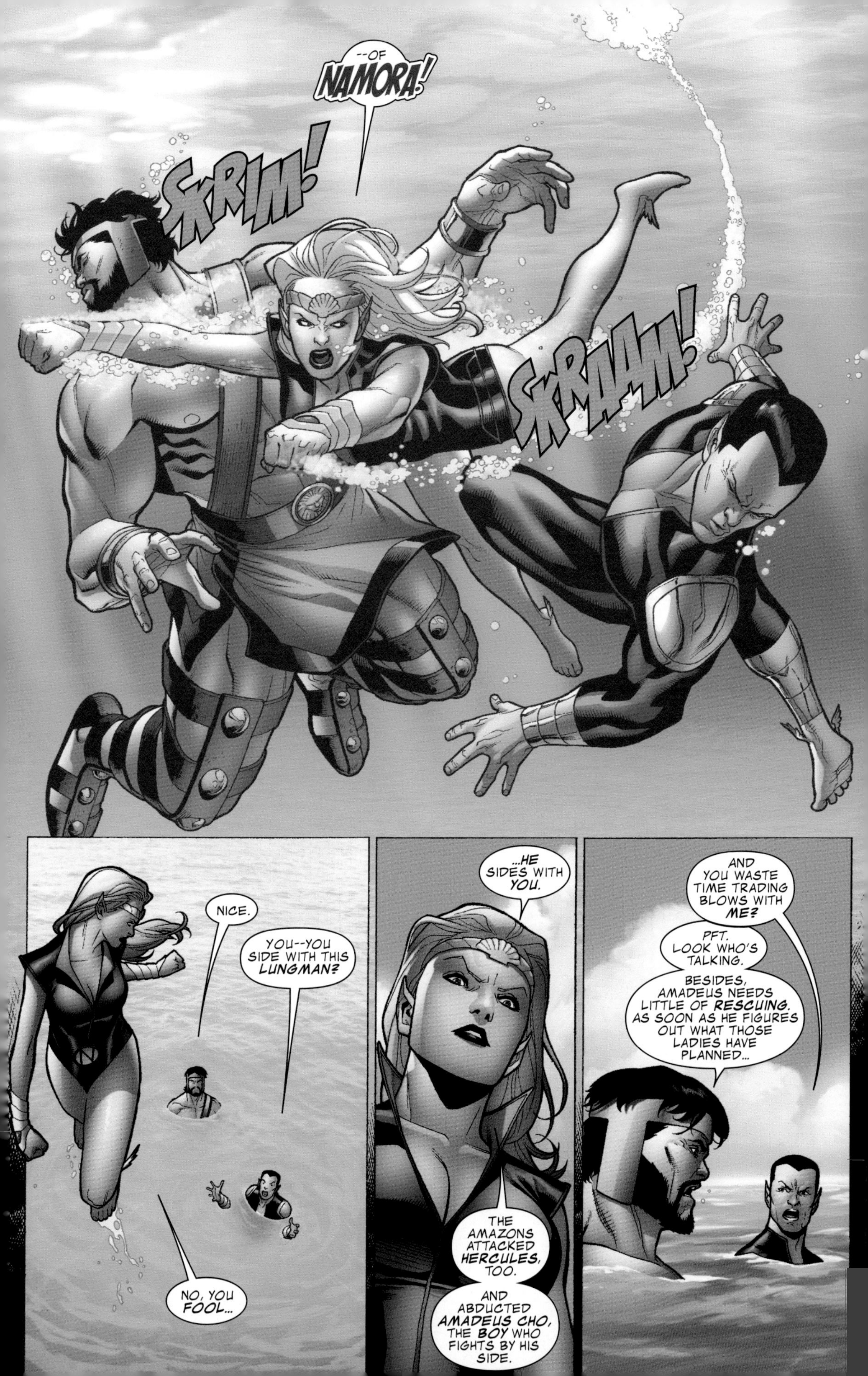
--OF NAMORA!
SKRIM!
SKRAAM!
NICE.
YOU--YOU SIDE WITH THIS LUNGMAN?
NO, YOU FOOL...
...HE SIDES WITH YOU.
THE AMAZONS ATTACKED HERCULES, TOO.
AND ABDUCTED AMADEUS CHO, THE BOY WHO FIGHTS BY HIS SIDE.
AND YOU WASTE TIME TRADING BLOWS WITH ME?
PFT. LOOK WHO'S TALKING.
BESIDES, AMADEUS NEEDS LITTLE OF RESCUING. AS SOON AS HE FIGURES OUT WHAT THOSE LADIES HAVE PLANNED...

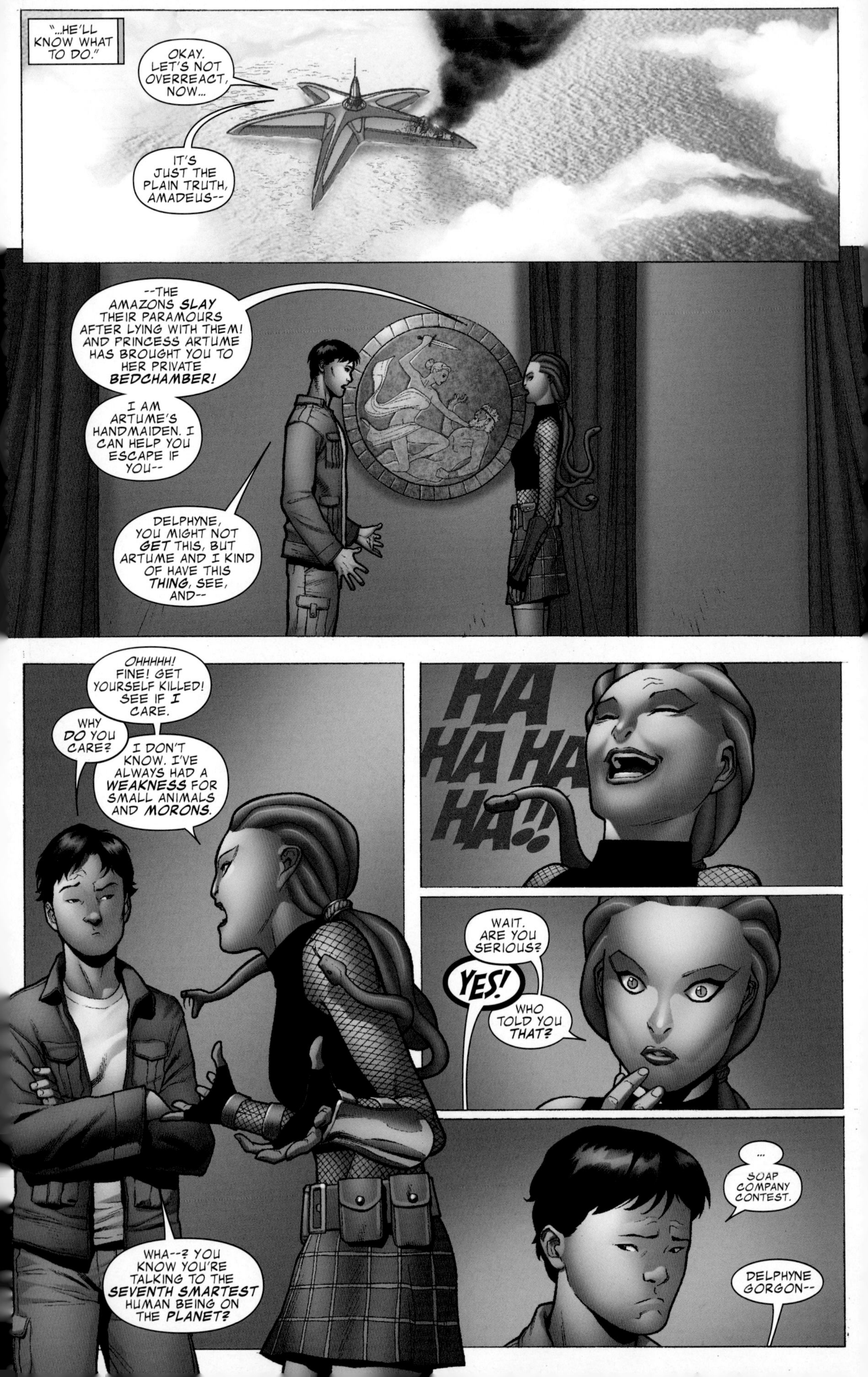
"...HE'LL KNOW WHAT TO DO."
OKAY. LET'S NOT OVERREACT, NOW...
IT'S JUST THE PLAIN TRUTH, AMADEUS--
--THE AMAZONS SLAY THEIR PARAMOURS AFTER LYING WITH THEM! AND PRINCESS ARTUME HAS BROUGHT YOU TO HER PRIVATE BEDCHAMBER!
I AM ARTUME'S HANDMAIDEN. I CAN HELP YOU ESCAPE IF YOU--
DELPHYNE, YOU MIGHT NOT GET THIS, BUT ARTUME AND I KIND OF HAVE THIS THING, SEE, AND--
OHHHHH! FINE! GET YOURSELF KILLED! SEE IF I CARE.
WHY DO YOU CARE?
I DON'T KNOW. I'VE ALWAYS HAD A WEAKNESS FOR SMALL ANIMALS AND MORONS.
WHA--? YOU KNOW YOU'RE TALKING TO THE SEVENTH SMARTEST HUMAN BEING ON THE PLANET?
HA HA HA HA HA!!
WAIT. ARE YOU SERIOUS?
YES!
WHO TOLD YOU THAT?
... SOAP COMPANY CONTEST.
DELPHYNE GORGON--

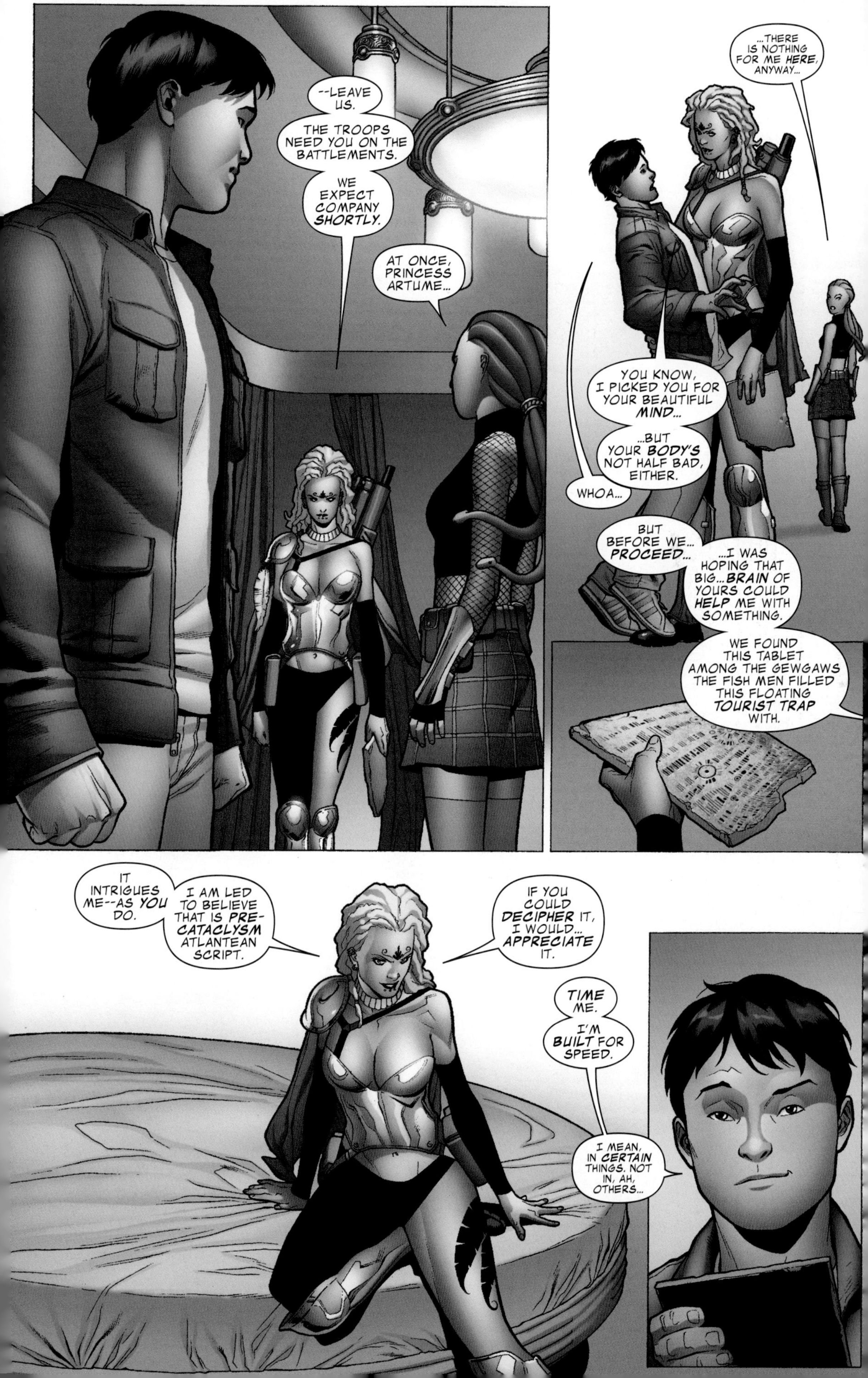
--LEAVE US.
THE TROOPS NEED YOU ON THE BATTLEMENTS.
WE EXPECT COMPANY SHORTLY.
AT ONCE, PRINCESS ARTUME...
...THERE IS NOTHING FOR ME HERE, ANYWAY...
YOU KNOW, I PICKED YOU FOR YOUR BEAUTIFUL MIND...
...BUT YOUR BODY'S NOT HALF BAD, EITHER.
WHOA...
BUT BEFORE WE... PROCEED...
...I WAS HOPING THAT BIG...BRAIN OF YOURS COULD HELP ME WITH SOMETHING.
WE FOUND THIS TABLET AMONG THE GEWGAWS THE FISH MEN FILLED THIS FLOATING TOURIST TRAP WITH.
IT INTRIGUES ME--AS YOU DO.
I AM LED TO BELIEVE THAT IS PRE-CATACLYSM ATLANTEAN SCRIPT.
IF YOU COULD DECIPHER IT, I WOULD... APPRECIATE IT.
TIME ME.
I'M BUILT FOR SPEED.
I MEAN, IN CERTAIN THINGS. NOT IN, AH, OTHERS...

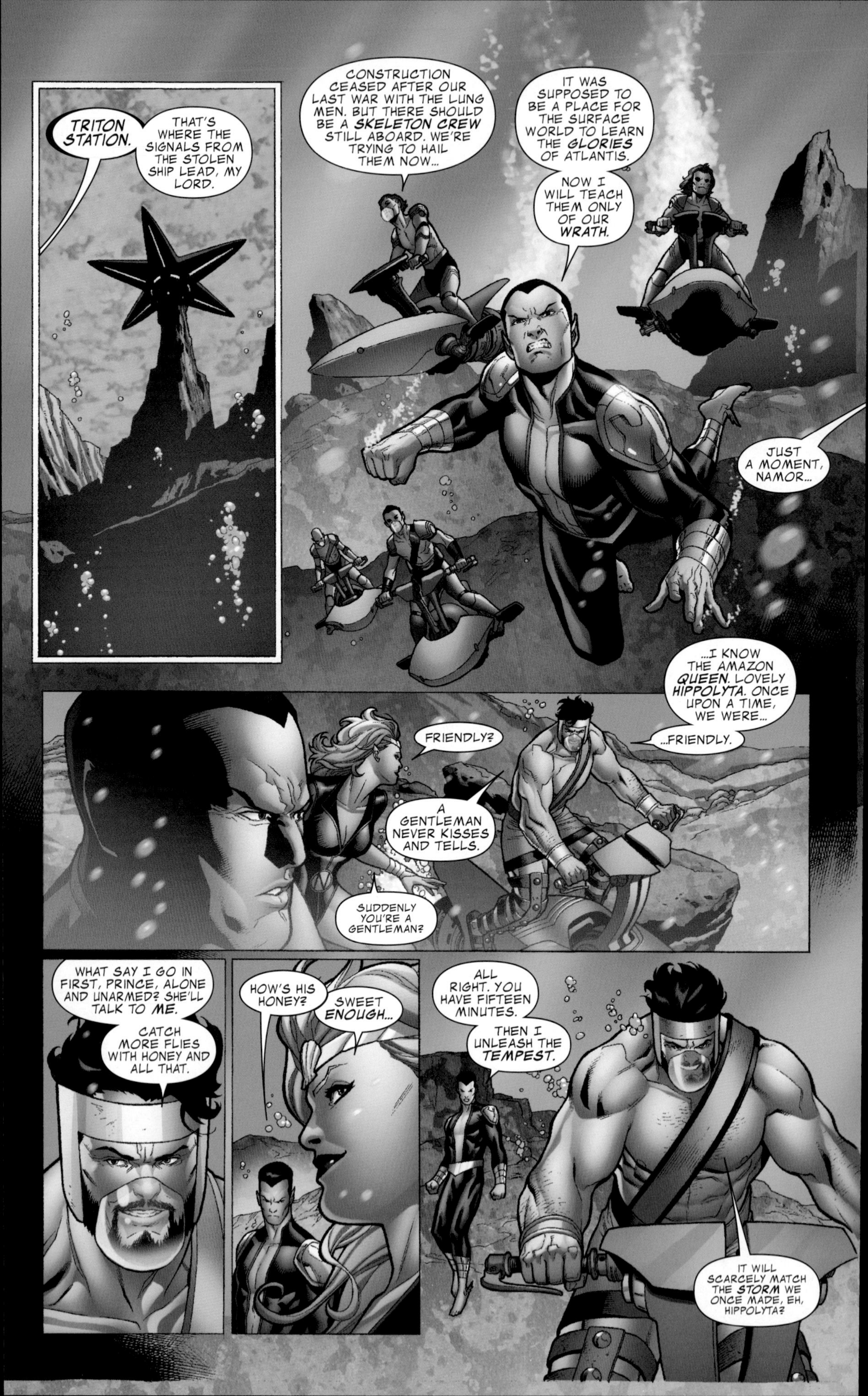
TRITON STATION.
THAT'S WHERE THE SIGNALS FROM THE STOLEN SHIP LEAD, MY LORD.
CONSTRUCTION CEASED AFTER OUR LAST WAR WITH THE LUNG MEN. BUT THERE SHOULD BE A SKELETON CREW STILL ABOARD. WE'RE TRYING TO HAIL THEM NOW...
IT WAS SUPPOSED TO BE A PLACE FOR THE SURFACE WORLD TO LEARN THE GLORIES OF ATLANTIS.
NOW I WILL TEACH THEM ONLY OF OUR WRATH.
JUST A MOMENT, NAMOR...
...I KNOW THE AMAZON QUEEN. LOVELY HIPPOLYTA. ONCE UPON A TIME, WE WERE...
...FRIENDLY.
FRIENDLY?
A GENTLEMAN NEVER KISSES AND TELLS.
SUDDENLY YOU'RE A GENTLEMAN?
WHAT SAY I GO IN FIRST, PRINCE, ALONE AND UNARMED? SHE'LL TALK TO ME.
CATCH MORE FLIES WITH HONEY AND ALL THAT.
HOW'S HIS HONEY?
SWEET ENOUGH...
ALL RIGHT. YOU HAVE FIFTEEN MINUTES.
THEN I UNLEASH THE TEMPEST.
IT WILL SCARCELY MATCH THE STORM WE ONCE MADE, EH, HIPPOLYTA?

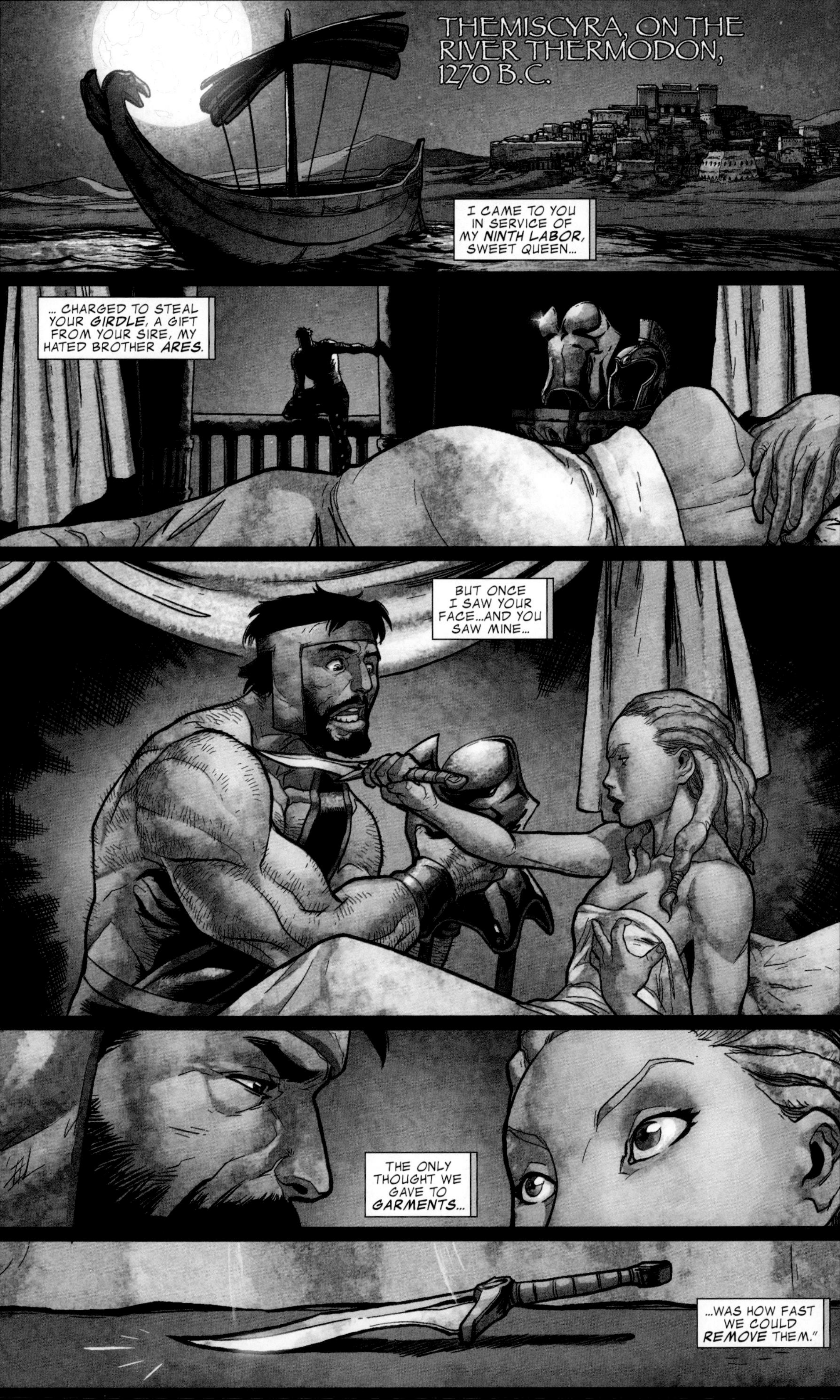

THEMISCYRA, ON THE RIVER THERMODON, 1270 B.C.
I CAME TO YOU IN SERVICE OF MY NINTH LABOR, SWEET QUEEN...
... CHARGED TO STEAL YOUR GIRDLE, A GIFT FROM YOUR SIRE, MY HATED BROTHER ARES.
BUT ONCE I SAW YOUR FACE...AND YOU SAW MINE...
THE ONLY THOUGHT WE GAVE TO GARMENTS...
...WAS HOW FAST WE COULD REMOVE THEM."

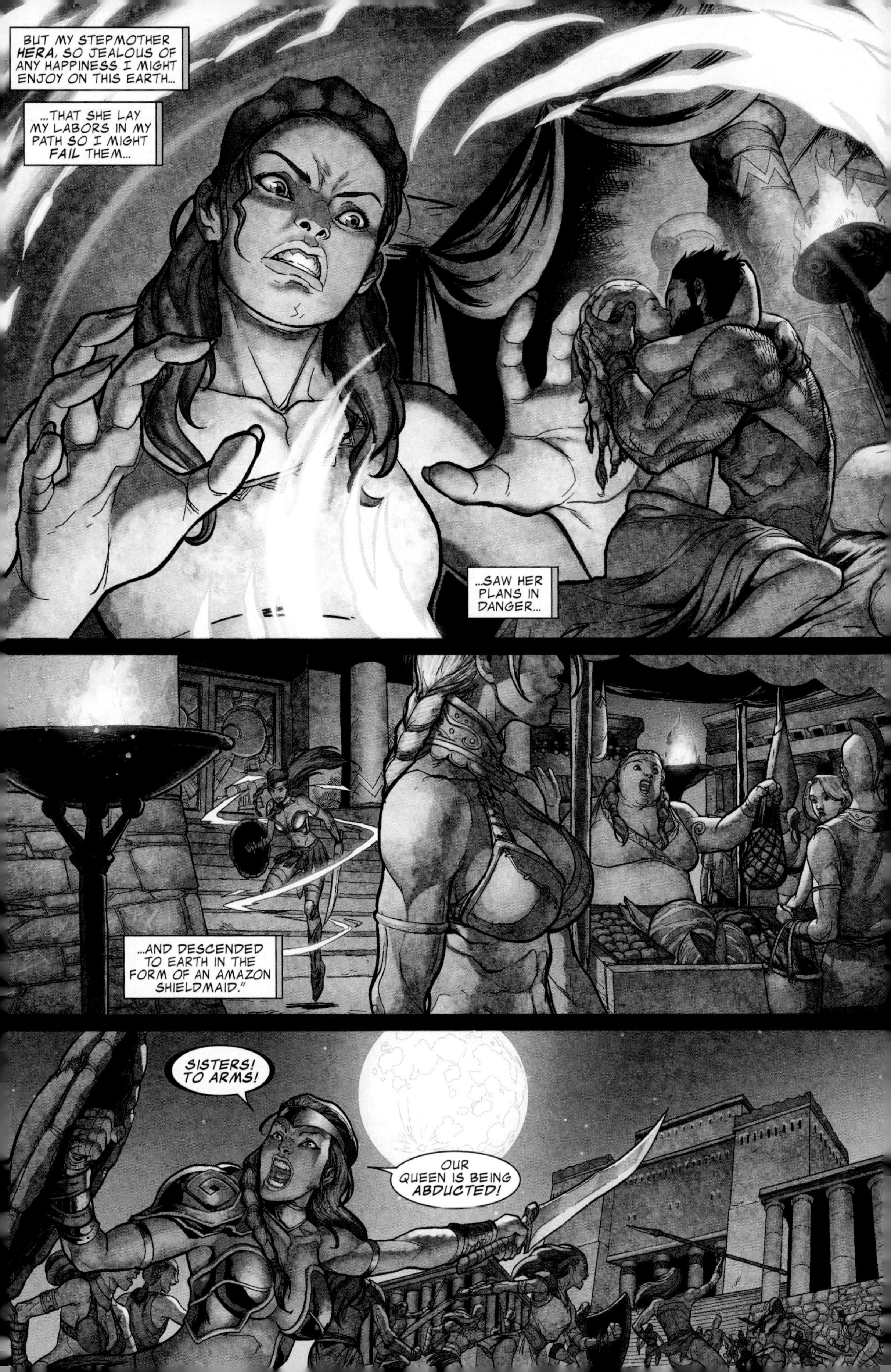
BUT MY STEPMOTHER HERA, SO JEALOUS OF ANY HAPPINESS I MIGHT ENJOY ON THIS EARTH...
...THAT SHE LAY MY LABORS IN MY PATH SO I MIGHT FAIL THEM...
...SAW HER PLANS IN DANGER...
...AND DESCENDED TO EARTH IN THE FORM OF AN AMAZON SHIELDMAID."
SISTERS! TO ARMS!
OUR QUEEN IS BEING ABDUCTED!

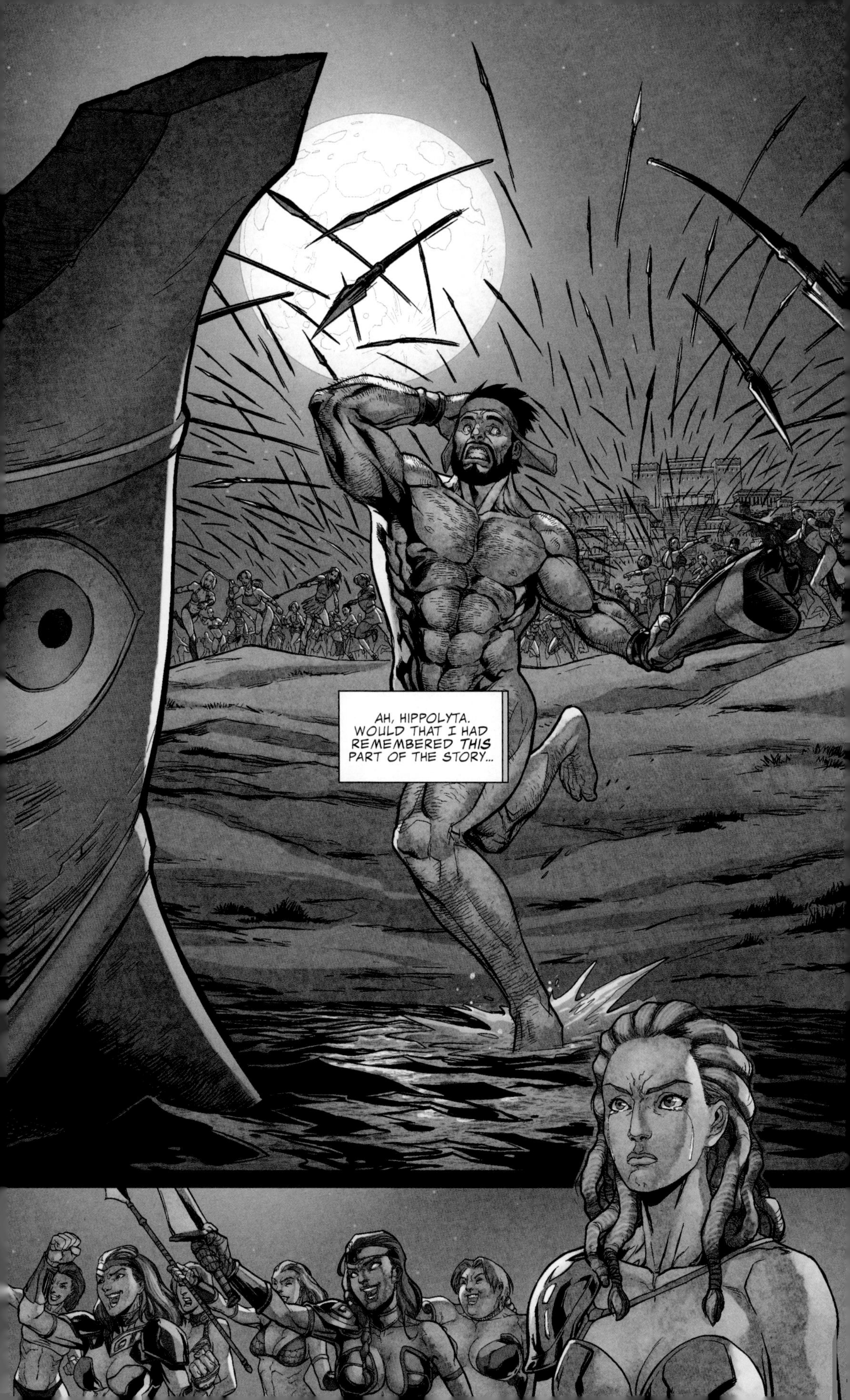
AH, HIPPOLYTA. WOULD THAT I HAD REMEMBERED THIS PART OF THE STORY...

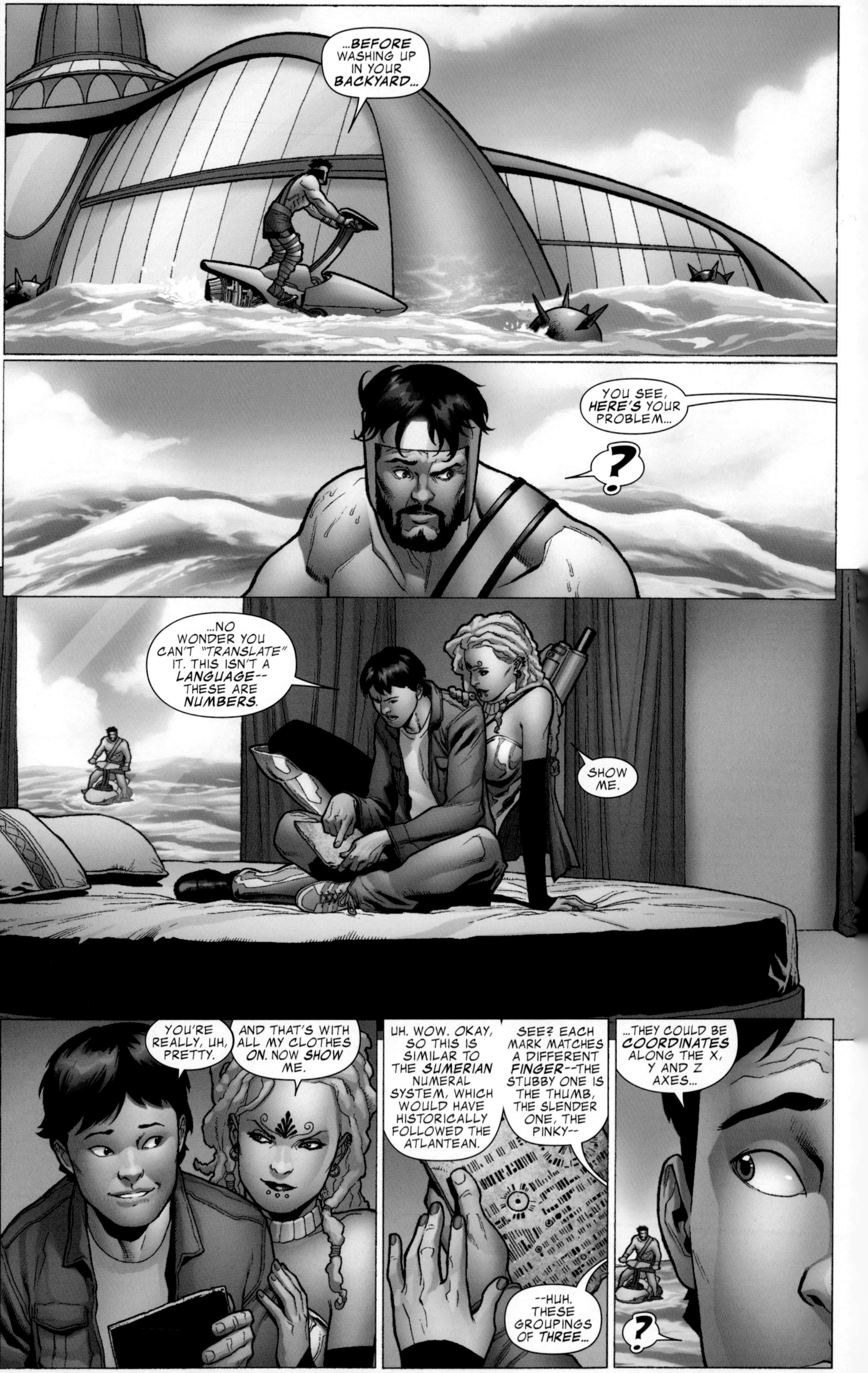
...BEFORE WASHING UP IN YOUR BACKYARD...
YOU SEE, HERE'S YOUR PROBLEM...
?
...NO WONDER YOU CAN'T "TRANSLATE" IT. THIS ISN'T A LANGUAGE-- THESE ARE NUMBERS.
SHOW ME.
YOU'RE REALLY, UH, PRETTY.
AND THAT'S WITH ALL MY CLOTHES ON. NOW SHOW ME.
UH. WOW. OKAY, SO THIS IS SIMILAR TO THE SUMERIAN NUMERAL SYSTEM, WHICH WOULD HAVE HISTORICALLY FOLLOWED THE ATLANTEAN.
SEE? EACH MARK MATCHES A DIFFERENT FINGER--THE STUBBY ONE IS THE THUMB, THE SLENDER ONE, THE PINKY--
--HUH. THESE GROUPINGS OF THREE...
...THEY COULD BE COORDINATES ALONG THE X, Y AND Z AXES...
?

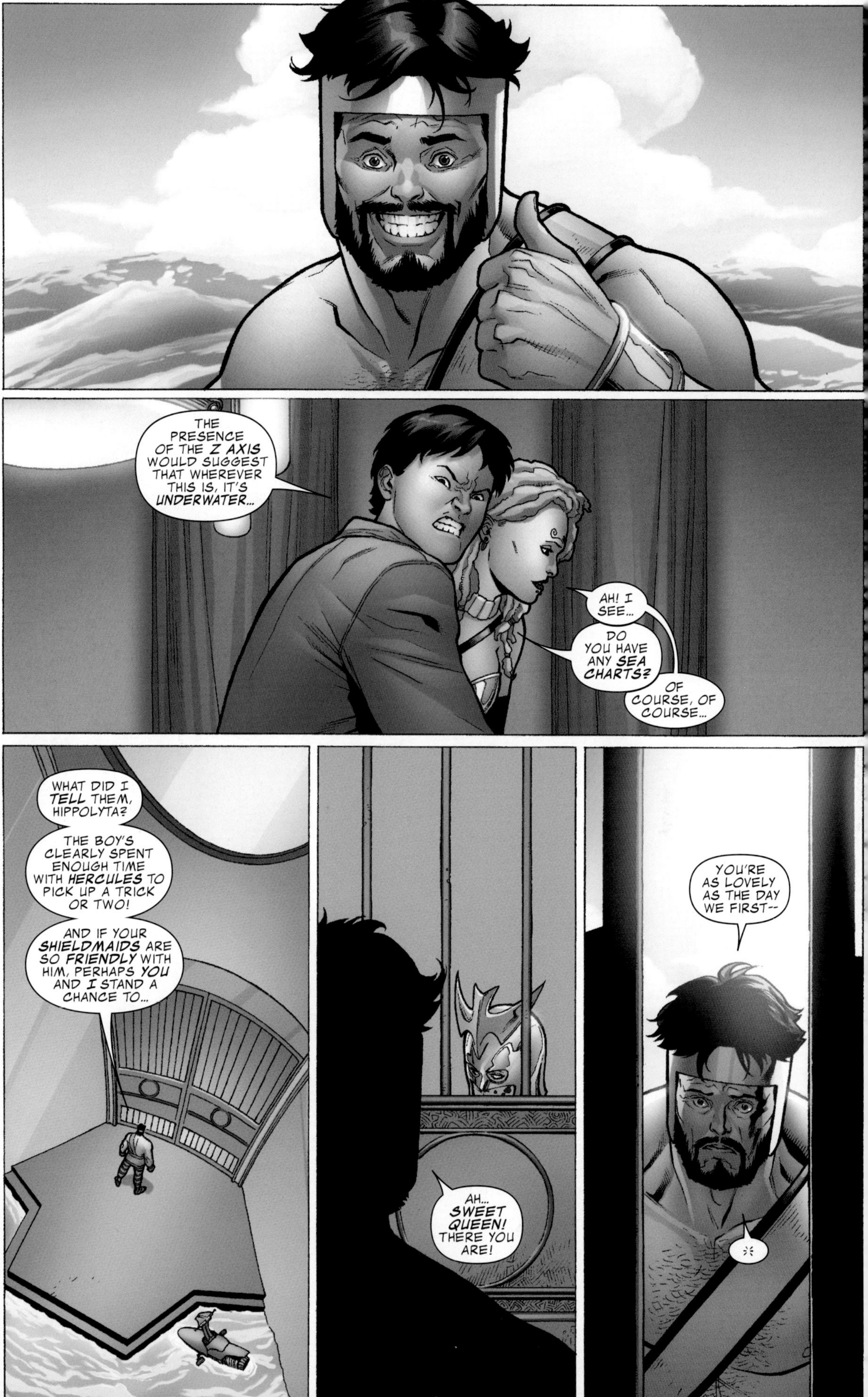
THE PRESENCE OF THE Z AXIS WOULD SUGGEST THAT WHEREVER THIS IS, IT'S UNDERWATER...
AH! I SEE...
DO YOU HAVE ANY SEA CHARTS?
OF COURSE, OF COURSE...
WHAT DID I TELL THEM, HIPPOLYTA?
THE BOY'S CLEARLY SPENT ENOUGH TIME WITH HERCULES TO PICK UP A TRICK OR TWO!
AND IF YOUR SHIELDMAIDS ARE SO FRIENDLY WITH HIM, PERHAPS YOU AND I STAND A CHANCE TO...
AH... SWEET QUEEN! THERE YOU ARE!
YOU'RE AS LOVELY AS THE DAY WE FIRST--

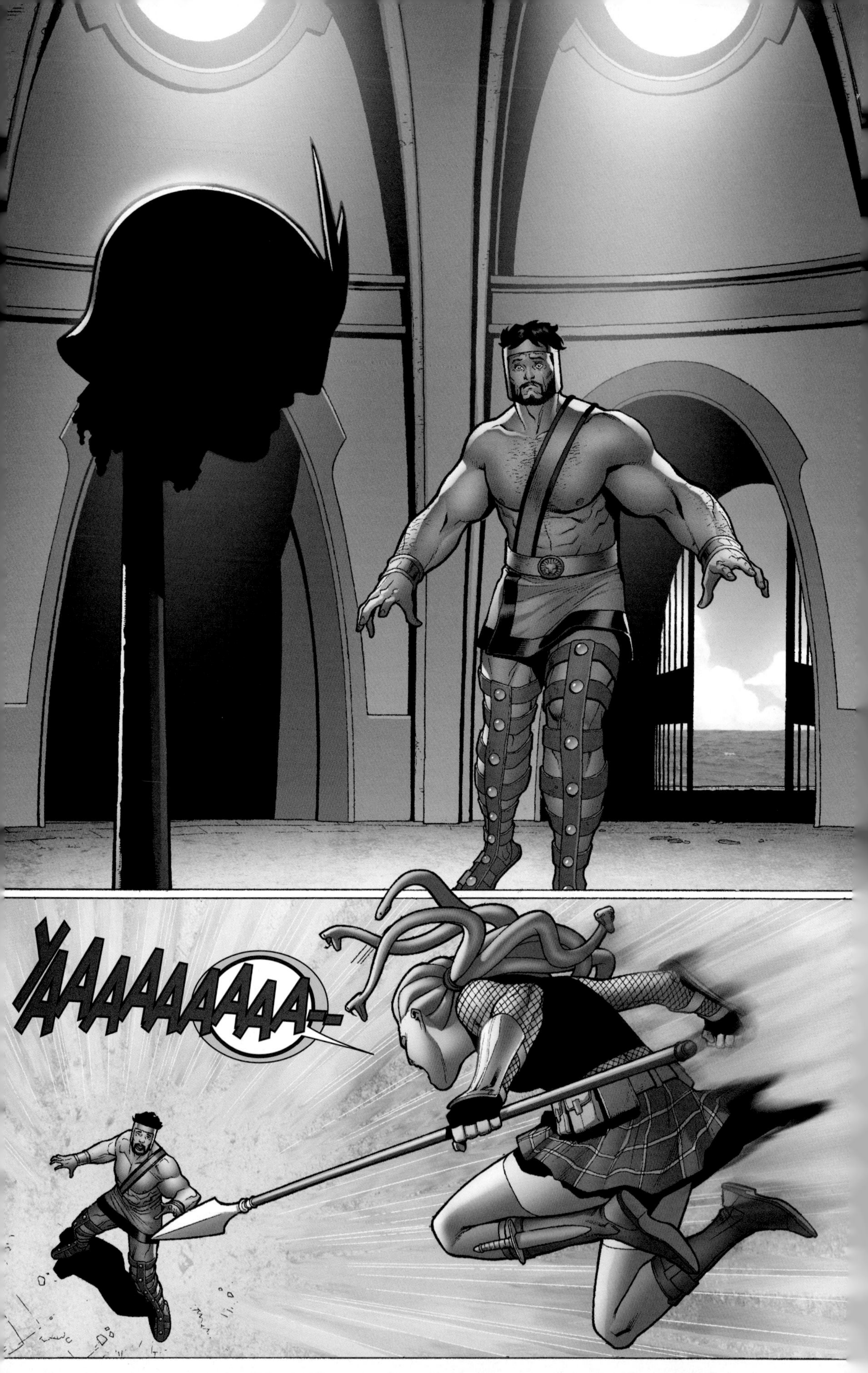
YAAAAAAAAA--

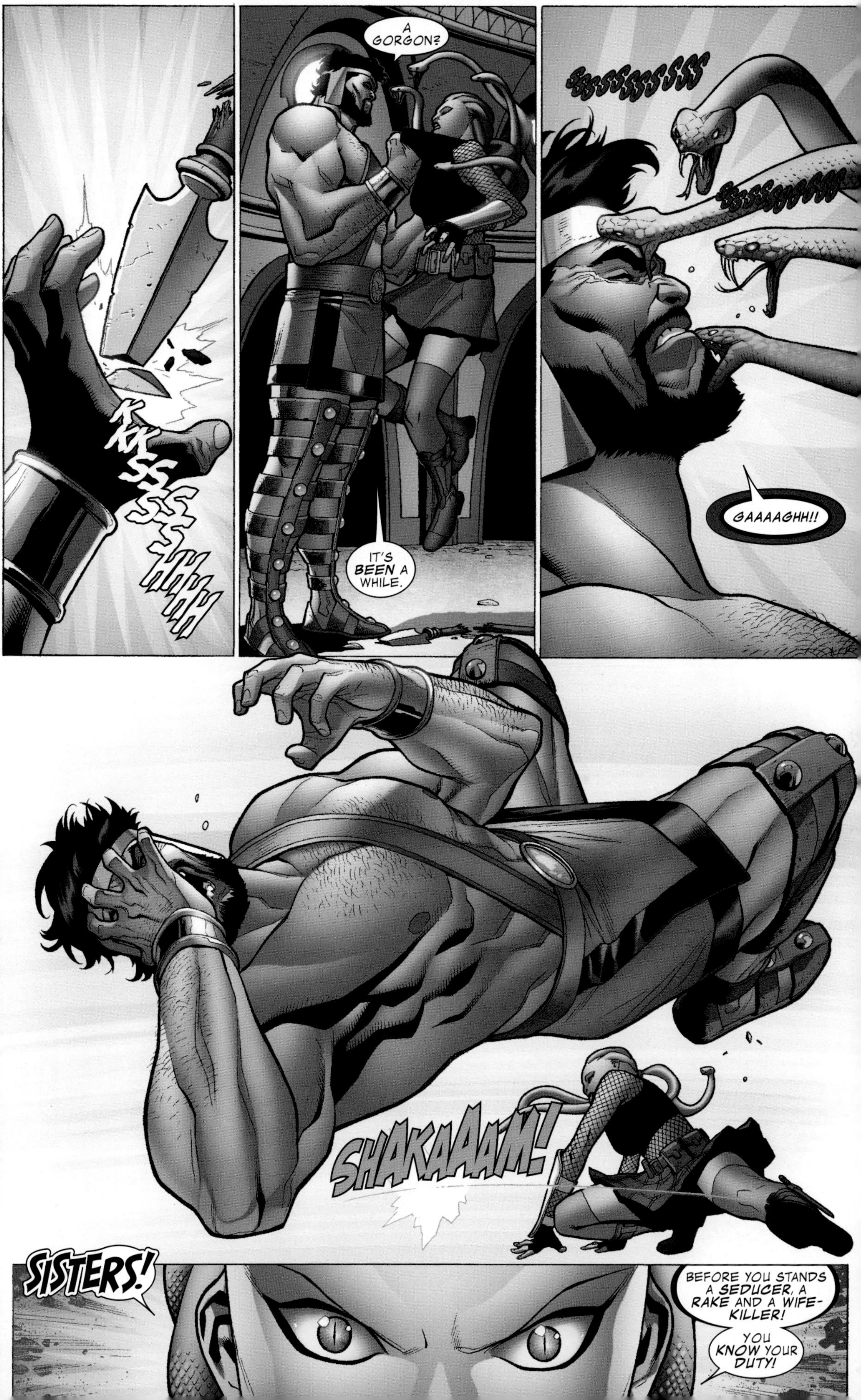
KKSSSSHHHH
A GORGON?
IT'S BEEN A WHILE.
SSSSSSSSSSSS
SSSSSSSSSSSS
GAAAAGHH!!
SHAKAAAM!
SISTERS!
BEFORE YOU STANDS A SEDUCER, A RAKE AND A WIFE-KILLER!
YOU KNOW YOUR DUTY!

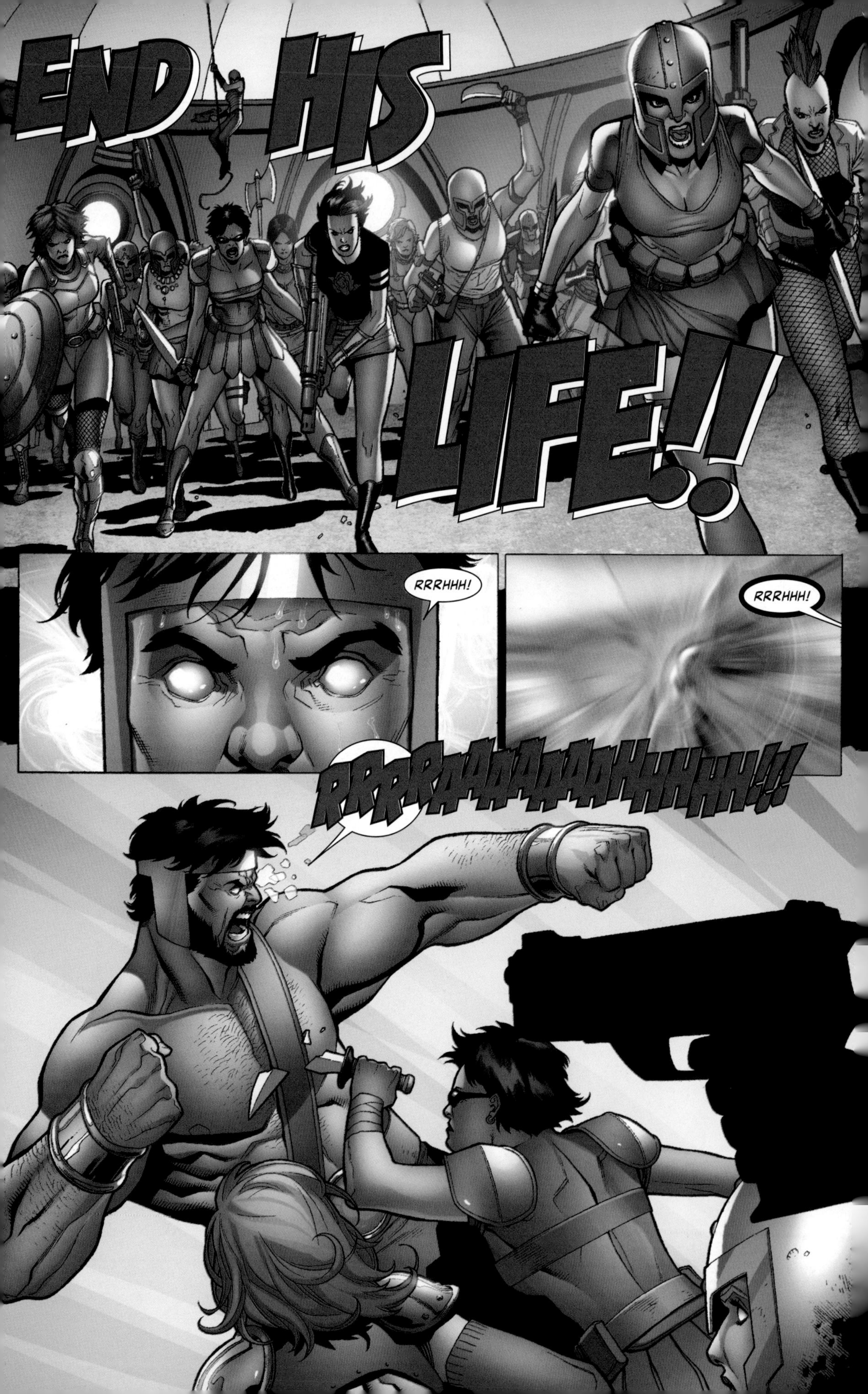
END HIS
LIFE!!
RRRHHH!
RRRHHH!
RRRRAAAAAAAAHHHHH!!!

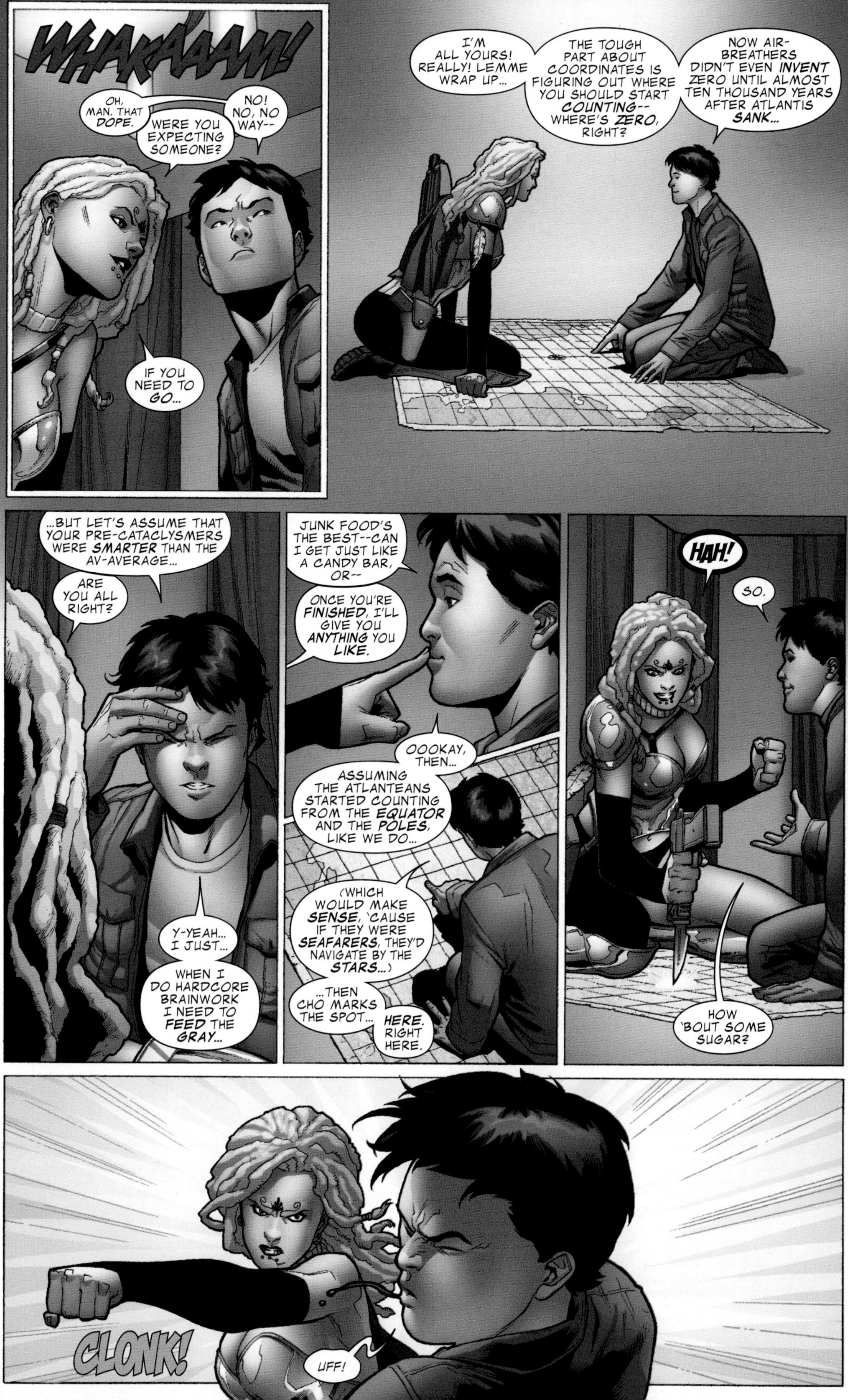
WHAKAAAM!
OH, MAN. THAT DOPE.
NO! NO, NO WAY--
WERE YOU EXPECTING SOMEONE?
IF YOU NEED TO GO...
I'M ALL YOURS! REALLY! LEMME WRAP UP...
THE TOUGH PART ABOUT COORDINATES IS FIGURING OUT WHERE YOU SHOULD START COUNTING-- WHERE'S ZERO, RIGHT?
NOW AIR-BREATHERS DIDN'T EVEN INVENT ZERO UNTIL ALMOST TEN THOUSAND YEARS AFTER ATLANTIS SANK...
...BUT LET'S ASSUME THAT YOUR PRE-CATACLYSMERS WERE SMARTER THAN THE AV-AVERAGE...
ARE YOU ALL RIGHT?
Y-YEAH... I JUST...
WHEN I DO HARDCORE BRAINWORK I NEED TO FEED THE GRAY...
JUNK FOOD'S THE BEST--CAN I GET JUST LIKE A CANDY BAR, OR--
ONCE YOU'RE FINISHED, I'LL GIVE YOU ANYTHING YOU LIKE.
OOOKAY, THEN...
ASSUMING THE ATLANTEANS STARTED COUNTING FROM THE EQUATOR AND THE POLES, LIKE WE DO...
(WHICH WOULD MAKE SENSE, 'CAUSE IF THEY WERE SEAFARERS, THEY'D NAVIGATE BY THE STARS...)
...THEN CHO MARKS THE SPOT...
HERE. RIGHT HERE.
HAH!
SO.
HOW 'BOUT SOME SUGAR?
CLONK!
UFF!

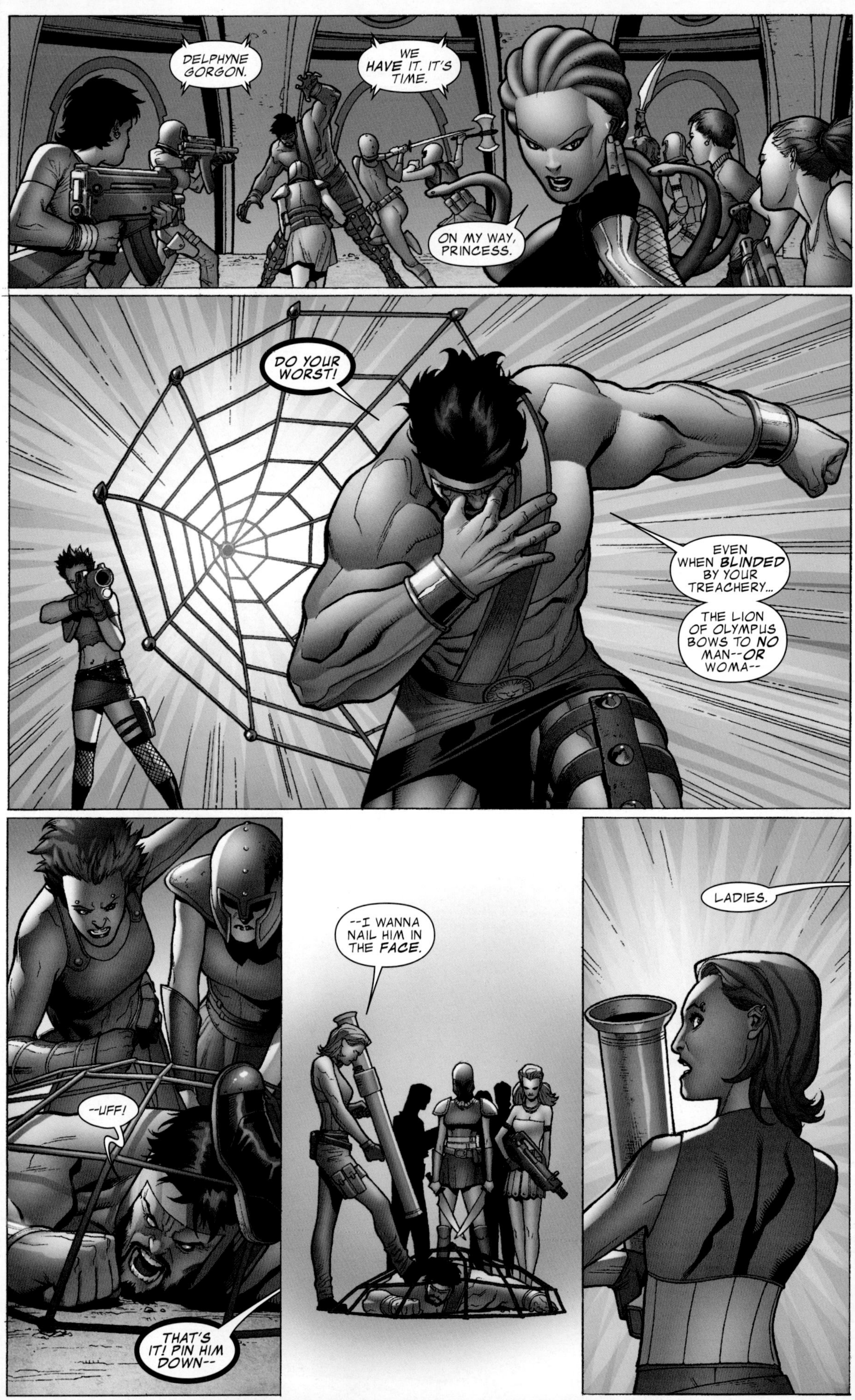
DELPHYNE GORGON.
WE HAVE IT. IT'S TIME.
ON MY WAY, PRINCESS.
DO YOUR WORST!
EVEN WHEN BLINDED BY YOUR TREACHERY...
THE LION OF OLYMPUS BOWS TO NO MAN--OR WOMA--
--UFF!
THAT'S IT! PIN HIM DOWN--
--I WANNA NAIL HIM IN THE FACE.
LADIES.

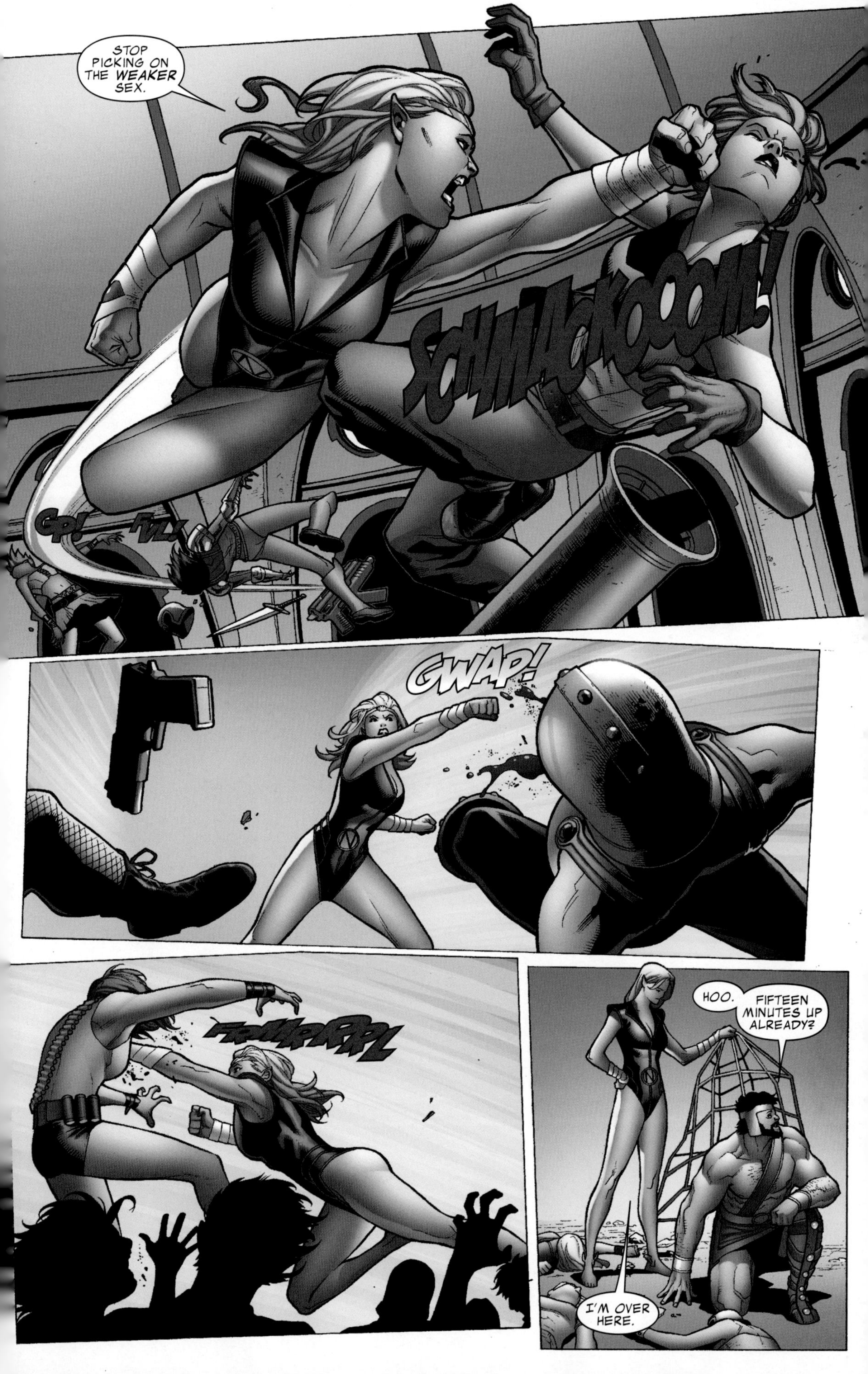
STOP PICKING ON THE WEAKER SEX.
SCHMACKOOOM!
GP!
FVL!
GWAP!
FRMMRRRL
HOO.
FIFTEEN MINUTES UP ALREADY?
I'M OVER HERE.

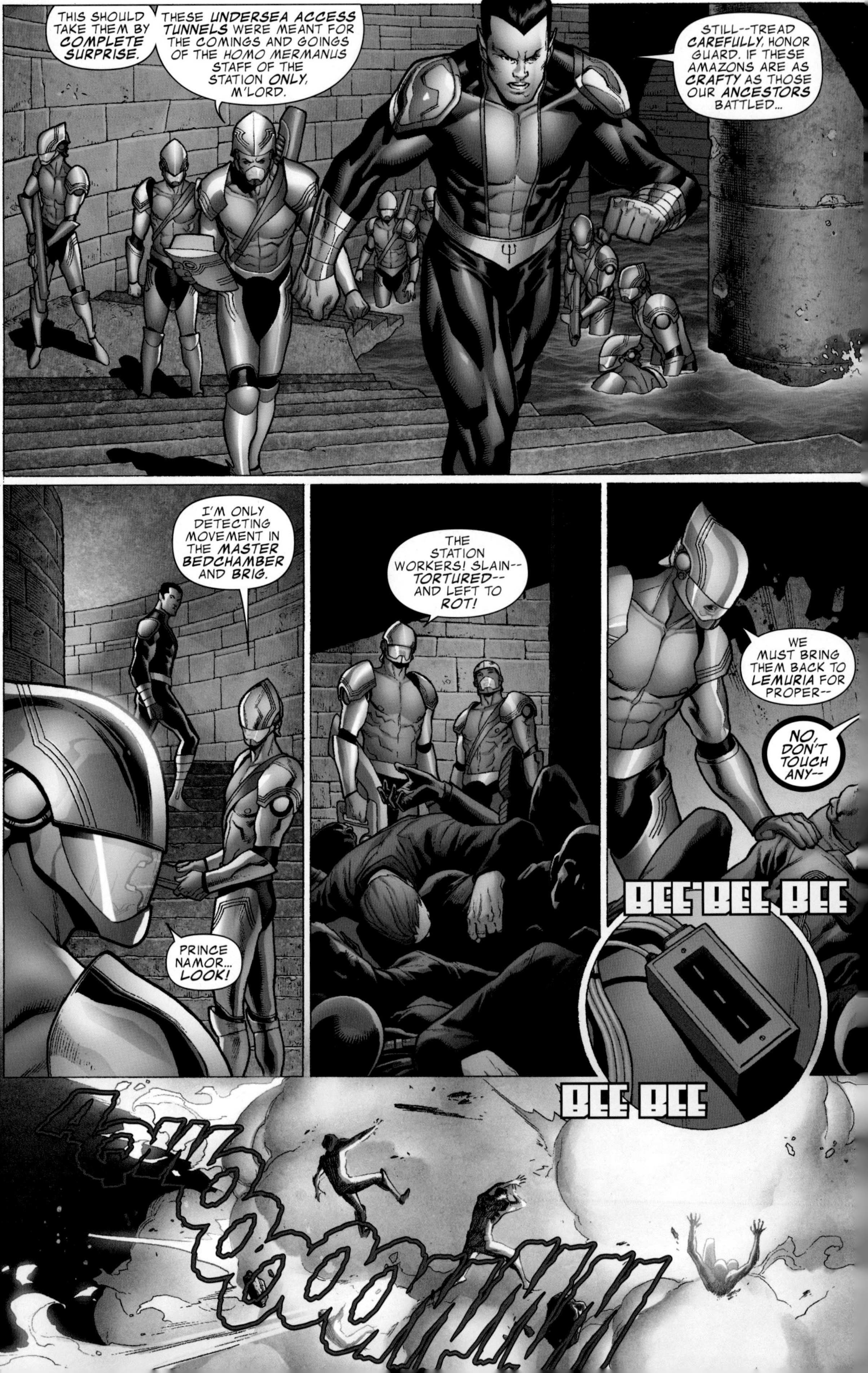

THIS SHOULD TAKE THEM BY COMPLETE SURPRISE.
THESE UNDERSEA ACCESS TUNNELS WERE MEANT FOR THE COMINGS AND GOINGS OF THE HOMO MERMANUS STAFF OF THE STATION ONLY, M'LORD.
STILL--TREAD CAREFULLY, HONOR GUARD. IF THESE AMAZONS ARE AS CRAFTY AS THOSE OUR ANCESTORS BATTLED...
I'M ONLY DETECTING MOVEMENT IN THE MASTER BEDCHAMBER AND BRIG.
PRINCE NAMOR... LOOK!
THE STATION WORKERS! SLAIN--TORTURED--AND LEFT TO ROT!
WE MUST BRING THEM BACK TO LEMURIA FOR PROPER--
NO, DON'T TOUCH ANY--
BEE BEE BEE
BEE BEE

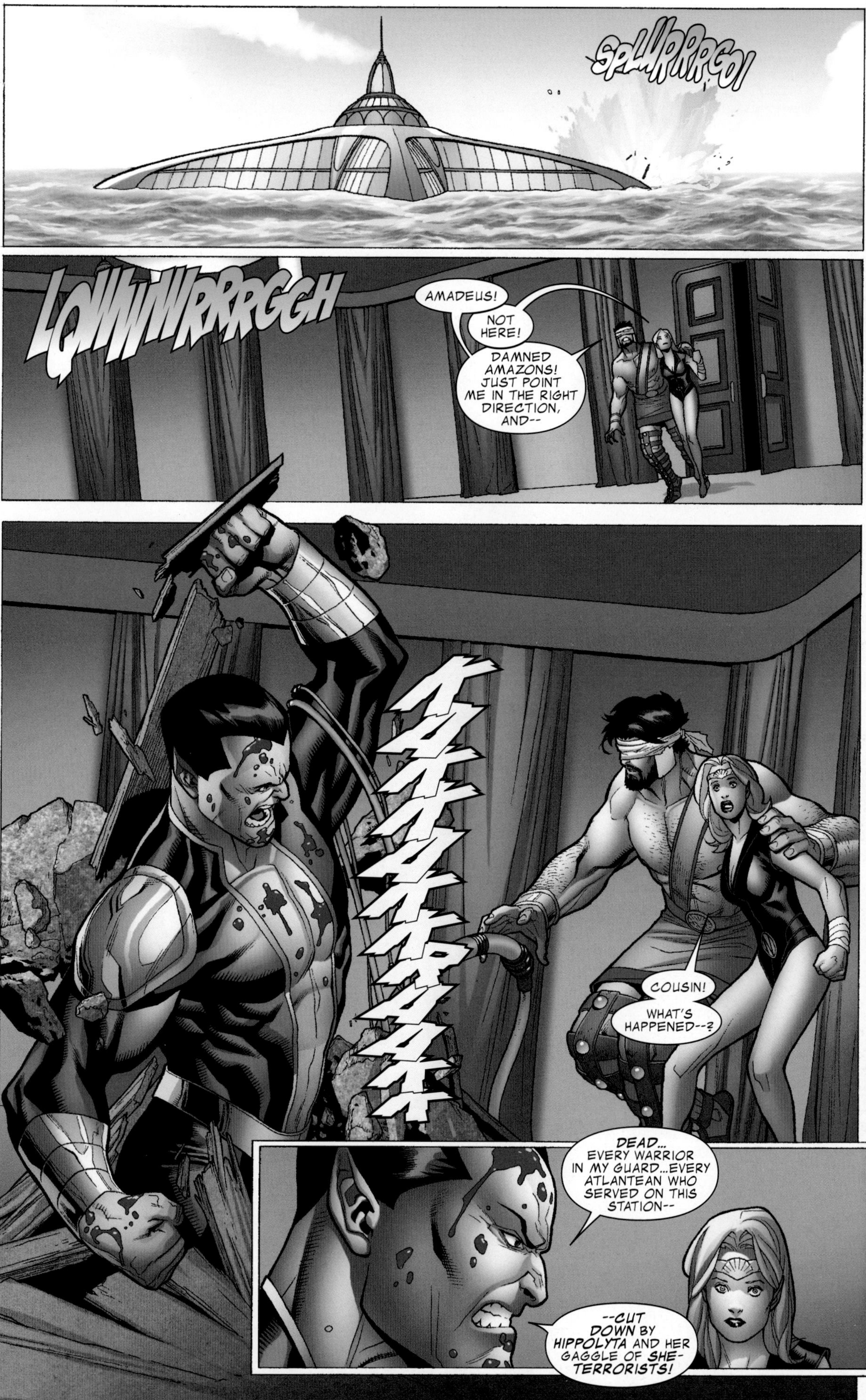
SPLUURRRGOI
LQWWWRRRGGH
AMADEUS!
NOT HERE!
DAMNED AMAZONS! JUST POINT ME IN THE RIGHT DIRECTION, AND--
COUSIN!
WHAT'S HAPPENED--?
DEAD... EVERY WARRIOR IN MY GUARD...EVERY ATLANTEAN WHO SERVED ON THIS STATION--
--CUT DOWN BY HIPPOLYTA AND HER GAGGLE OF SHE-TERRORISTS!

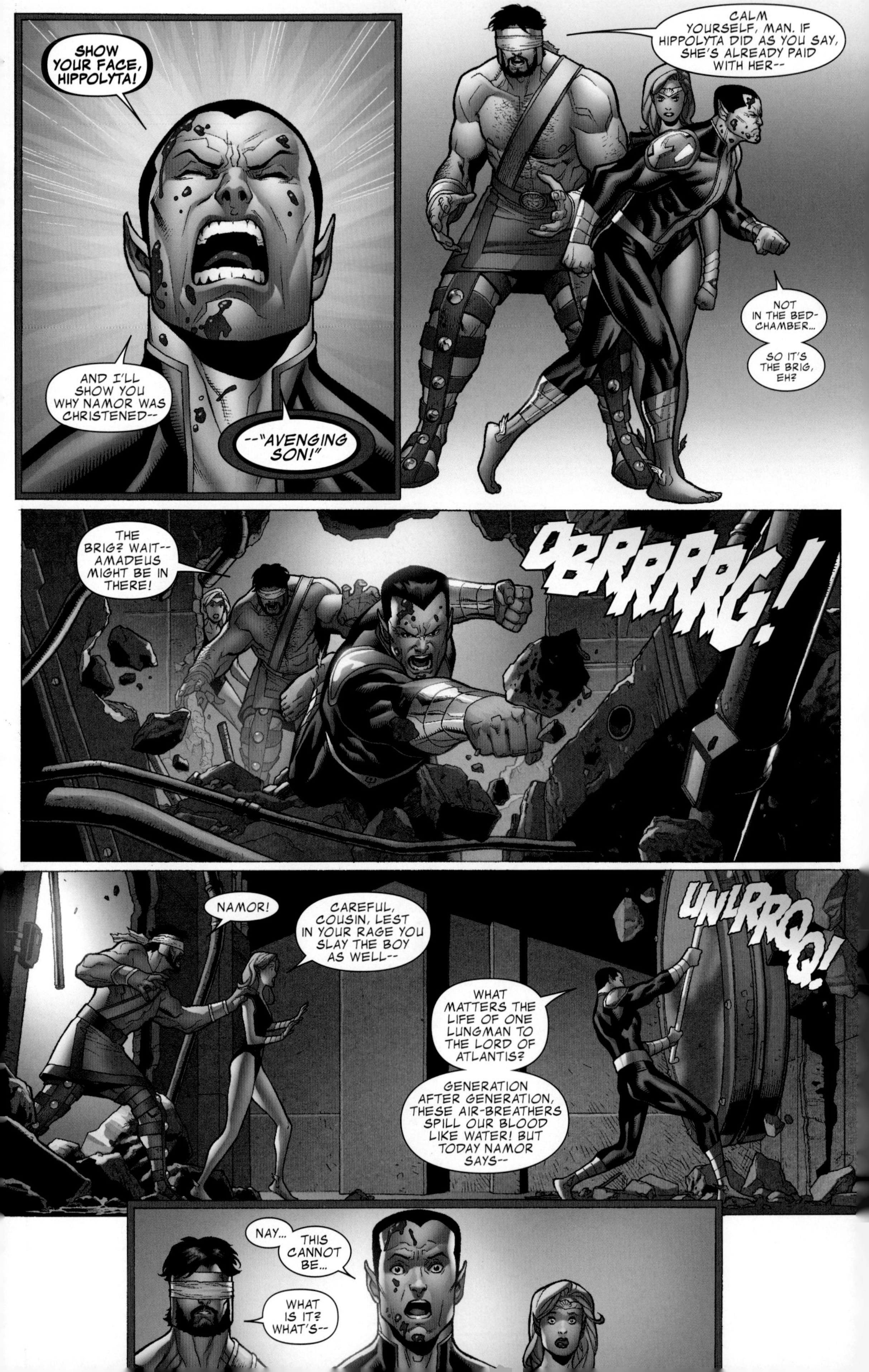
SHOW YOUR FACE, HIPPOLYTA!
AND I'LL SHOW YOU WHY NAMOR WAS CHRISTENED--
--"AVENGING SON!"
CALM YOURSELF, MAN. IF HIPPOLYTA DID AS YOU SAY, SHE'S ALREADY PAID WITH HER--
NOT IN THE BED-CHAMBER...
SO IT'S THE BRIG, EH?
THE BRIG? WAIT-- AMADEUS MIGHT BE IN THERE!
OBRRRRG!
NAMOR!
CAREFUL, COUSIN, LEST IN YOUR RAGE YOU SLAY THE BOY AS WELL--
UNLRROQ!
WHAT MATTERS THE LIFE OF ONE LUNGMAN TO THE LORD OF ATLANTIS?
GENERATION AFTER GENERATION, THESE AIR-BREATHERS SPILL OUR BLOOD LIKE WATER! BUT TODAY NAMOR SAYS--
NAY...
THIS CANNOT BE...
WHAT IS IT? WHAT'S--

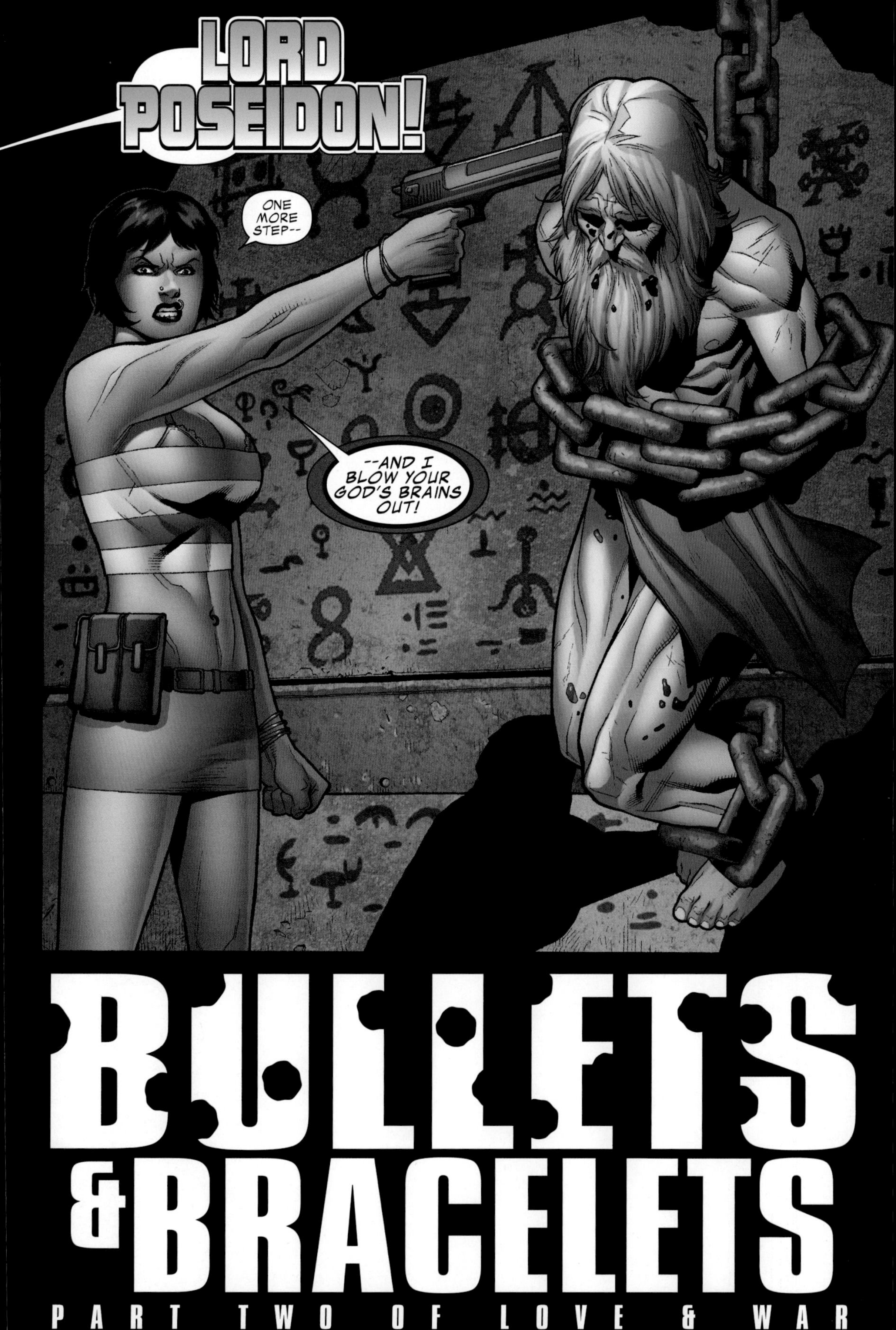
LORD POSEIDON!
ONE MORE STEP--
--AND I BLOW YOUR GOD'S BRAINS OUT!
BULLETS & BRACELETS
PART TWO OF LOVE & WAR

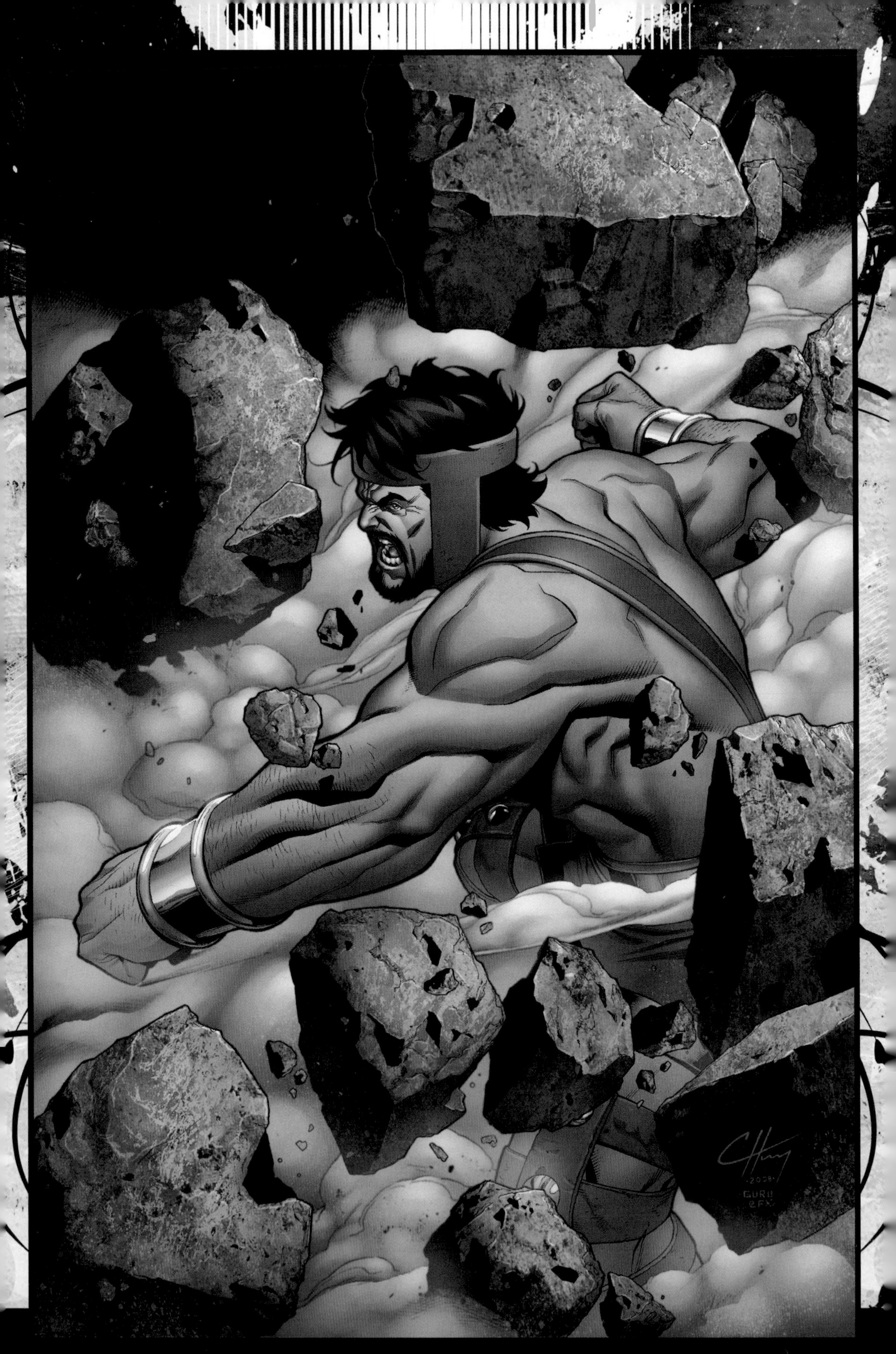

INCREDIBLE HERCULES #123

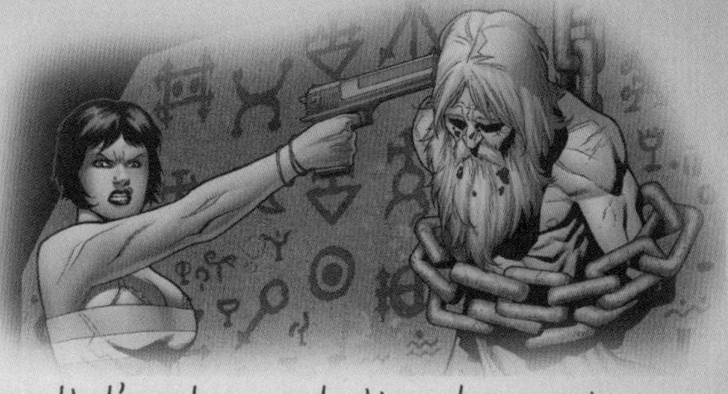

TO POSEIDON WITH LOVE

By ~~Anonymous,~~ Anonmadeus Cho

that's got a gun to his watery noggin...

I begin to sing about Poseidon, the great god,

mover of the earth and fruitless sea,

(I thought I'd be bearing some fruit, but the crazy-hot Amazons that wanted to breed with me...didn't actually want to breed with me)

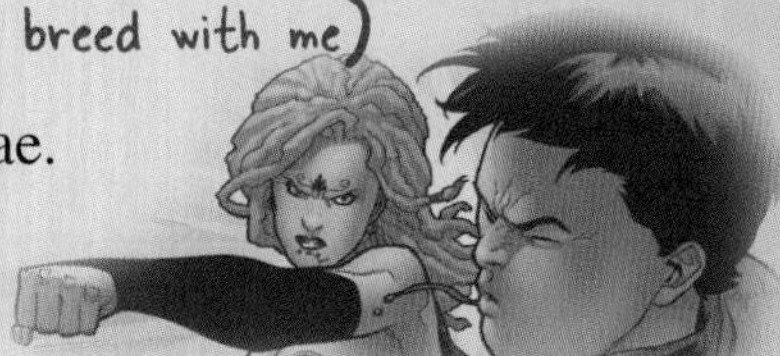

god of ~~the deep~~ Namor & Namora who is also lord of Helicon and wide Aegae.

A two-fold office the gods allotted you, O Shaker of Earth, to be a tamer of horses and ~~a saviour of ships~~!

Herc's uncle. Guess what? Herc can't see (which sucks when all you're fighting is Amazonian babeishness)

Hail, Poseidon, Holder of the Earth, ~~dark-haired~~ blue-skinned lord!

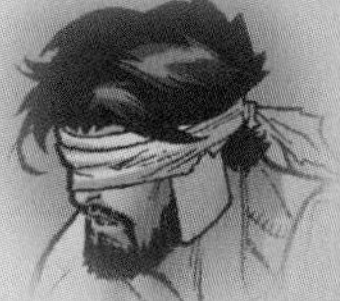

O blessed one, be kindly in heart and help those who voyage in ships!

and if you've got a second maybe save me from the psycho-femmes that won't give me any candy...

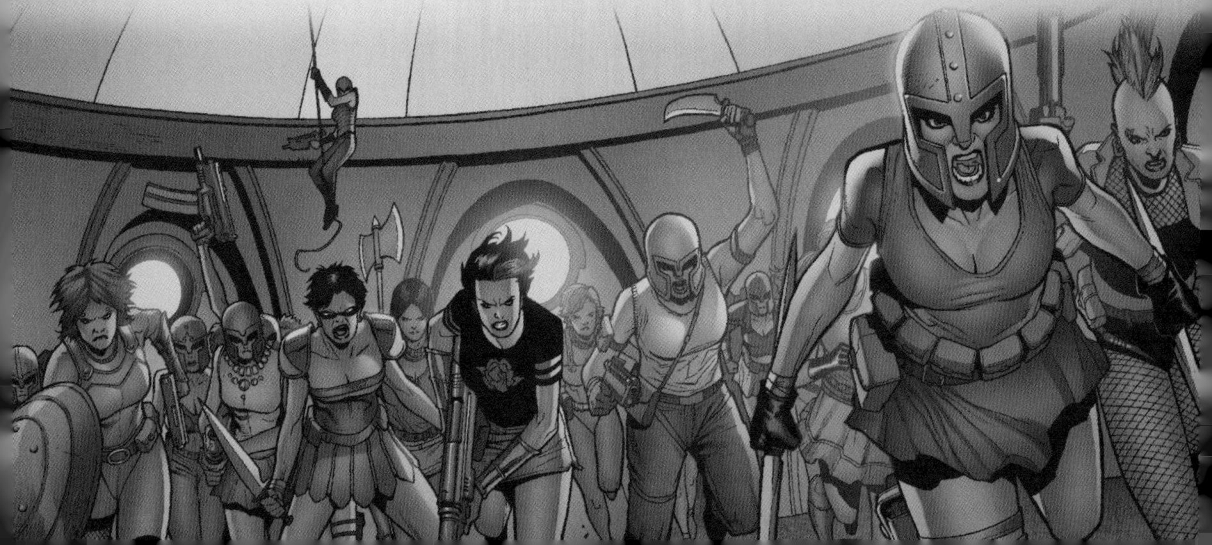

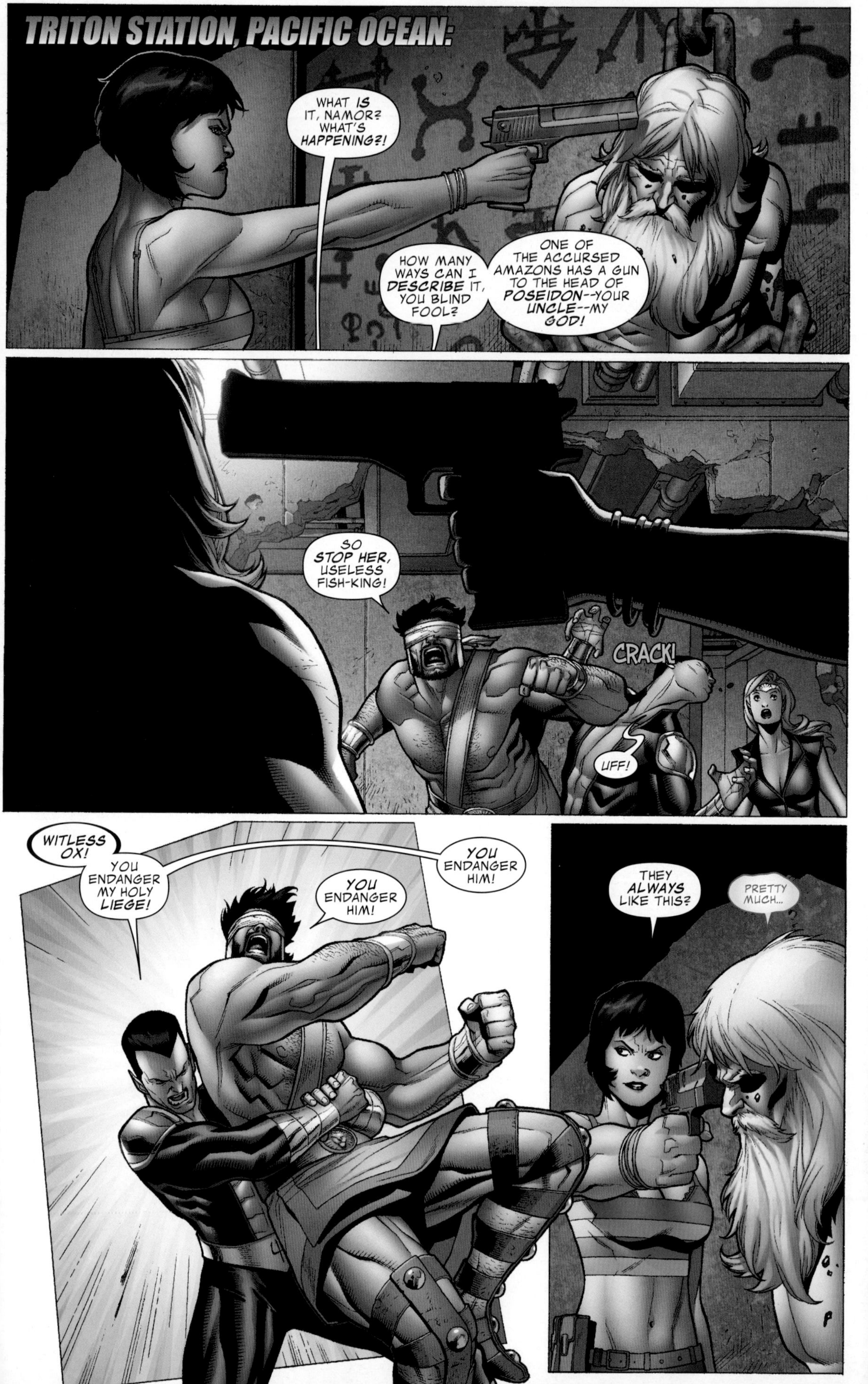
TRITON STATION, PACIFIC OCEAN:
WHAT IS IT, NAMOR? WHAT'S HAPPENING?!
HOW MANY WAYS CAN I DESCRIBE IT, YOU BLIND FOOL?
ONE OF THE ACCURSED AMAZONS HAS A GUN TO THE HEAD OF POSEIDON--YOUR UNCLE--MY GOD!
SO STOP HER, USELESS FISH-KING!
CRACK!
UFF!
WITLESS OX! YOU ENDANGER MY HOLY LIEGE!
YOU ENDANGER HIM!
YOU ENDANGER HIM!
THEY ALWAYS LIKE THIS?
PRETTY MUCH...

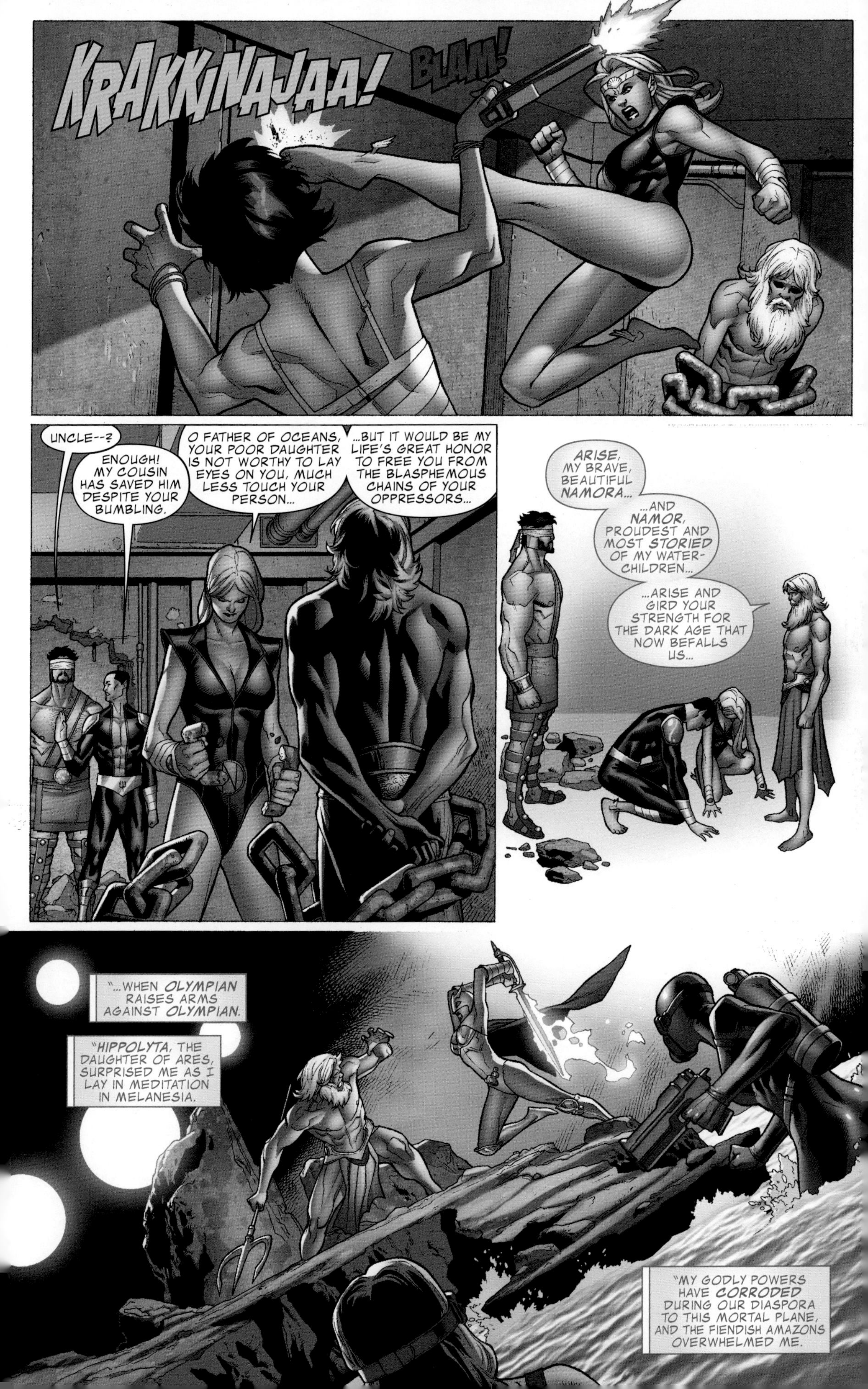
KRAKKNAJAA!
BLAM!
UNCLE--?
ENOUGH! MY COUSIN HAS SAVED HIM DESPITE YOUR BUMBLING.
O FATHER OF OCEANS, YOUR POOR DAUGHTER IS NOT WORTHY TO LAY EYES ON YOU, MUCH LESS TOUCH YOUR PERSON...
...BUT IT WOULD BE MY LIFE'S GREAT HONOR TO FREE YOU FROM THE BLASPHEMOUS CHAINS OF YOUR OPPRESSORS...
ARISE, MY BRAVE, BEAUTIFUL NAMORA...
...AND NAMOR, PROUDEST AND MOST STORIED OF MY WATER-CHILDREN...
...ARISE AND GIRD YOUR STRENGTH FOR THE DARK AGE THAT NOW BEFALLS US...
"...WHEN OLYMPIAN RAISES ARMS AGAINST OLYMPIAN.
"HIPPOLYTA, THE DAUGHTER OF ARES, SURPRISED ME AS I LAY IN MEDITATION IN MELANESIA.
"MY GODLY POWERS HAVE CORRODED DURING OUR DIASPORA TO THIS MORTAL PLANE, AND THE FIENDISH AMAZONS OVERWHELMED ME.

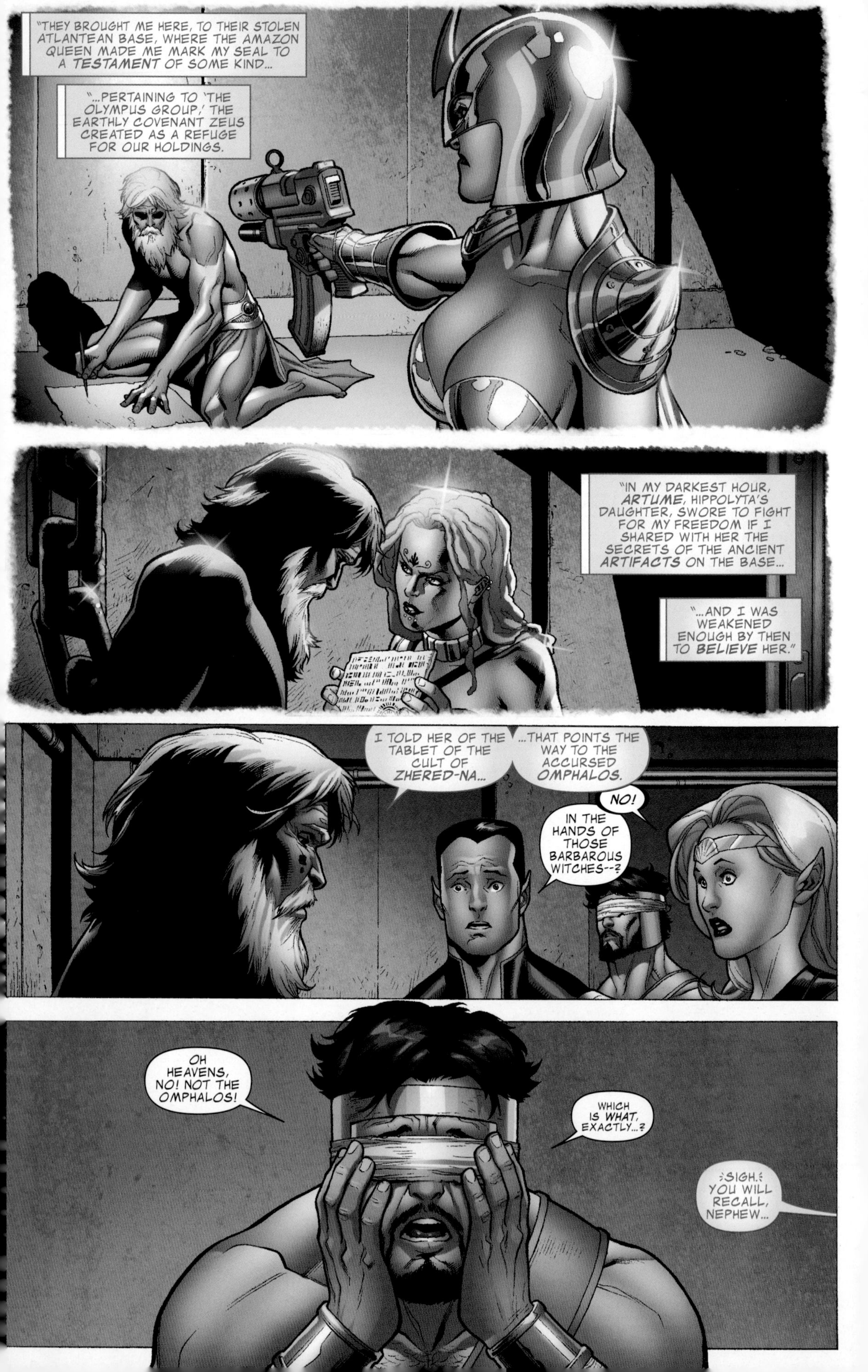
"THEY BROUGHT ME HERE, TO THEIR STOLEN ATLANTEAN BASE, WHERE THE AMAZON QUEEN MADE ME MARK MY SEAL TO A TESTAMENT OF SOME KIND...
"...PERTAINING TO 'THE OLYMPUS GROUP,' THE EARTHLY COVENANT ZEUS CREATED AS A REFUGE FOR OUR HOLDINGS.
"IN MY DARKEST HOUR, ARTUME, HIPPOLYTA'S DAUGHTER, SWORE TO FIGHT FOR MY FREEDOM IF I SHARED WITH HER THE SECRETS OF THE ANCIENT ARTIFACTS ON THE BASE...
"...AND I WAS WEAKENED ENOUGH BY THEN TO BELIEVE HER."
I TOLD HER OF THE TABLET OF THE CULT OF ZHERED-NA...
...THAT POINTS THE WAY TO THE ACCURSED OMPHALOS.
NO!
IN THE HANDS OF THOSE BARBAROUS WITCHES--?
OH HEAVENS, NO! NOT THE OMPHALOS!
WHICH IS WHAT, EXACTLY...?
SIGH. YOU WILL RECALL, NEPHEW...

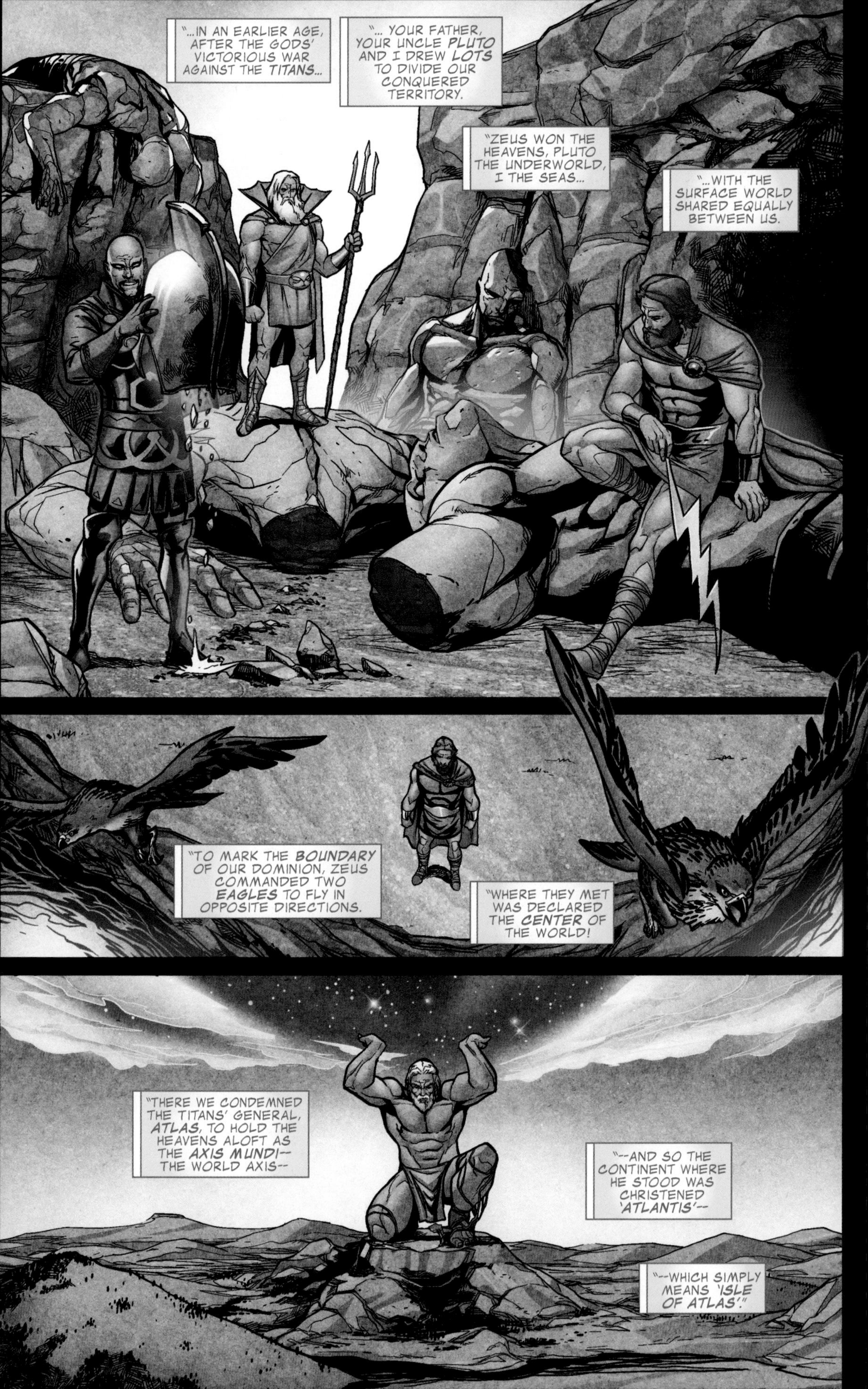
"...IN AN EARLIER AGE, AFTER THE GODS' VICTORIOUS WAR AGAINST THE TITANS...
"... YOUR FATHER, YOUR UNCLE PLUTO AND I DREW LOTS TO DIVIDE OUR CONQUERED TERRITORY.
"ZEUS WON THE HEAVENS, PLUTO THE UNDERWORLD, I THE SEAS...
"...WITH THE SURFACE WORLD SHARED EQUALLY BETWEEN US.
"TO MARK THE BOUNDARY OF OUR DOMINION, ZEUS COMMANDED TWO EAGLES TO FLY IN OPPOSITE DIRECTIONS.
"WHERE THEY MET WAS DECLARED THE CENTER OF THE WORLD!
"THERE WE CONDEMNED THE TITANS' GENERAL, ATLAS, TO HOLD THE HEAVENS ALOFT AS THE AXIS MUNDI-- THE WORLD AXIS--
"--AND SO THE CONTINENT WHERE HE STOOD WAS CHRISTENED 'ATLANTIS'--
"--WHICH SIMPLY MEANS 'ISLE OF ATLAS'."

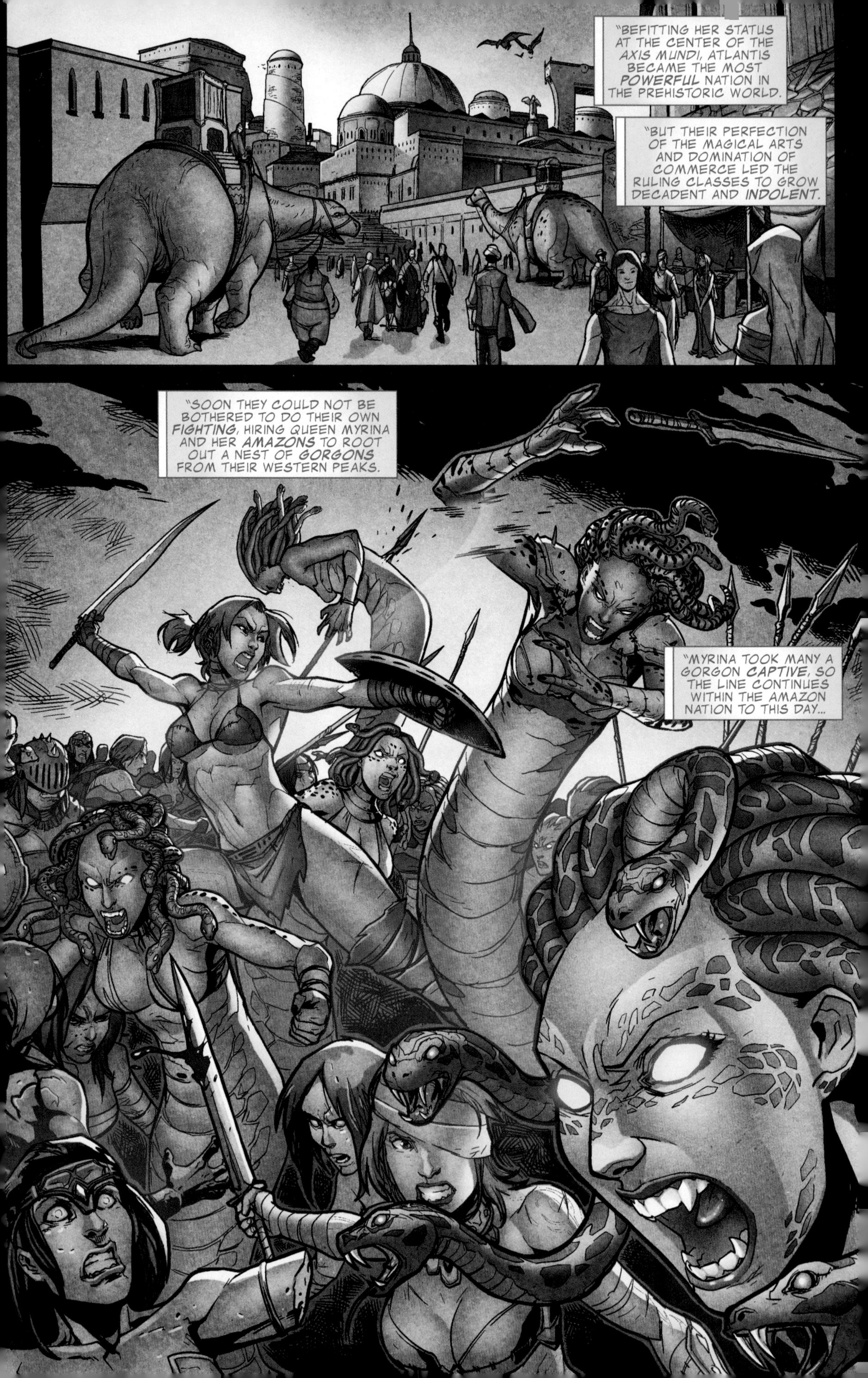
"BEFITTING HER STATUS AT THE CENTER OF THE AXIS MUNDI, ATLANTIS BECAME THE MOST POWERFUL NATION IN THE PREHISTORIC WORLD.
"BUT THEIR PERFECTION OF THE MAGICAL ARTS AND DOMINATION OF COMMERCE LED THE RULING CLASSES TO GROW DECADENT AND INDOLENT.
"SOON THEY COULD NOT BE BOTHERED TO DO THEIR OWN FIGHTING, HIRING QUEEN MYRINA AND HER AMAZONS TO ROOT OUT A NEST OF GORGONS FROM THEIR WESTERN PEAKS.
"MYRINA TOOK MANY A GORGON CAPTIVE, SO THE LINE CONTINUES WITHIN THE AMAZON NATION TO THIS DAY...

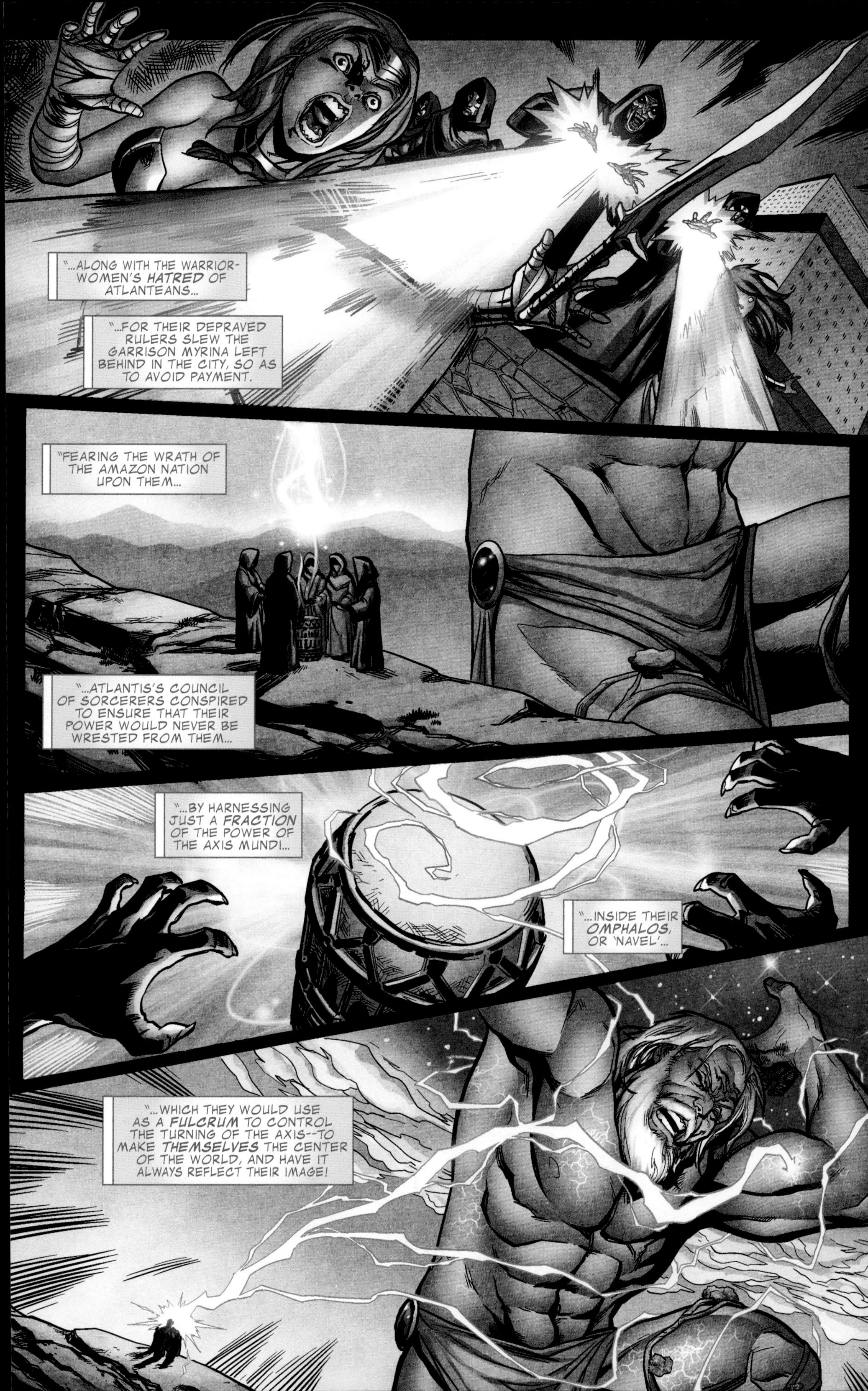
"...ALONG WITH THE WARRIOR-WOMEN'S HATRED OF ATLANTEANS...
"...FOR THEIR DEPRAVED RULERS SLEW THE GARRISON MYRINA LEFT BEHIND IN THE CITY, SO AS TO AVOID PAYMENT.
"FEARING THE WRATH OF THE AMAZON NATION UPON THEM...
"...ATLANTIS'S COUNCIL OF SORCERERS CONSPIRED TO ENSURE THAT THEIR POWER WOULD NEVER BE WRESTED FROM THEM...
"...BY HARNESSING JUST A FRACTION OF THE POWER OF THE AXIS MUNDI...
"...INSIDE THEIR OMPHALOS, OR 'NAVEL'...
"...WHICH THEY WOULD USE AS A FULCRUM TO CONTROL THE TURNING OF THE AXIS--TO MAKE THEMSELVES THE CENTER OF THE WORLD, AND HAVE IT ALWAYS REFLECT THEIR IMAGE!

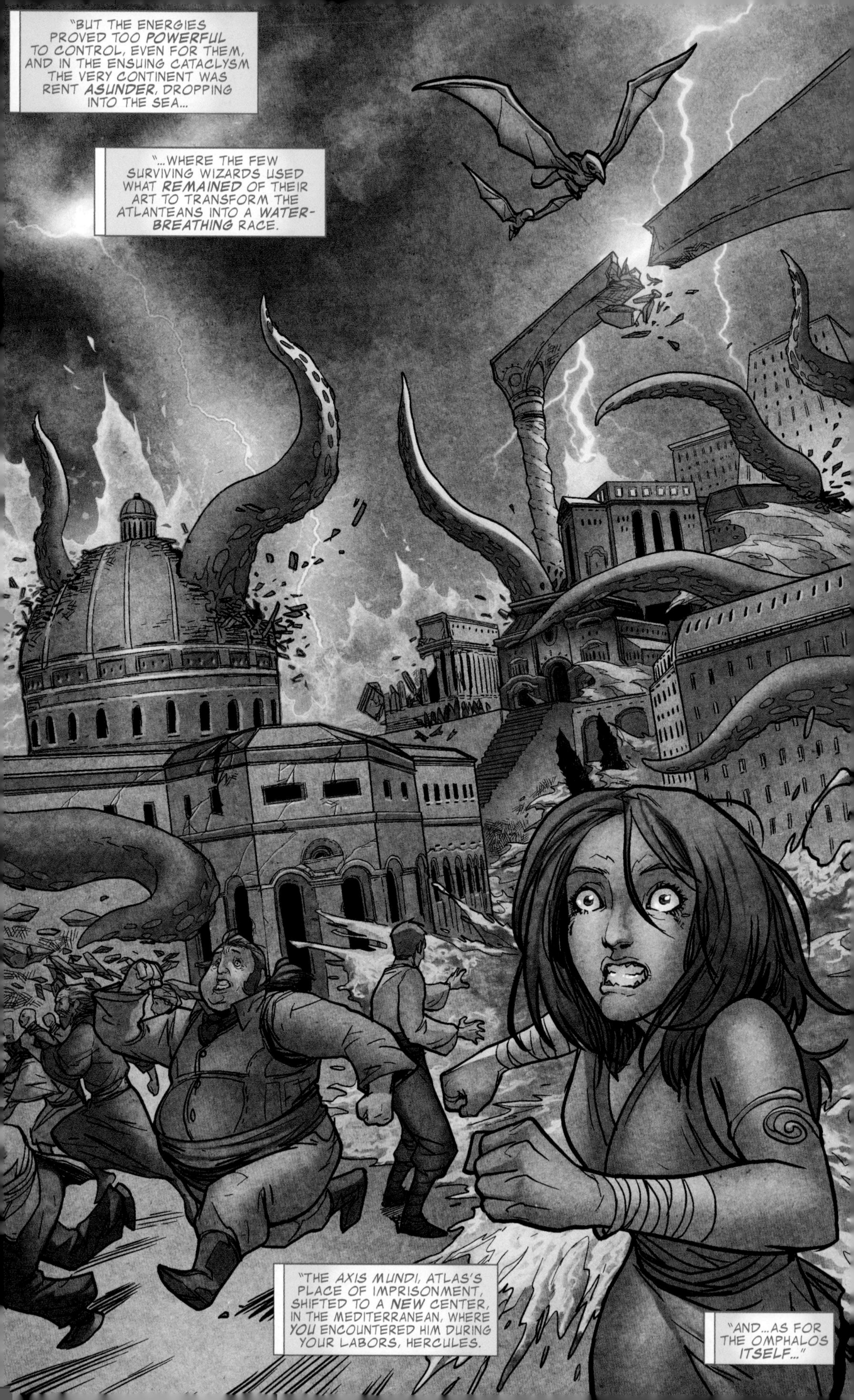
"BUT THE ENERGIES PROVED TOO POWERFUL TO CONTROL, EVEN FOR THEM, AND IN THE ENSUING CATACLYSM THE VERY CONTINENT WAS RENT ASUNDER, DROPPING INTO THE SEA...
"...WHERE THE FEW SURVIVING WIZARDS USED WHAT REMAINED OF THEIR ART TO TRANSFORM THE ATLANTEANS INTO A WATER-BREATHING RACE.
"THE AXIS MUNDI, ATLAS'S PLACE OF IMPRISONMENT, SHIFTED TO A NEW CENTER, IN THE MEDITERRANEAN, WHERE YOU ENCOUNTERED HIM DURING YOUR LABORS, HERCULES.
"AND...AS FOR THE OMPHALOS ITSELF..."

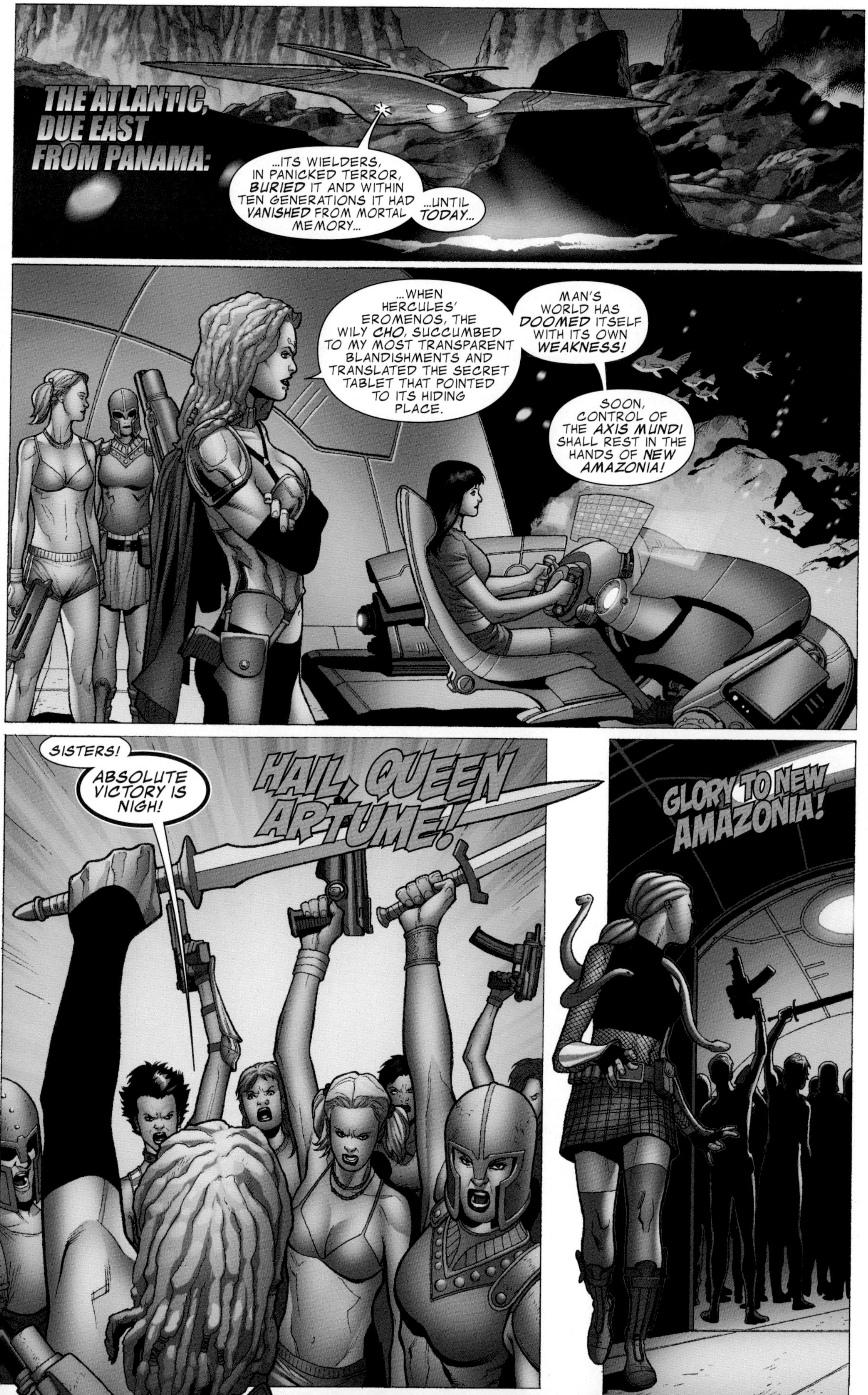
THE ATLANTIC, DUE EAST FROM PANAMA:
...ITS WIELDERS, IN PANICKED TERROR, BURIED IT AND WITHIN TEN GENERATIONS IT HAD VANISHED FROM MORTAL MEMORY...
...UNTIL TODAY...
...WHEN HERCULES' EROMENOS, THE WILY CHO, SUCCUMBED TO MY MOST TRANSPARENT BLANDISHMENTS AND TRANSLATED THE SECRET TABLET THAT POINTED TO ITS HIDING PLACE.
MAN'S WORLD HAS DOOMED ITSELF WITH ITS OWN WEAKNESS!
SOON, CONTROL OF THE AXIS MUNDI SHALL REST IN THE HANDS OF NEW AMAZONIA!
SISTERS!
ABSOLUTE VICTORY IS NIGH!
HAIL, QUEEN ARTUME!
GLORY TO NEW AMAZONIA!

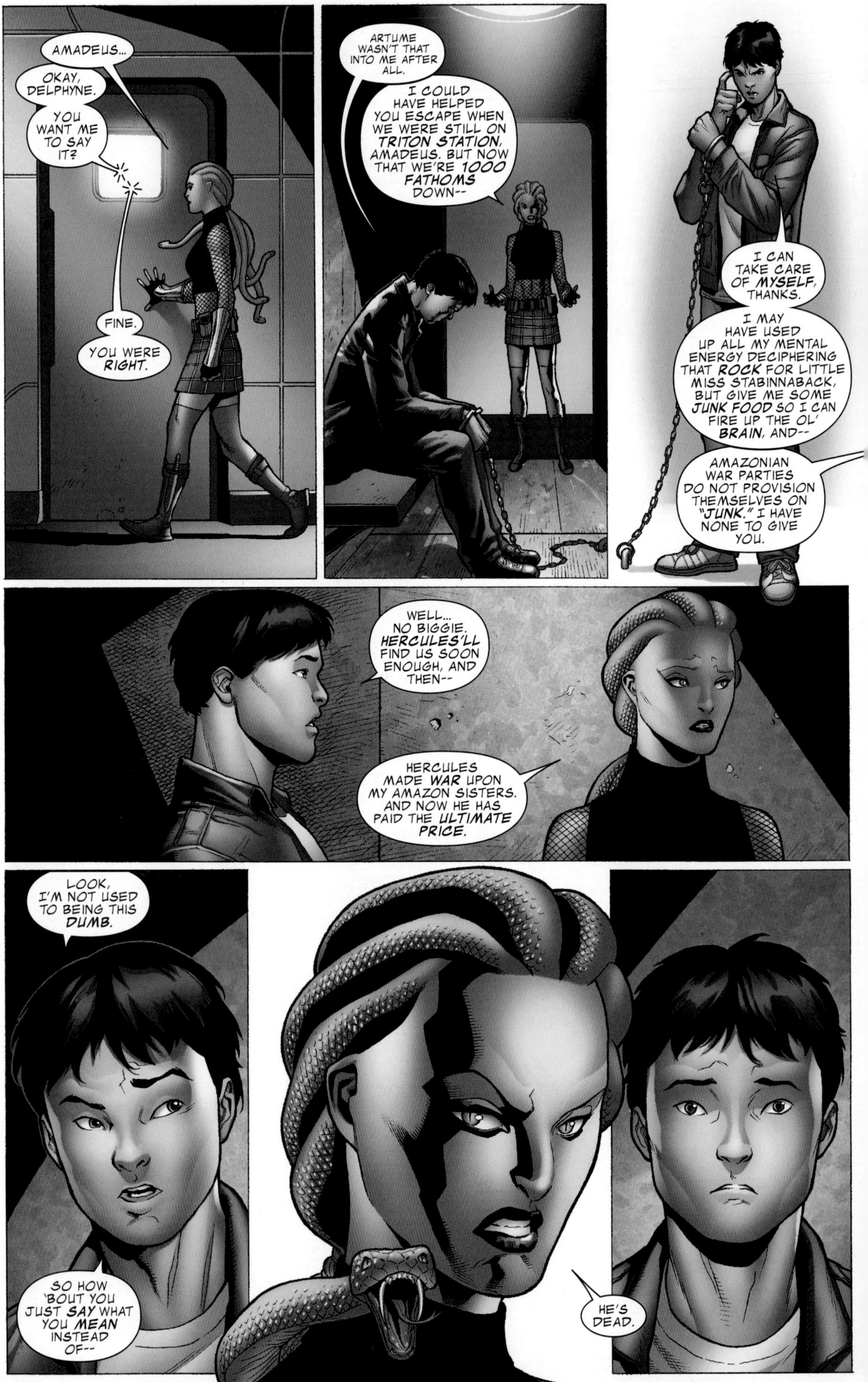
AMADEUS...
OKAY, DELPHYNE.
YOU WANT ME TO SAY IT?
FINE.
YOU WERE RIGHT.
ARTUME WASN'T THAT INTO ME AFTER ALL.
I COULD HAVE HELPED YOU ESCAPE WHEN WE WERE STILL ON TRITON STATION, AMADEUS. BUT NOW THAT WE'RE 1000 FATHOMS DOWN--
I CAN TAKE CARE OF MYSELF, THANKS.
I MAY HAVE USED UP ALL MY MENTAL ENERGY DECIPHERING THAT ROCK FOR LITTLE MISS STABINNABACK, BUT GIVE ME SOME JUNK FOOD SO I CAN FIRE UP THE OL' BRAIN, AND--
AMAZONIAN WAR PARTIES DO NOT PROVISION THEMSELVES ON "JUNK." I HAVE NONE TO GIVE YOU.
WELL... NO BIGGIE. HERCULES'LL FIND US SOON ENOUGH, AND THEN--
HERCULES MADE WAR UPON MY AMAZON SISTERS. AND NOW HE HAS PAID THE ULTIMATE PRICE.
LOOK, I'M NOT USED TO BEING THIS DUMB.
SO HOW 'BOUT YOU JUST SAY WHAT YOU MEAN INSTEAD OF--
HE'S DEAD.

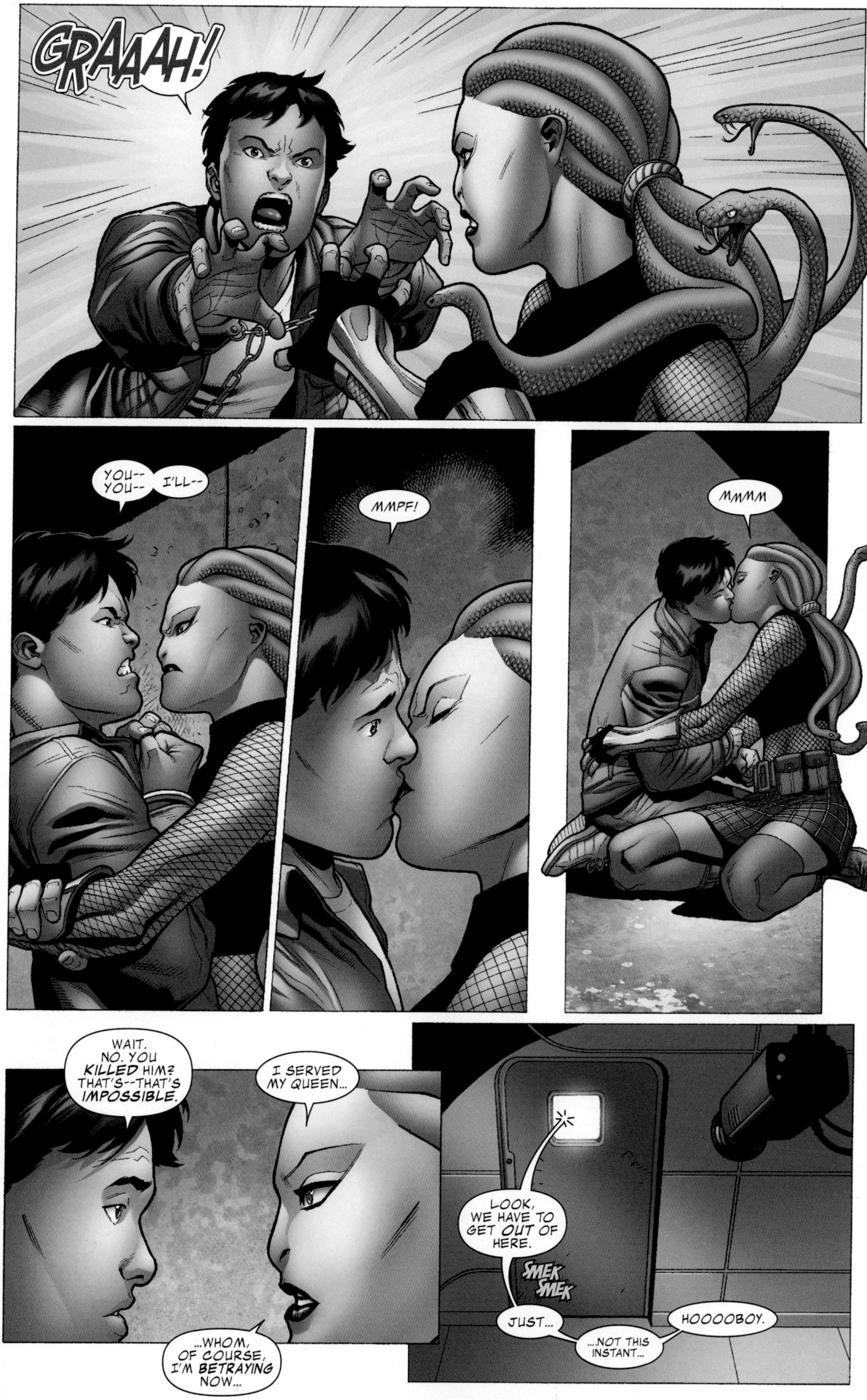
GRAAAH!
YOU-- YOU--
I'LL--
MMPF!
MMMM
WAIT. NO. YOU KILLED HIM? THAT'S--THAT'S IMPOSSIBLE.
I SERVED MY QUEEN...
...WHOM, OF COURSE, I'M BETRAYING NOW...
LOOK, WE HAVE TO GET OUT OF HERE.
SMEK SMEK
JUST...
...NOT THIS INSTANT...
HOOOOBOY.

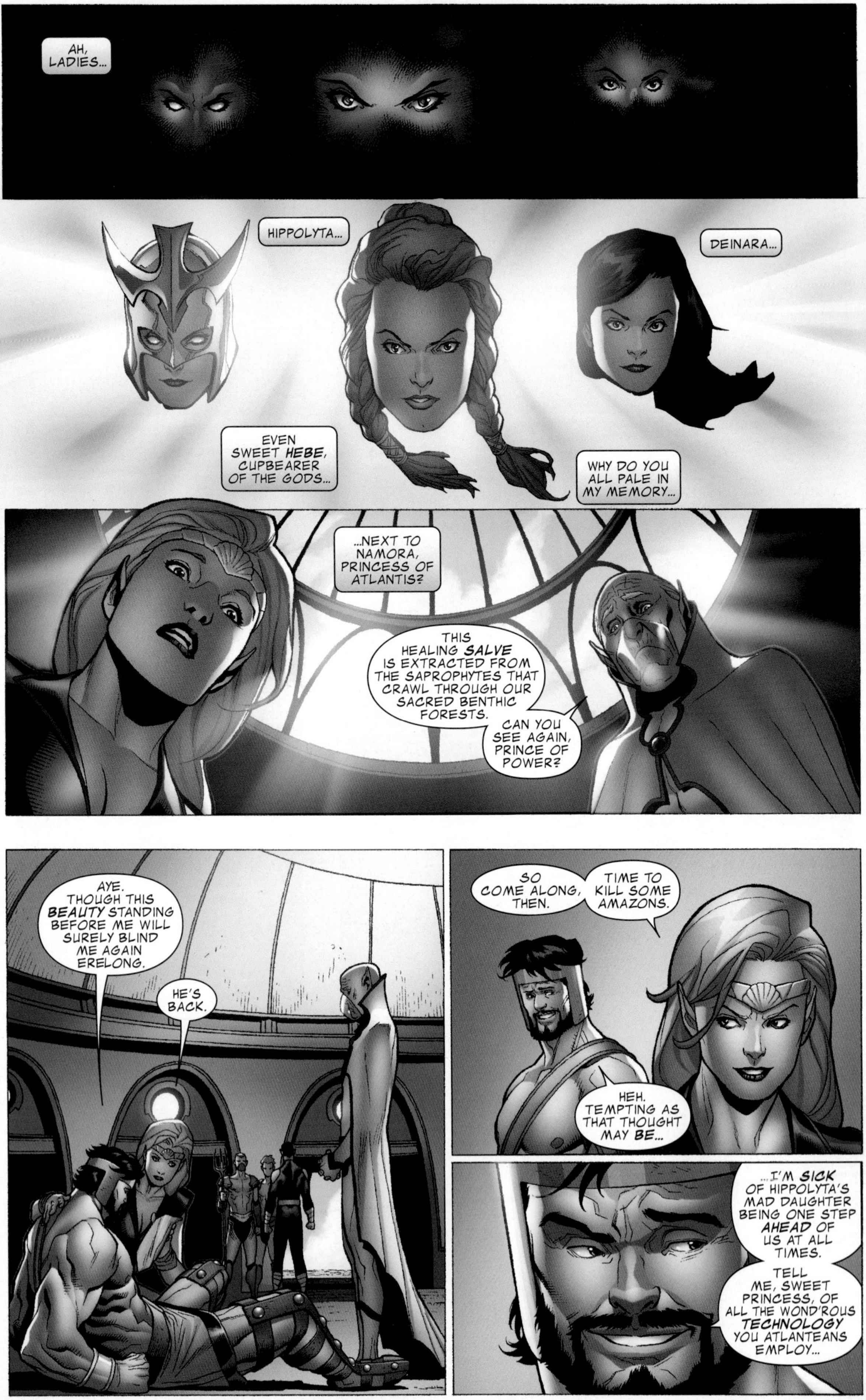

AH, LADIES...
HIPPOLYTA...
DEINARA...
EVEN SWEET HEBE, CUPBEARER OF THE GODS...
WHY DO YOU ALL PALE IN MY MEMORY...
...NEXT TO NAMORA, PRINCESS OF ATLANTIS?
THIS HEALING SALVE IS EXTRACTED FROM THE SAPROPHYTES THAT CRAWL THROUGH OUR SACRED BENTHIC FORESTS.
CAN YOU SEE AGAIN, PRINCE OF POWER?
AYE. THOUGH THIS BEAUTY STANDING BEFORE ME WILL SURELY BLIND ME AGAIN ERELONG.
HE'S BACK.
SO COME ALONG, THEN.
TIME TO KILL SOME AMAZONS.
HEH. TEMPTING AS THAT THOUGHT MAY BE...
...I'M SICK OF HIPPOLYTA'S MAD DAUGHTER BEING ONE STEP AHEAD OF US AT ALL TIMES.
TELL ME, SWEET PRINCESS, OF ALL THE WOND'ROUS TECHNOLOGY YOU ATLANTEANS EMPLOY...

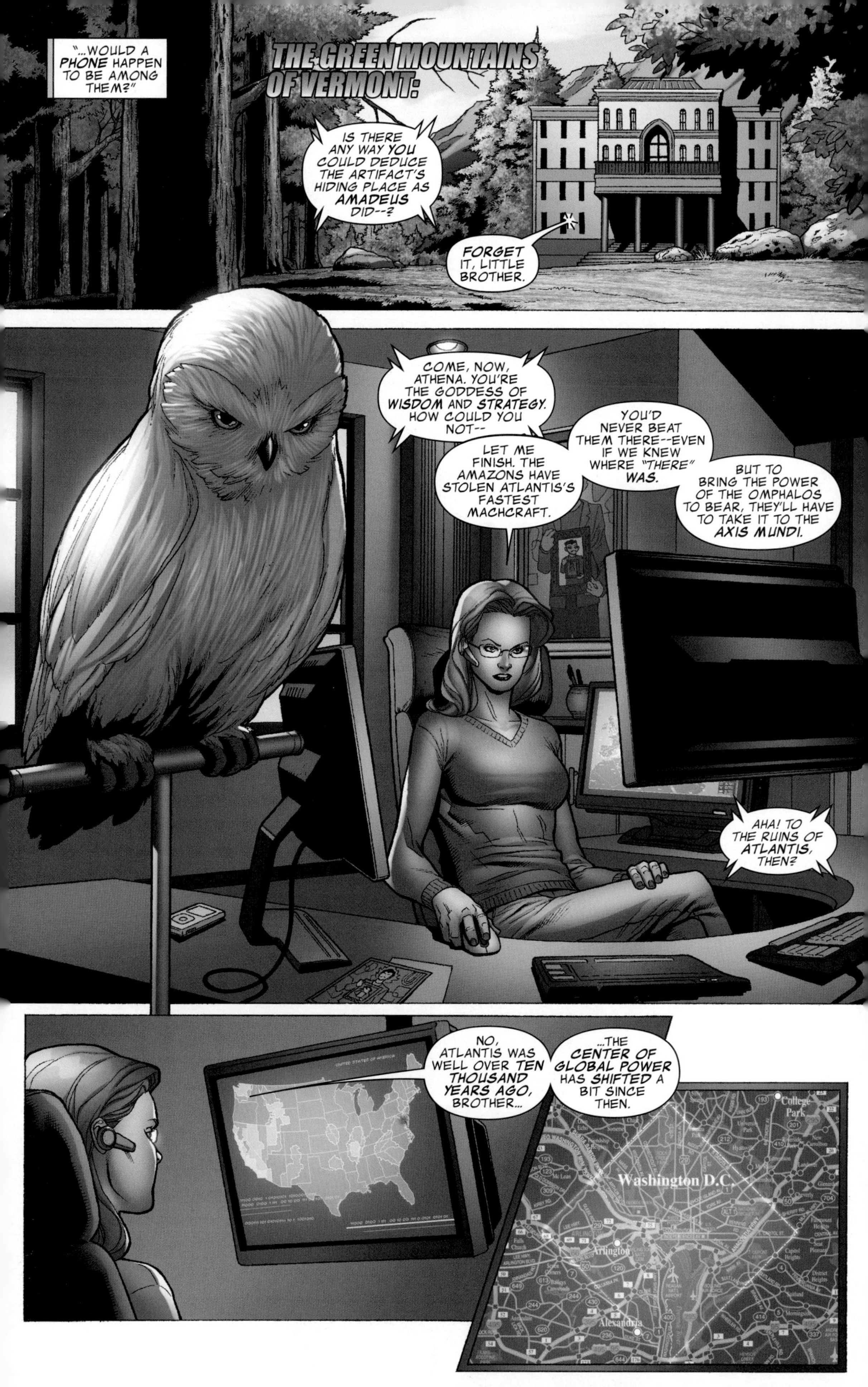
"...WOULD A PHONE HAPPEN TO BE AMONG THEM?"
THE GREEN MOUNTAINS OF VERMONT:
IS THERE ANY WAY YOU COULD DEDUCE THE ARTIFACT'S HIDING PLACE AS AMADEUS DID--?
FORGET IT, LITTLE BROTHER.
COME, NOW, ATHENA. YOU'RE THE GODDESS OF WISDOM AND STRATEGY. HOW COULD YOU NOT--
LET ME FINISH. THE AMAZONS HAVE STOLEN ATLANTIS'S FASTEST MACHCRAFT.
YOU'D NEVER BEAT THEM THERE--EVEN IF WE KNEW WHERE "THERE" WAS.
BUT TO BRING THE POWER OF THE OMPHALOS TO BEAR, THEY'LL HAVE TO TAKE IT TO THE AXIS MUNDI.
AHA! TO THE RUINS OF ATLANTIS, THEN?
NO, ATLANTIS WAS WELL OVER TEN THOUSAND YEARS AGO, BROTHER...
...THE CENTER OF GLOBAL POWER HAS SHIFTED A BIT SINCE THEN.
College Park
Washington D.C.
Arlington
Alexandria

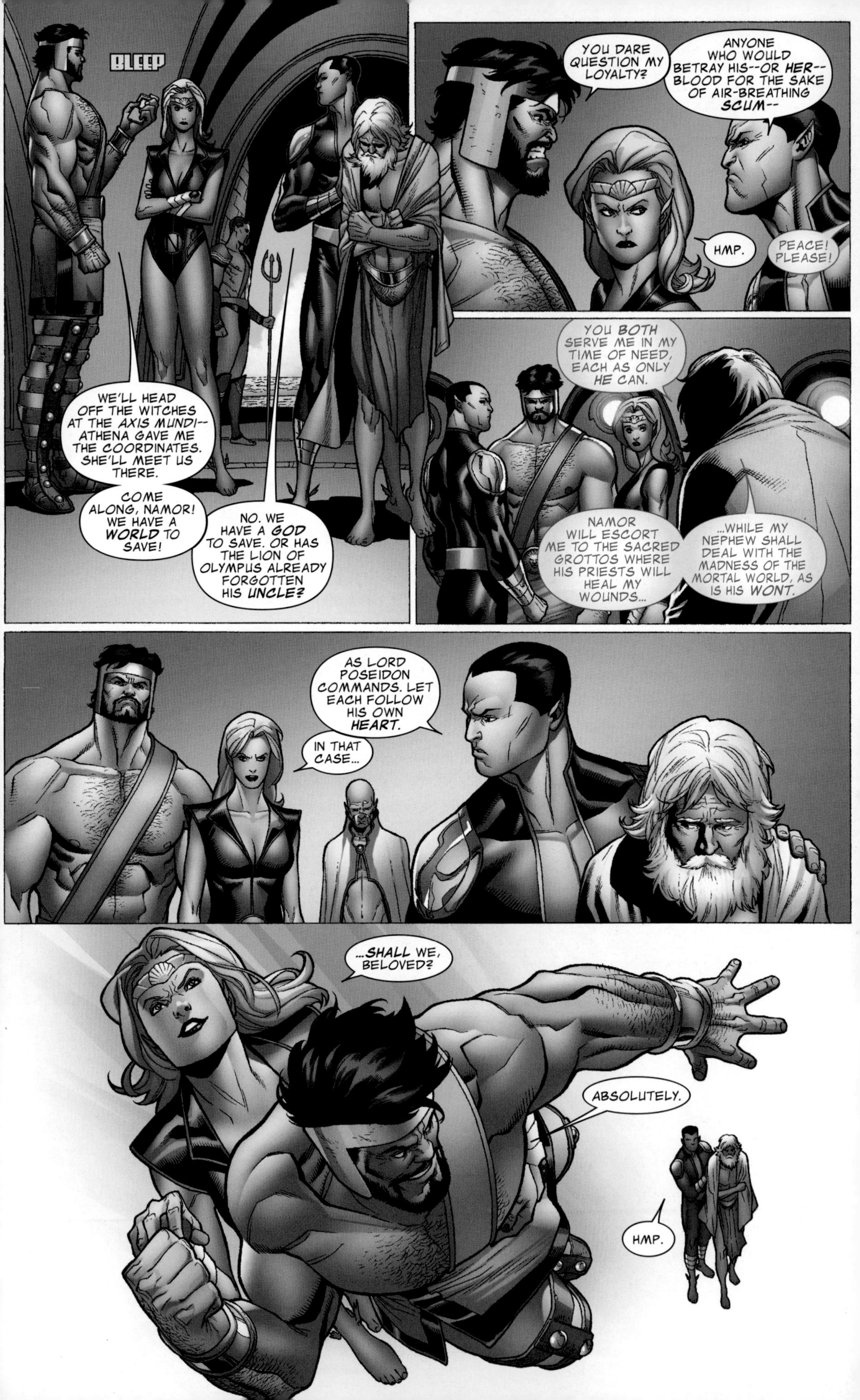
BLEEP
WE'LL HEAD OFF THE WITCHES AT THE AXIS MUNDI-- ATHENA GAVE ME THE COORDINATES. SHE'LL MEET US THERE.
COME ALONG, NAMOR! WE HAVE A WORLD TO SAVE!
NO. WE HAVE A GOD TO SAVE. OR HAS THE LION OF OLYMPUS ALREADY FORGOTTEN HIS UNCLE?
YOU DARE QUESTION MY LOYALTY?
ANYONE WHO WOULD BETRAY HIS--OR HER-- BLOOD FOR THE SAKE OF AIR-BREATHING SCUM--
HMP.
PEACE! PLEASE!
YOU BOTH SERVE ME IN MY TIME OF NEED, EACH AS ONLY HE CAN.
NAMOR WILL ESCORT ME TO THE SACRED GROTTOS WHERE HIS PRIESTS WILL HEAL MY WOUNDS...
...WHILE MY NEPHEW SHALL DEAL WITH THE MADNESS OF THE MORTAL WORLD, AS IS HIS WONT.
AS LORD POSEIDON COMMANDS. LET EACH FOLLOW HIS OWN HEART.
IN THAT CASE...
...SHALL WE, BELOVED?
ABSOLUTELY.
HMP.

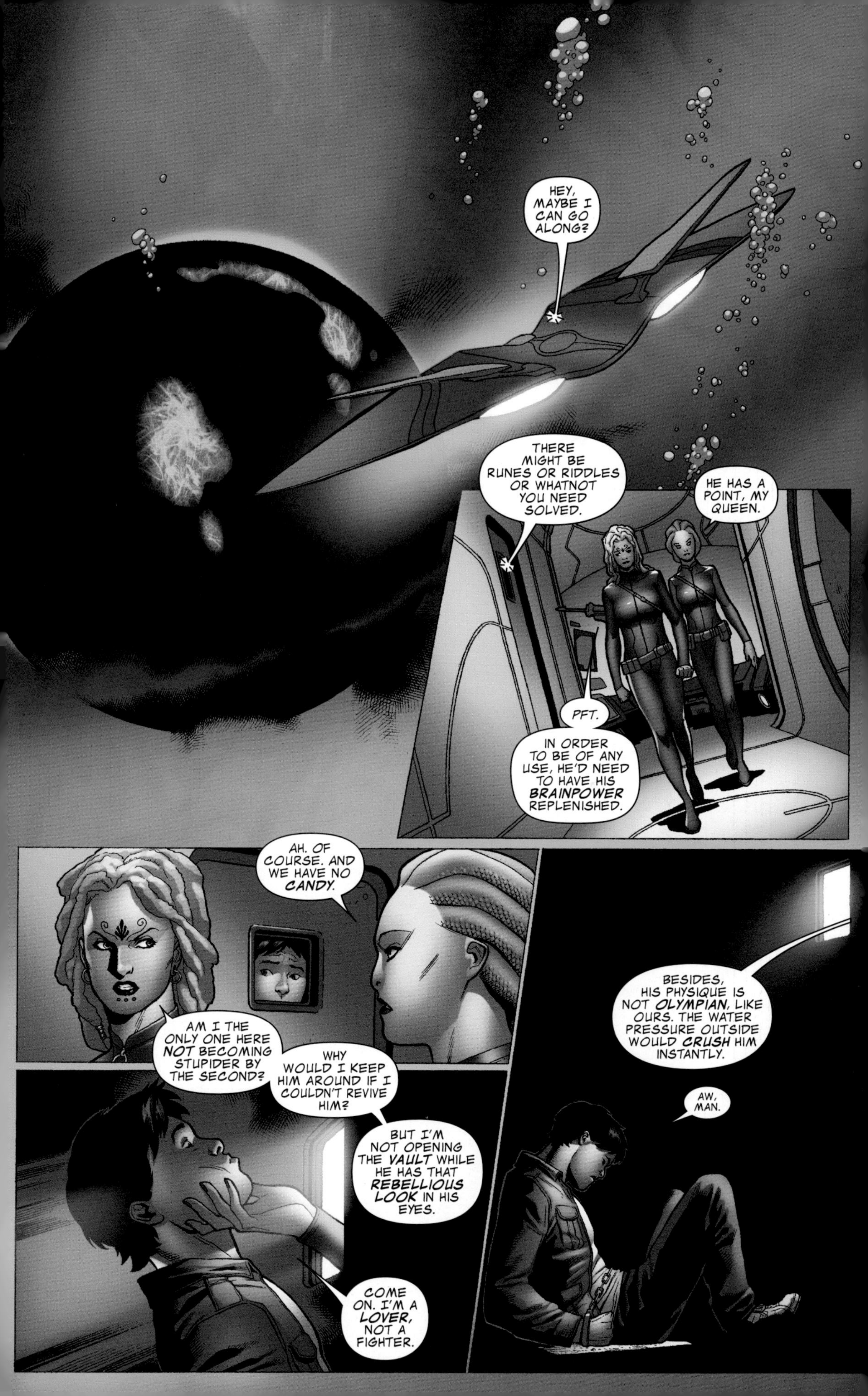

HEY, MAYBE I CAN GO ALONG?
THERE MIGHT BE RUNES OR RIDDLES OR WHATNOT YOU NEED SOLVED.
HE HAS A POINT, MY QUEEN.
PFT.
IN ORDER TO BE OF ANY USE, HE'D NEED TO HAVE HIS BRAINPOWER REPLENISHED.
AH. OF COURSE. AND WE HAVE NO CANDY.
AM I THE ONLY ONE HERE NOT BECOMING STUPIDER BY THE SECOND?
WHY WOULD I KEEP HIM AROUND IF I COULDN'T REVIVE HIM?
BUT I'M NOT OPENING THE VAULT WHILE HE HAS THAT REBELLIOUS LOOK IN HIS EYES.
COME ON. I'M A LOVER, NOT A FIGHTER.
BESIDES, HIS PHYSIQUE IS NOT OLYMPIAN, LIKE OURS. THE WATER PRESSURE OUTSIDE WOULD CRUSH HIM INSTANTLY.
AW, MAN.

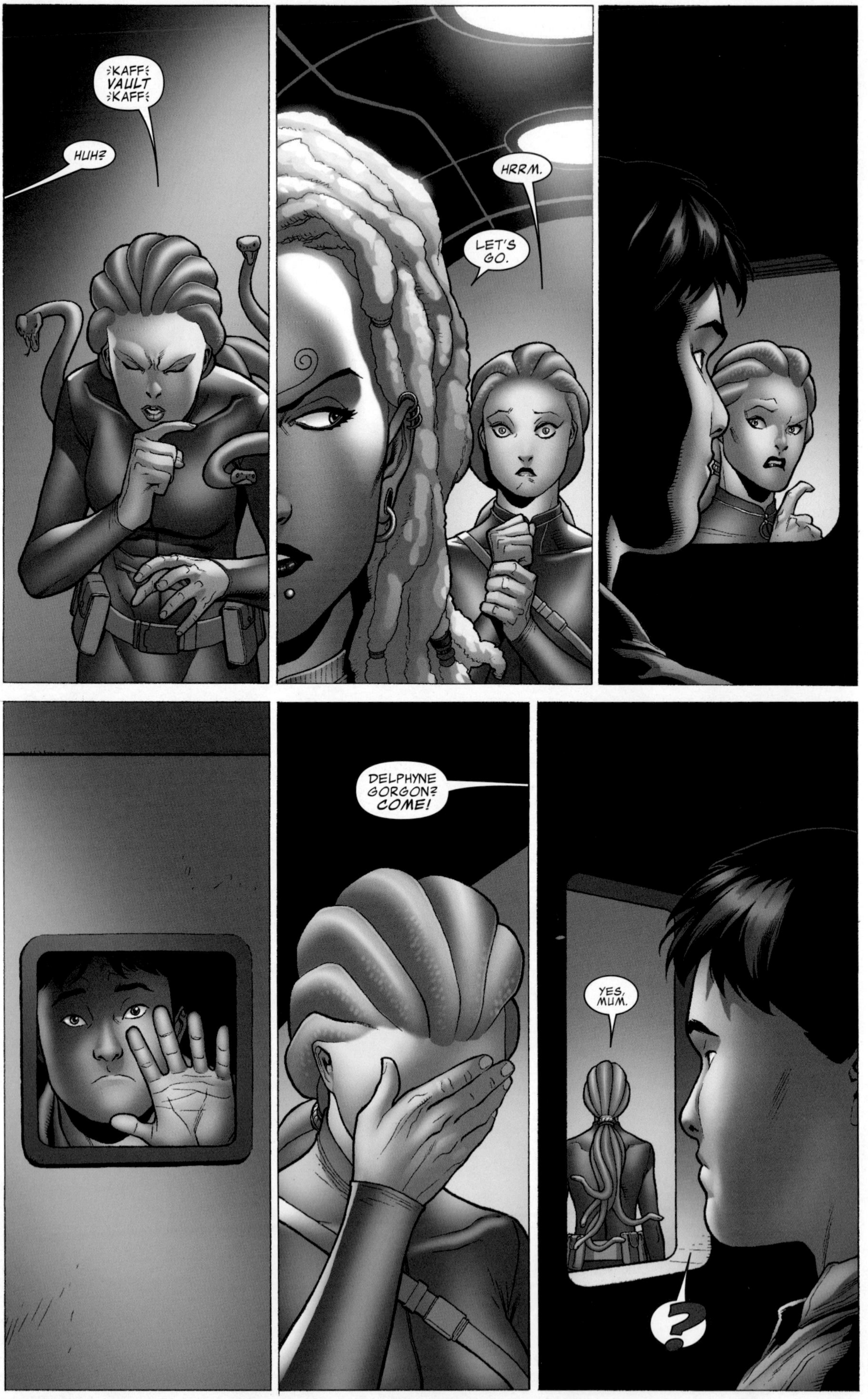

KAFF VAULT KAFF
HUH?
HRRM.
LET'S GO.
DELPHYNE GORGON? COME!
YES, MUM.
?

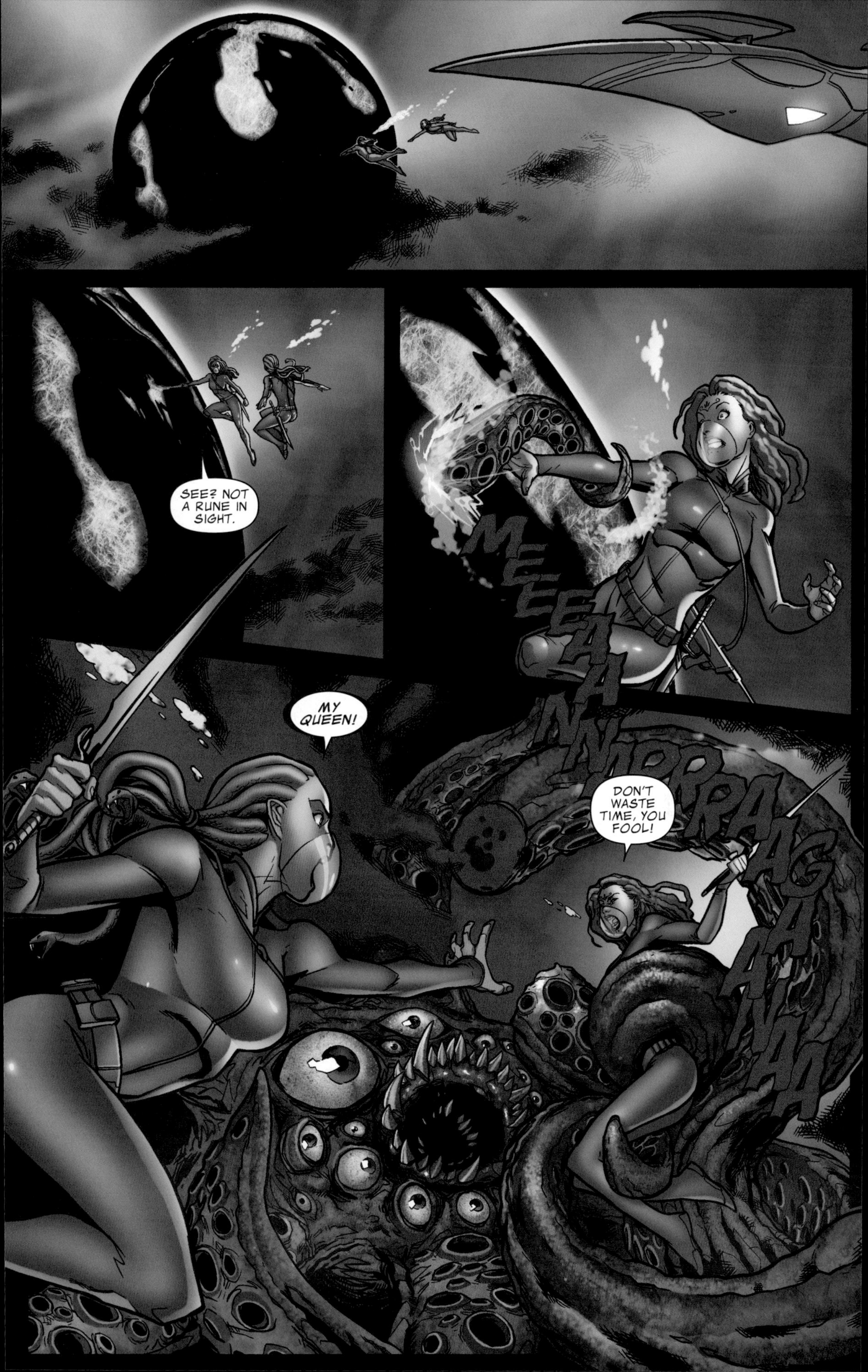
SEE? NOT A RUNE IN SIGHT.
MEEEAANNRRAAGAAAA
MY QUEEN!
DON'T WASTE TIME, YOU FOOL!

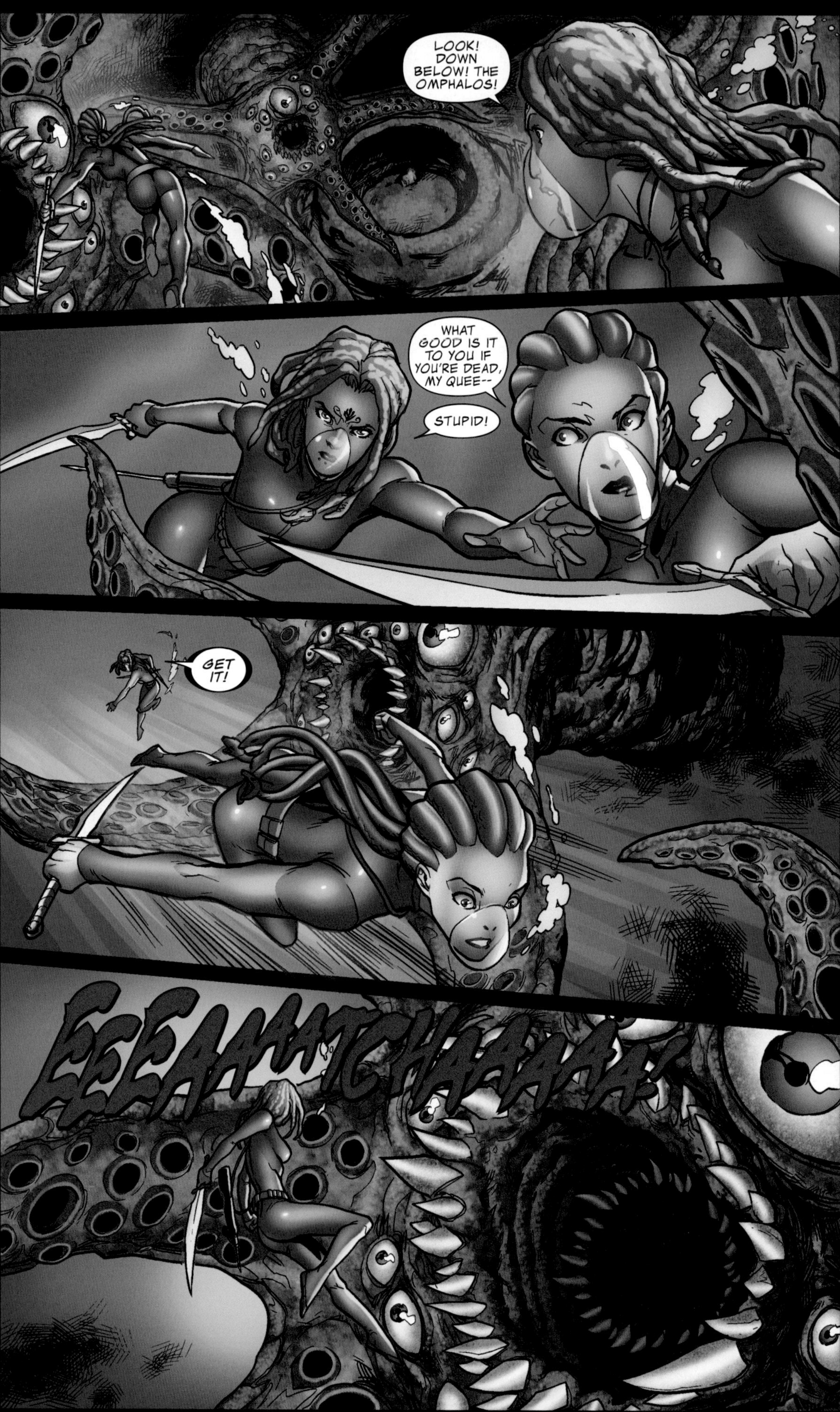
LOOK! DOWN BELOW! THE OMPHALOS!
WHAT GOOD IS IT TO YOU IF YOU'RE DEAD, MY QUEE--
STUPID!
GET IT!
EEEAAAATCHAAAAA!

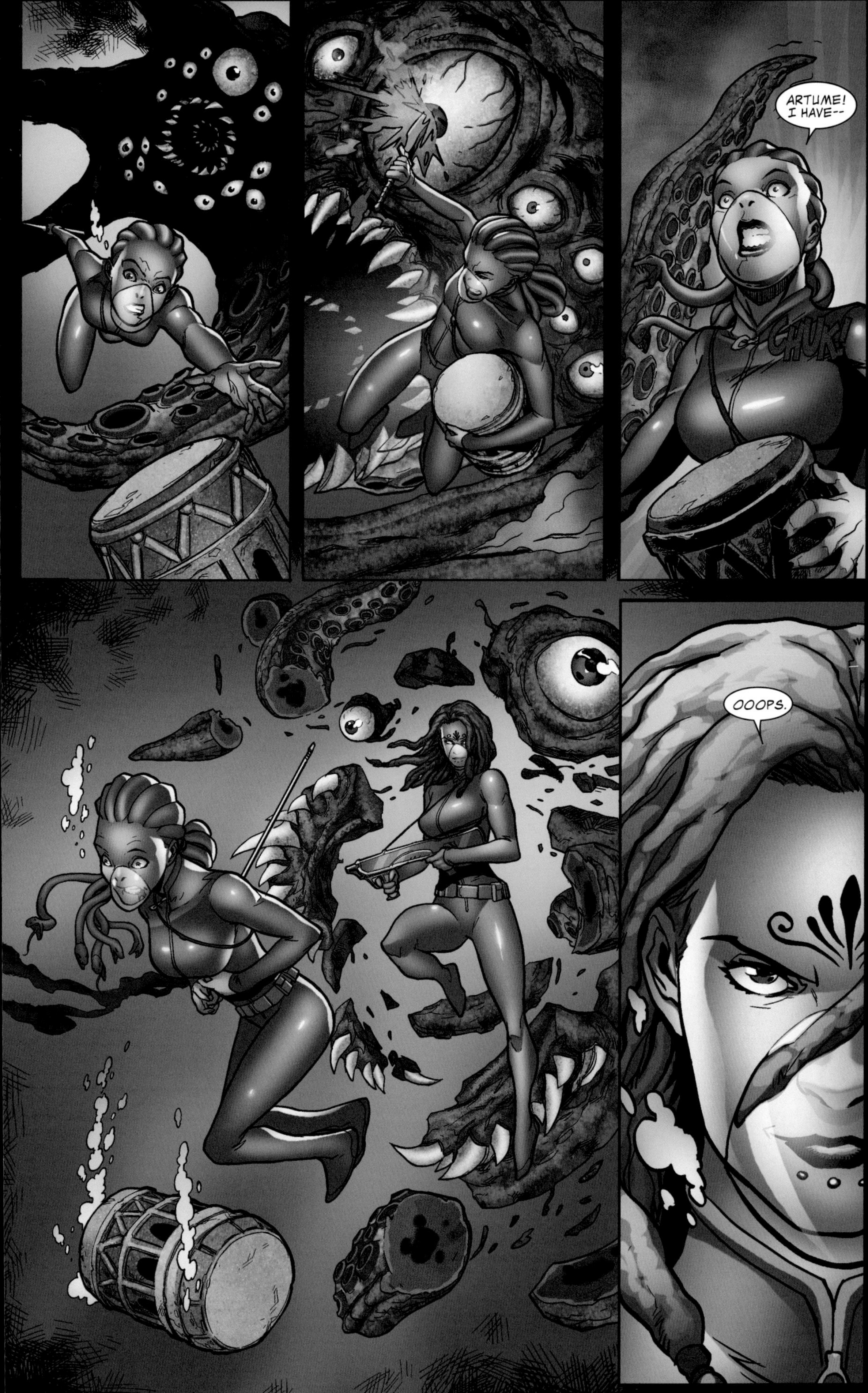
ARTUME! I HAVE--
CHUK!
OOOPS.

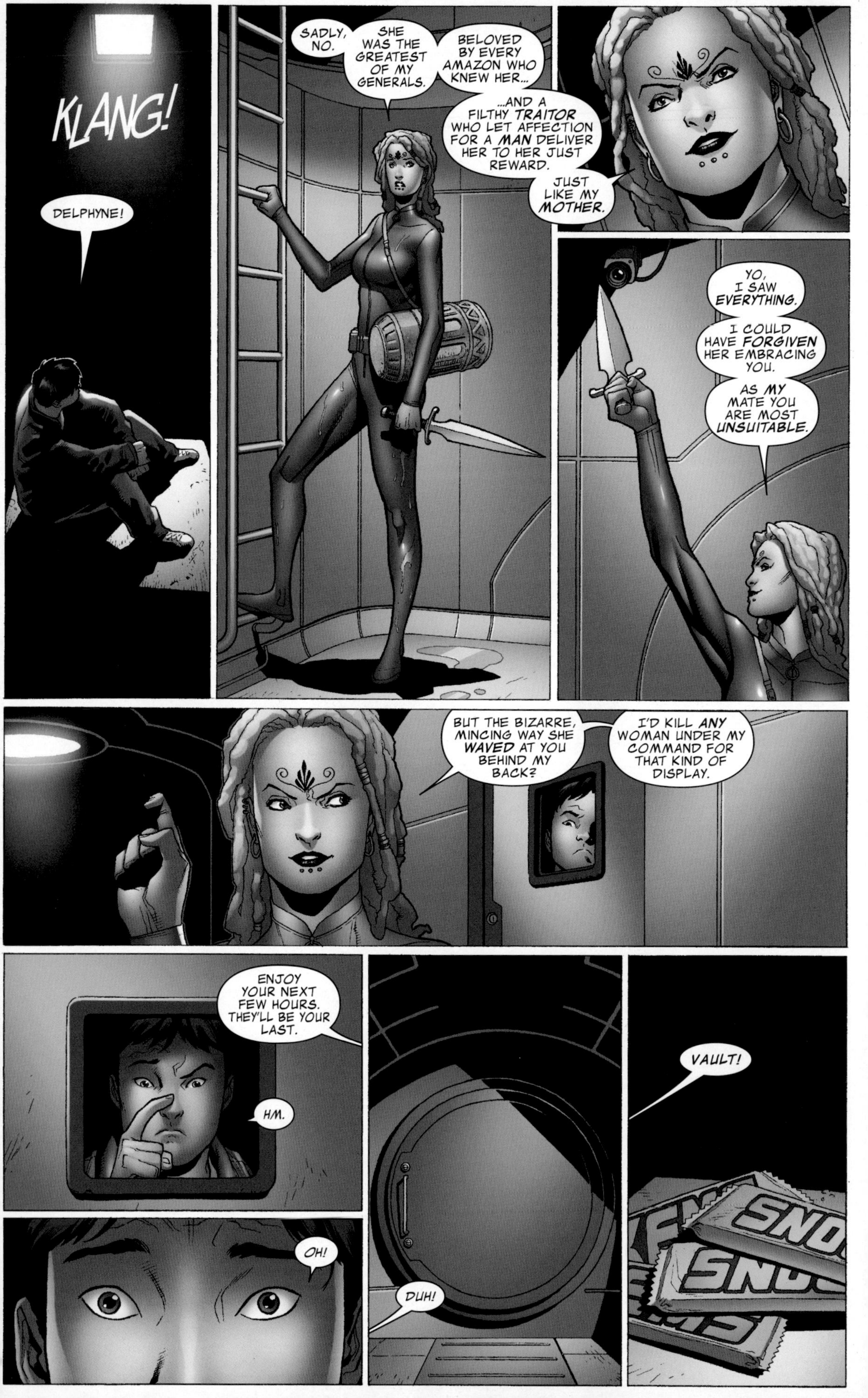
KLANG!
DELPHYNE!
SADLY, NO.
SHE WAS THE GREATEST OF MY GENERALS.
BELOVED BY EVERY AMAZON WHO KNEW HER...
...AND A FILTHY TRAITOR WHO LET AFFECTION FOR A MAN DELIVER HER TO HER JUST REWARD.
JUST LIKE MY MOTHER.
YO, I SAW EVERYTHING.
I COULD HAVE FORGIVEN HER EMBRACING YOU.
AS MY MATE YOU ARE MOST UNSUITABLE.
BUT THE BIZARRE, MINCING WAY SHE WAVED AT YOU BEHIND MY BACK?
I'D KILL ANY WOMAN UNDER MY COMMAND FOR THAT KIND OF DISPLAY.
ENJOY YOUR NEXT FEW HOURS. THEY'LL BE YOUR LAST.
HM.
OH!
DUH!
VAULT!

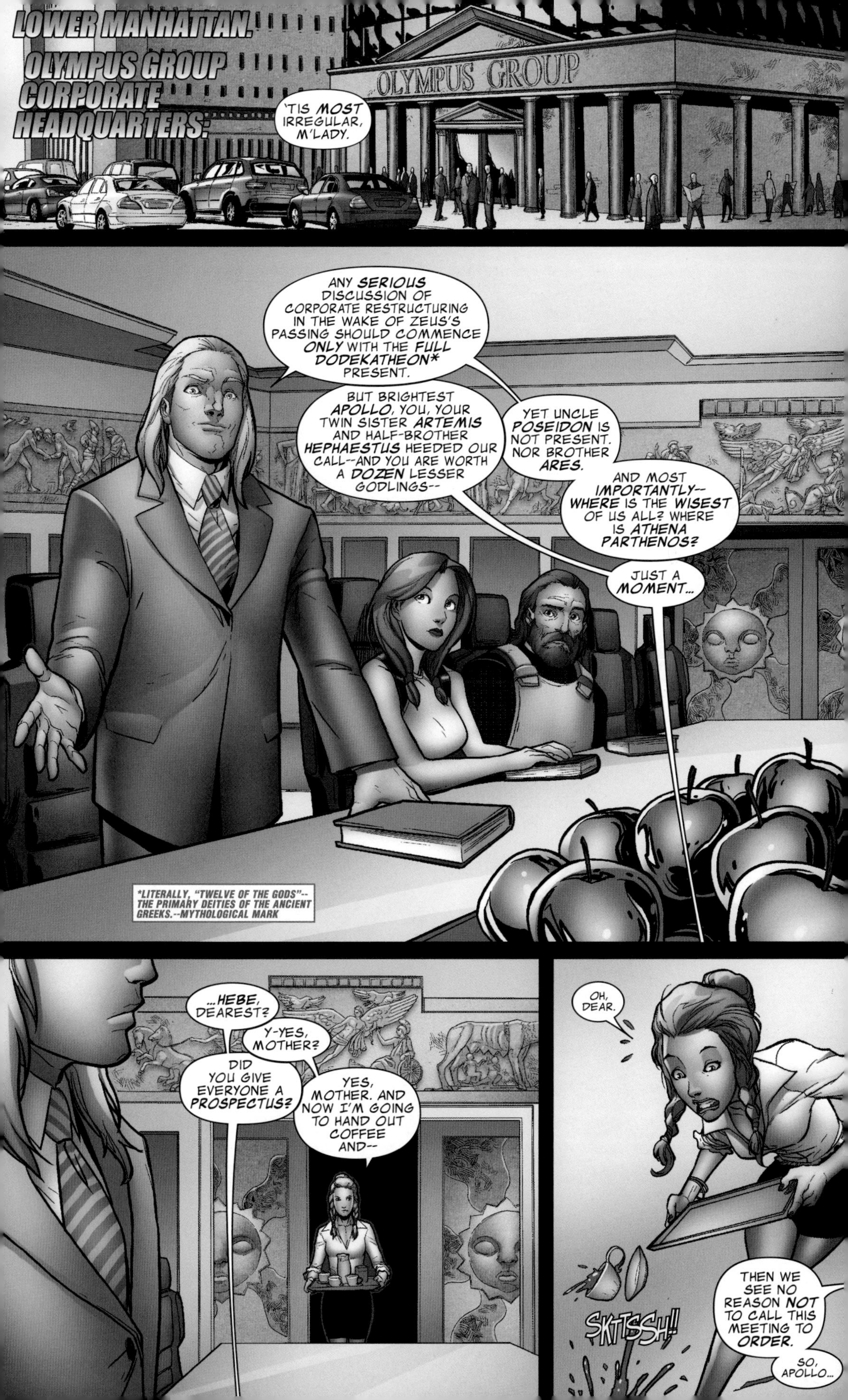
LOWER MANHATTAN.
OLYMPUS GROUP CORPORATE HEADQUARTERS:
OLYMPUS GROUP
'TIS MOST IRREGULAR, M'LADY.
ANY SERIOUS DISCUSSION OF CORPORATE RESTRUCTURING IN THE WAKE OF ZEUS'S PASSING SHOULD COMMENCE ONLY WITH THE FULL DODEKATHEON* PRESENT.
BUT BRIGHTEST APOLLO, YOU, YOUR TWIN SISTER ARTEMIS AND HALF-BROTHER HEPHAESTUS HEEDED OUR CALL--AND YOU ARE WORTH A DOZEN LESSER GODLINGS--
YET UNCLE POSEIDON IS NOT PRESENT. NOR BROTHER ARES.
AND MOST IMPORTANTLY--WHERE IS THE WISEST OF US ALL? WHERE IS ATHENA PARTHENOS?
JUST A MOMENT...
*LITERALLY, "TWELVE OF THE GODS"--THE PRIMARY DEITIES OF THE ANCIENT GREEKS.--MYTHOLOGICAL MARK
...HEBE, DEAREST?
Y-YES, MOTHER?
DID YOU GIVE EVERYONE A PROSPECTUS?
YES, MOTHER. AND NOW I'M GOING TO HAND OUT COFFEE AND--
OH, DEAR.
SKTSSH!!
THEN WE SEE NO REASON NOT TO CALL THIS MEETING TO ORDER.
SO, APOLLO...

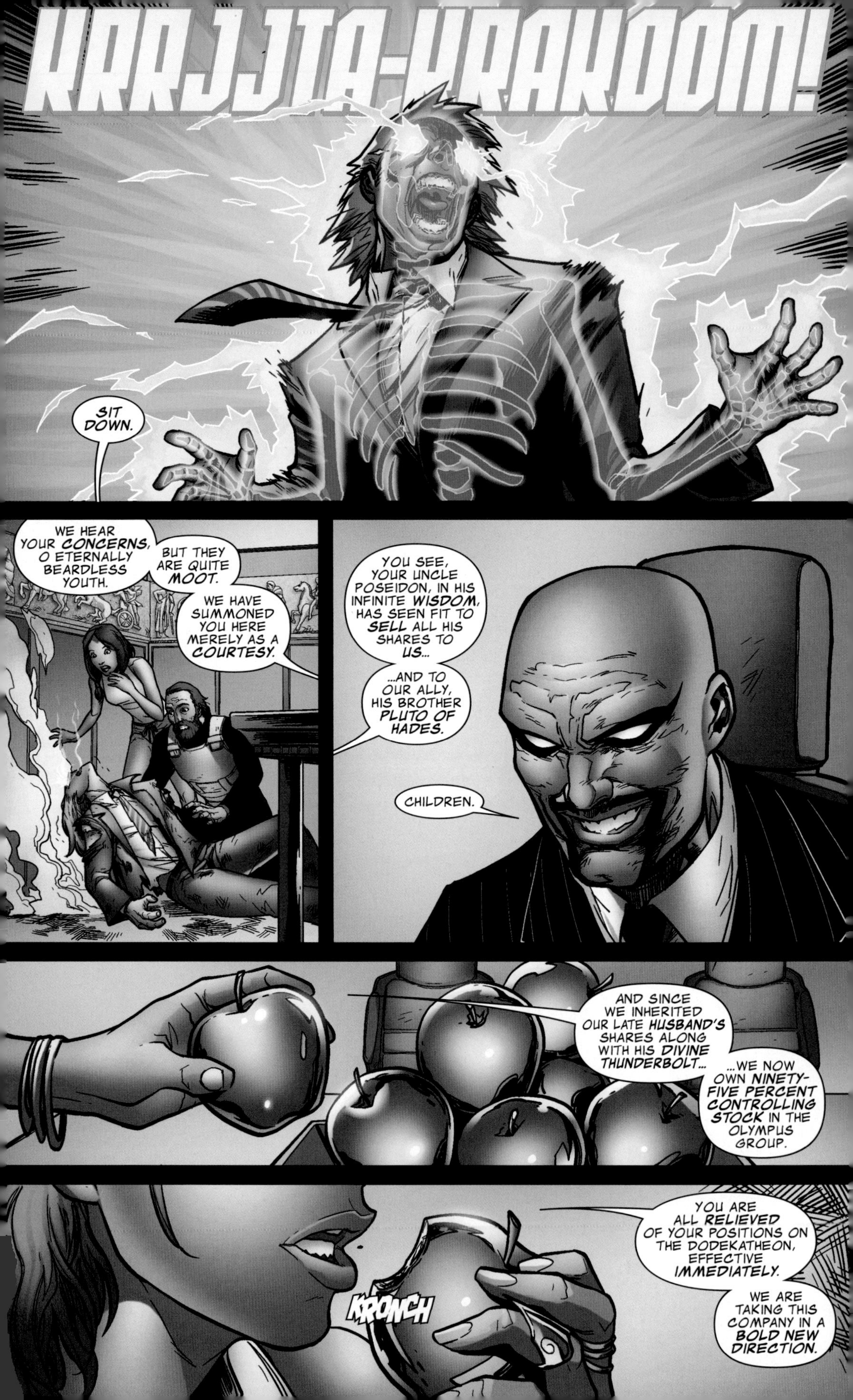
KRRJJTA-KRAKOOM!
SIT DOWN.
WE HEAR YOUR CONCERNS, O ETERNALLY BEARDLESS YOUTH.
BUT THEY ARE QUITE MOOT.
WE HAVE SUMMONED YOU HERE MERELY AS A COURTESY.
YOU SEE, YOUR UNCLE POSEIDON, IN HIS INFINITE WISDOM, HAS SEEN FIT TO SELL ALL HIS SHARES TO US...
...AND TO OUR ALLY, HIS BROTHER PLUTO OF HADES.
CHILDREN.
AND SINCE WE INHERITED OUR LATE HUSBAND'S SHARES ALONG WITH HIS DIVINE THUNDERBOLT...
...WE NOW OWN NINETY-FIVE PERCENT CONTROLLING STOCK IN THE OLYMPUS GROUP.
YOU ARE ALL RELIEVED OF YOUR POSITIONS ON THE DODEKATHEON, EFFECTIVE IMMEDIATELY.
KRONCH
WE ARE TAKING THIS COMPANY IN A BOLD NEW DIRECTION.

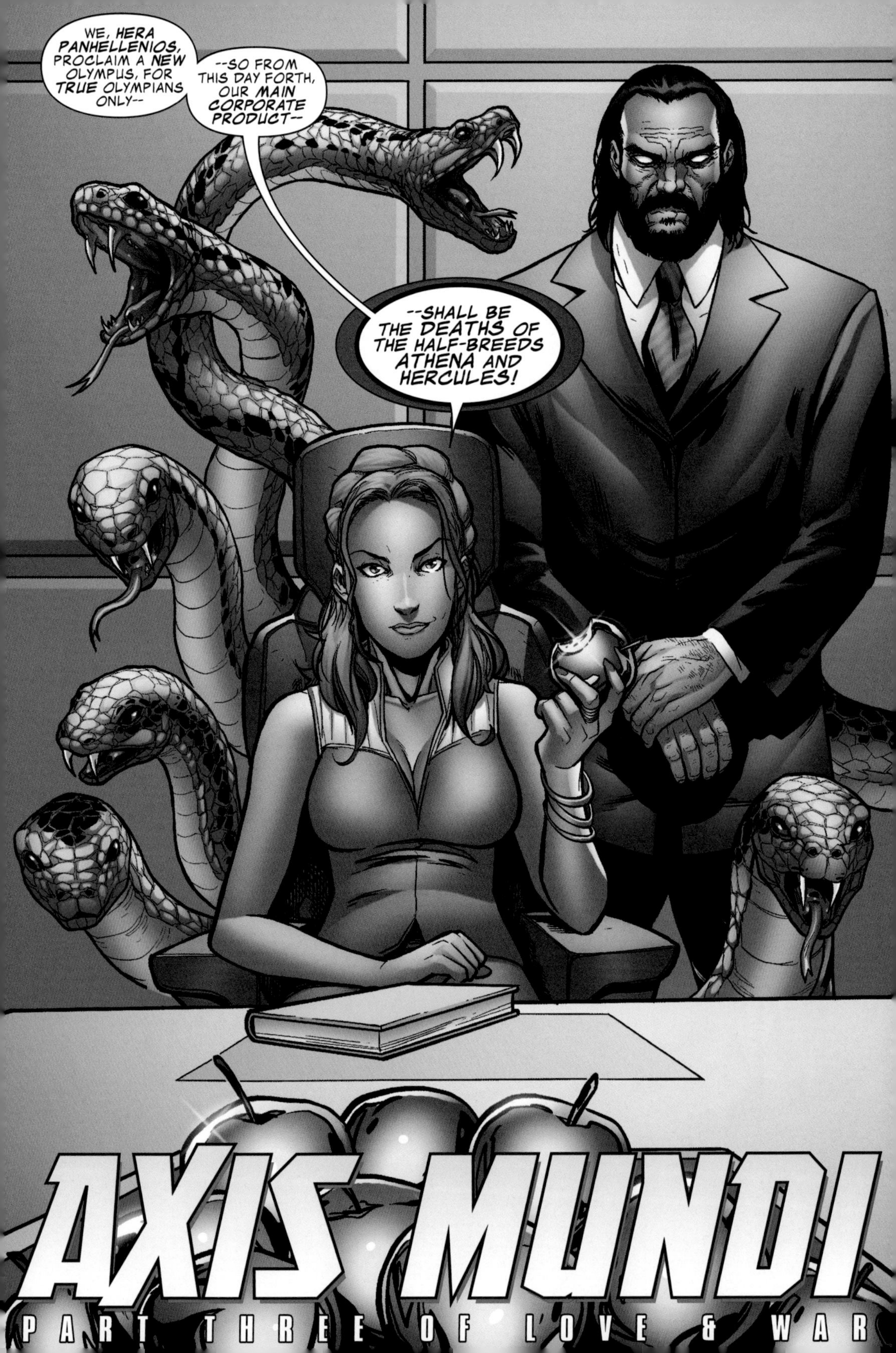
WE, HERA PANHELLENIOS, PROCLAIM A NEW OLYMPUS, FOR TRUE OLYMPIANS ONLY--
--SO FROM THIS DAY FORTH, OUR MAIN CORPORATE PRODUCT--
--SHALL BE THE DEATHS OF THE HALF-BREEDS ATHENA AND HERCULES!
AXIS MUNDI
PART THREE OF LOVE & WAR

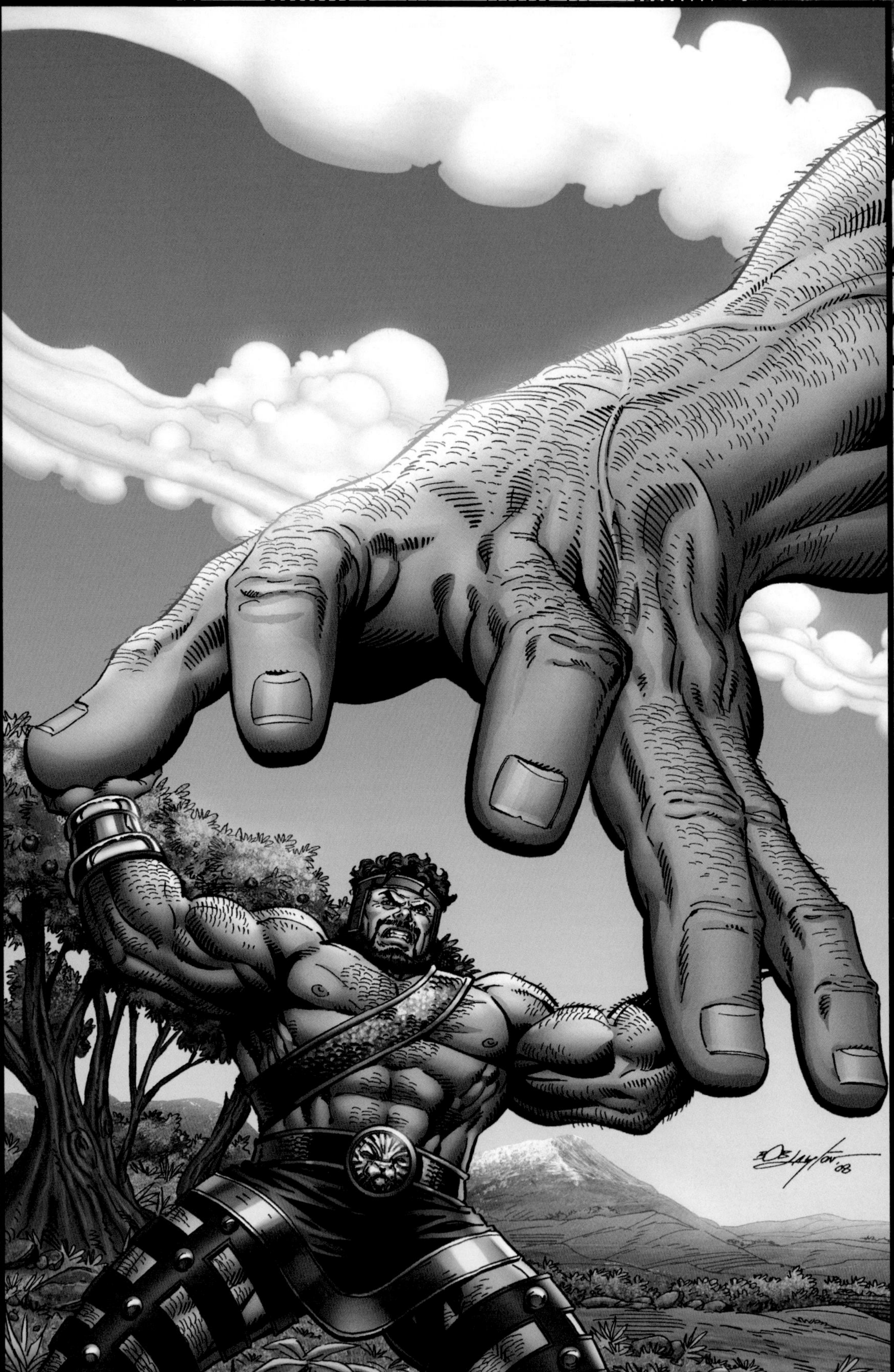

INCREDIBLE HERCULES #134

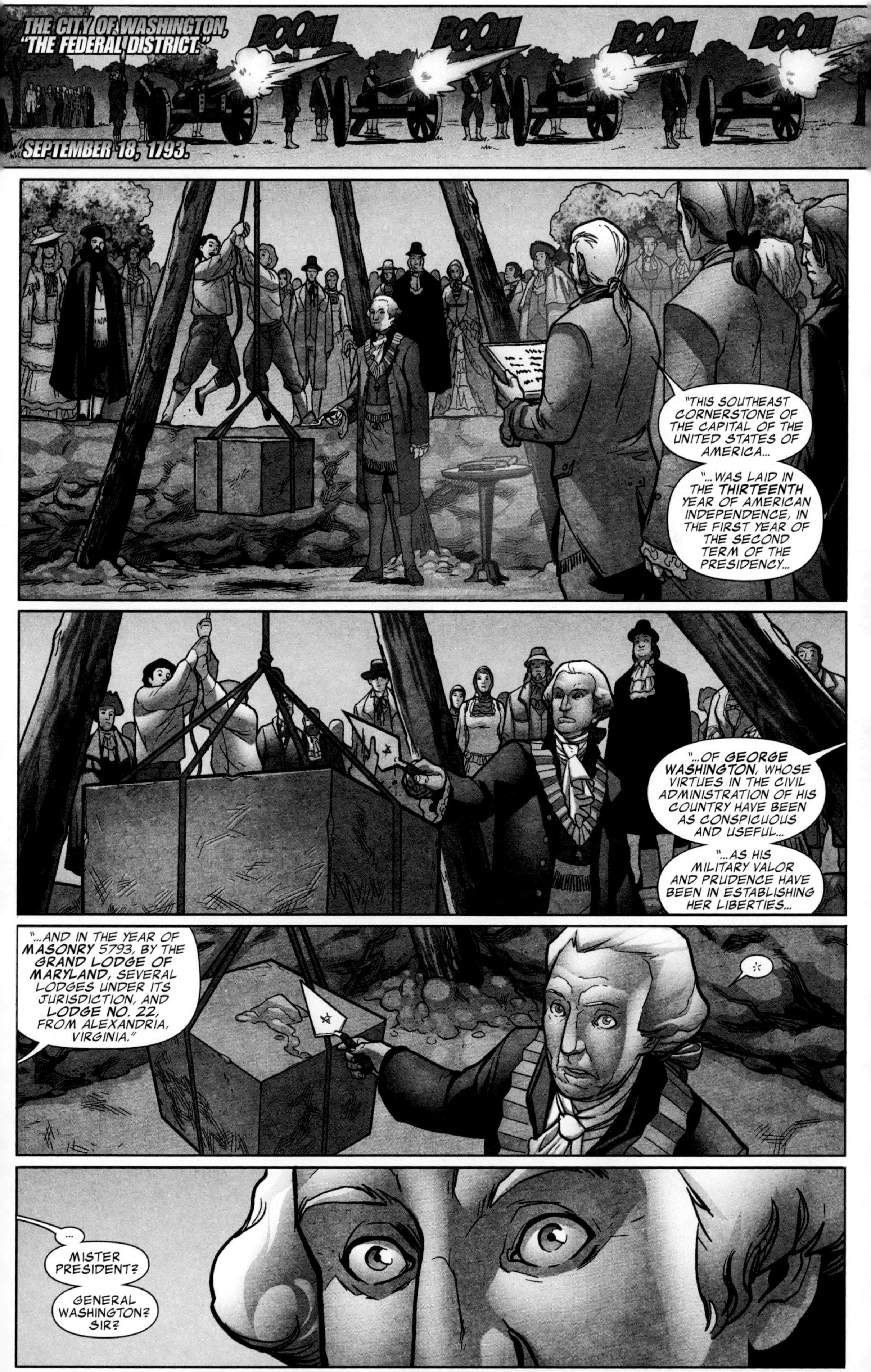
THE CITY OF WASHINGTON, "THE FEDERAL DISTRICT."
BOOM! BOOM! BOOM! BOOM!
SEPTEMBER 18, 1793.
"THIS SOUTHEAST CORNERSTONE OF THE CAPITAL OF THE UNITED STATES OF AMERICA...
"...WAS LAID IN THE THIRTEENTH YEAR OF AMERICAN INDEPENDENCE, IN THE FIRST YEAR OF THE SECOND TERM OF THE PRESIDENCY...
"...OF GEORGE WASHINGTON, WHOSE VIRTUES IN THE CIVIL ADMINISTRATION OF HIS COUNTRY HAVE BEEN AS CONSPICUOUS AND USEFUL...
"...AS HIS MILITARY VALOR AND PRUDENCE HAVE BEEN IN ESTABLISHING HER LIBERTIES...
"...AND IN THE YEAR OF MASONRY 5793, BY THE GRAND LODGE OF MARYLAND, SEVERAL LODGES UNDER ITS JURISDICTION, AND LODGE NO. 22, FROM ALEXANDRIA, VIRGINIA."
...
MISTER PRESIDENT?
GENERAL WASHINGTON? SIR?

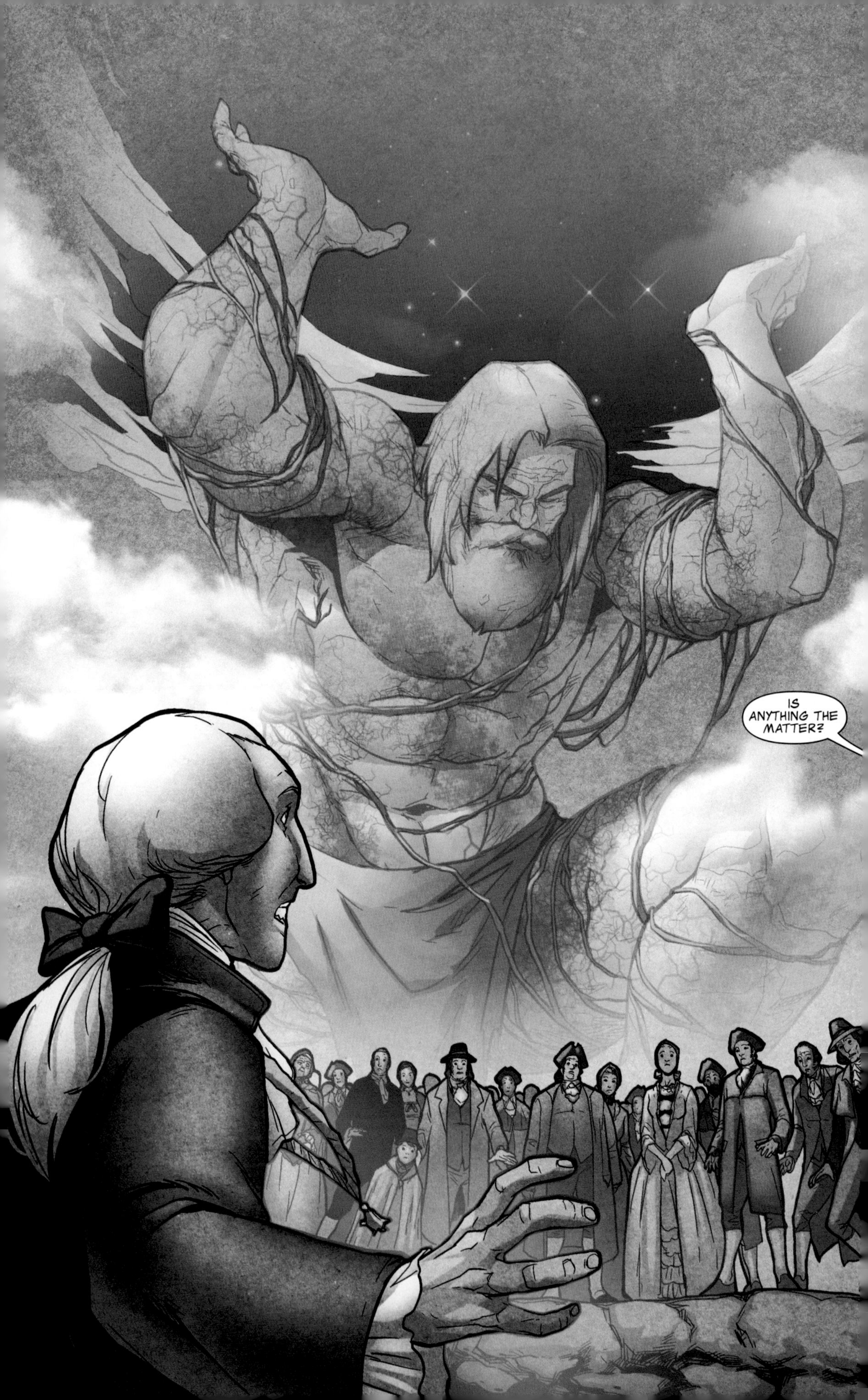
IS ANYTHING THE MATTER?

Shout-out Chorge Amadashington

Second Inaugural ~~Address~~ of ~~George Washington~~

Amazonian Holding Cell, Flying Around

P~~hiladelphia, Pennsylvan~~ia

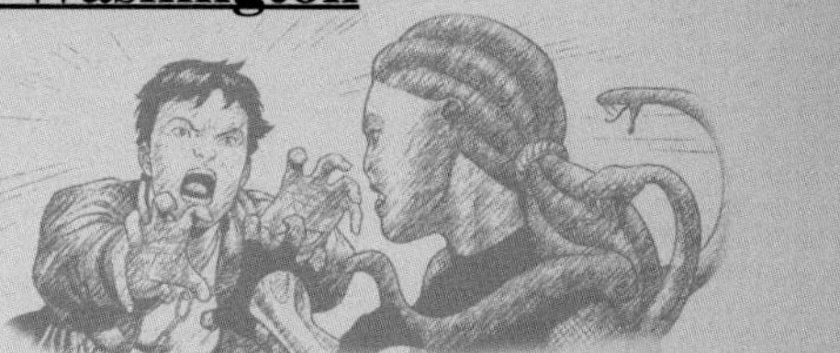

Monday, March 4, 1793 or... now

Yo, people that aren't as smart as me,

~~Fellow Citizens~~,

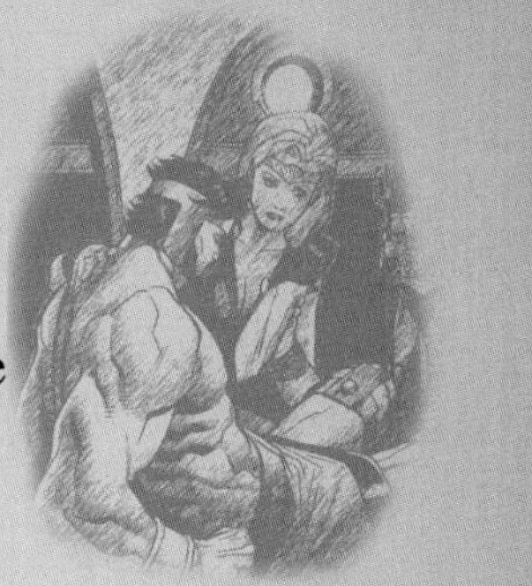

depending on my (maybe-dead) sidekick, Hercules, to save the day before Amazons

I am again ~~called upon by the voice of my country to~~ execute ~~the functions of its Chief Magistrate~~ me.

OMPHALOS (whatever that is)

When the ~~occasion proper for it~~ shall arrive, I shall endeavor to express the high sense I entertain of this distinguished honor, and of the confidence which has been reposed in me by the ~~people of united America.~~ murder-happy chicks that've trapped me.

(even though my super-charged brain's fritzing due to lack of junk food)

Previous to the execution of ~~any offical act of the President the Constitution requires an oath of offic~~e.

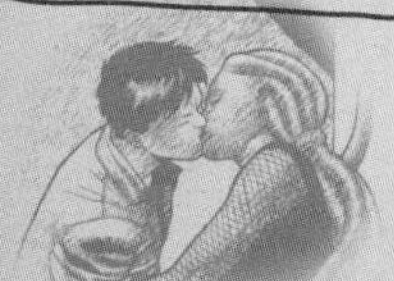

the mega-HOT snaked-headed Delphyne, she wanted to rock the Amadeus. But Artume got her stab on.

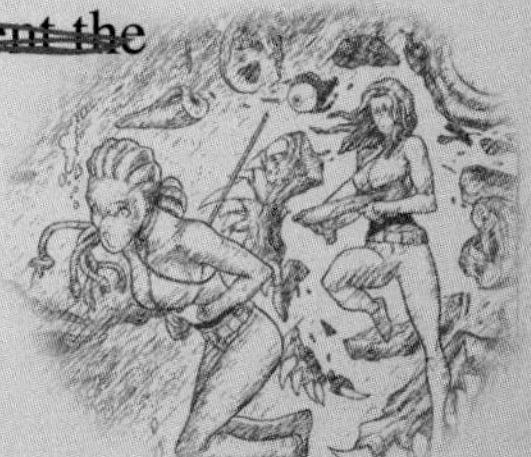

This Oath I am now about to take, and in your presence: That if it shall be found ~~during my administration of the Government I have in any instance violated willingly or knowingly the injunctions thereof~~, I may (besides incurring constitutional pubishment) be subject to ~~the upbraidings of all who are now witnesses of the present solemn ceremony~~.

all sorts of unfun killing-related activities...

that the AmaZANYans don't need any more info from me

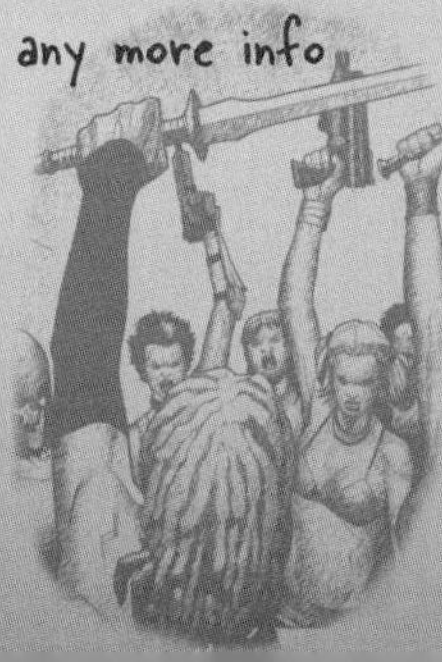

Yay adventure.

I want my puppy.

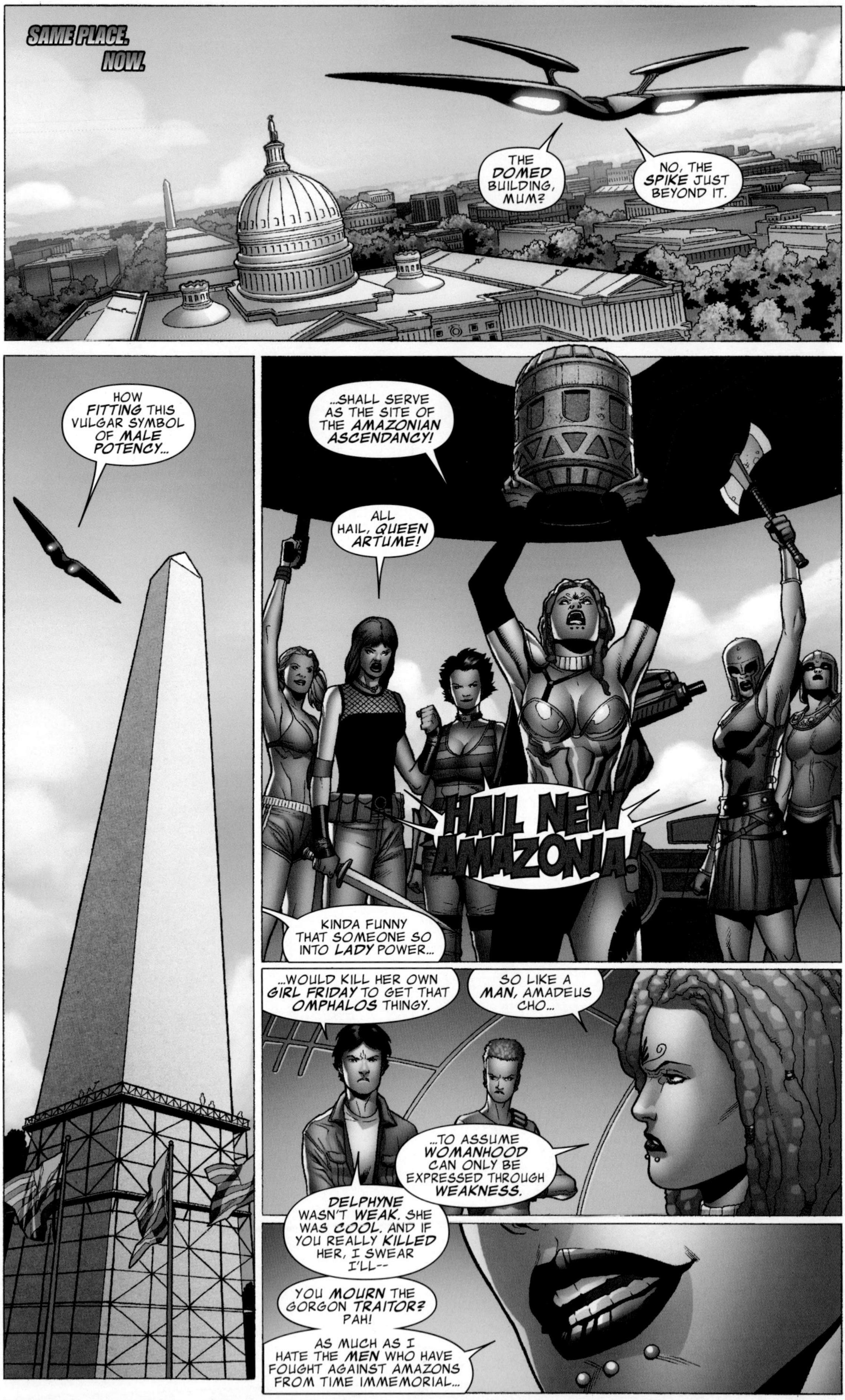
SAME PLACE. NOW.
THE DOMED BUILDING, MUM?
NO, THE SPIKE JUST BEYOND IT.
HOW FITTING THIS VULGAR SYMBOL OF MALE POTENCY...
...SHALL SERVE AS THE SITE OF THE AMAZONIAN ASCENDANCY!
ALL HAIL, QUEEN ARTUME!
HAIL NEW AMAZONIA!
KINDA FUNNY THAT SOMEONE SO INTO LADY POWER...
...WOULD KILL HER OWN GIRL FRIDAY TO GET THAT OMPHALOS THINGY.
SO LIKE A MAN, AMADEUS CHO...
...TO ASSUME WOMANHOOD CAN ONLY BE EXPRESSED THROUGH WEAKNESS.
DELPHYNE WASN'T WEAK. SHE WAS COOL. AND IF YOU REALLY KILLED HER, I SWEAR I'LL--
YOU MOURN THE GORGON TRAITOR? PAH!
AS MUCH AS I HATE THE MEN WHO HAVE FOUGHT AGAINST AMAZONS FROM TIME IMMEMORIAL...

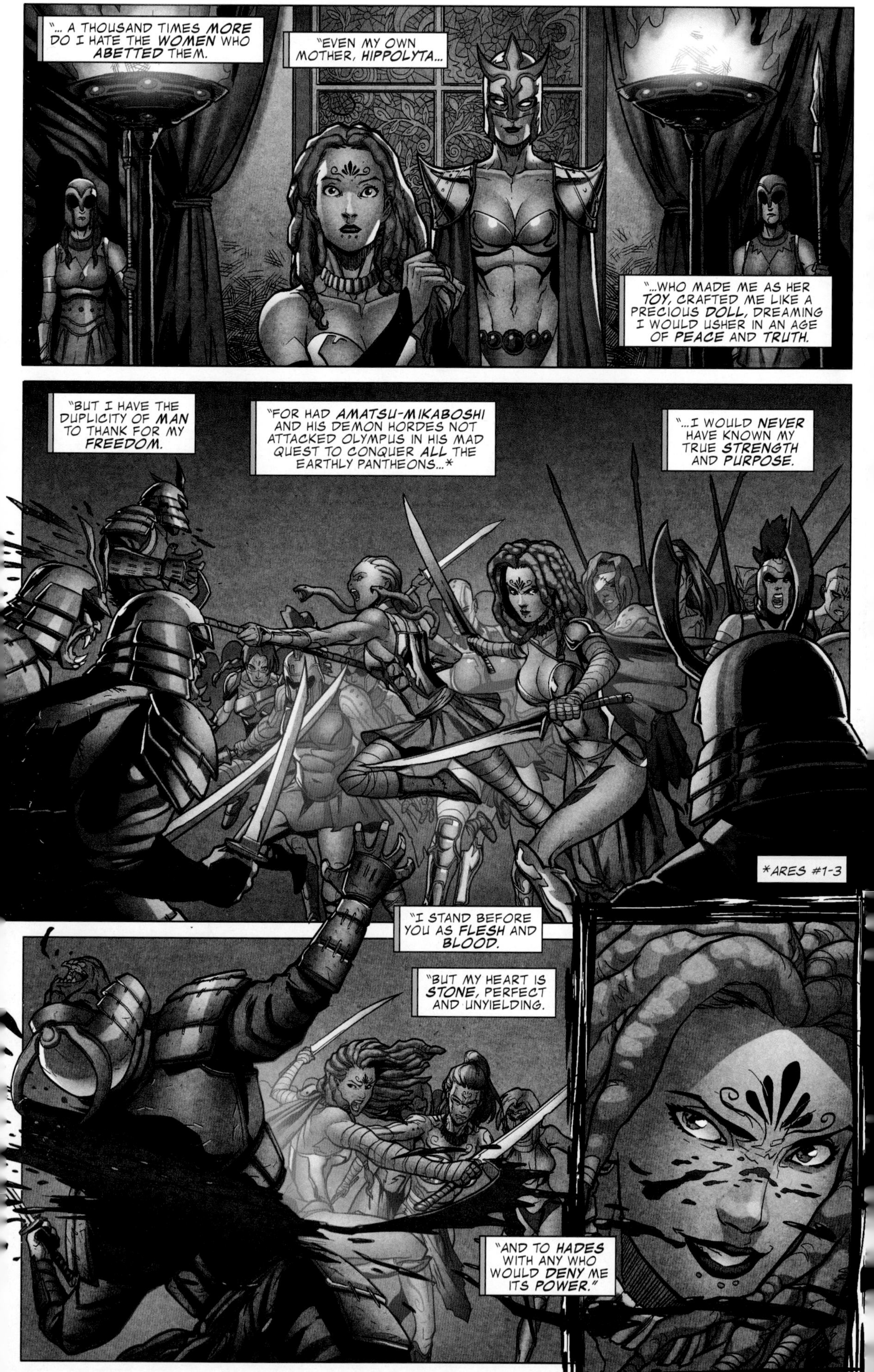
"... A THOUSAND TIMES MORE DO I HATE THE WOMEN WHO ABETTED THEM.
"EVEN MY OWN MOTHER, HIPPOLYTA...
"...WHO MADE ME AS HER TOY, CRAFTED ME LIKE A PRECIOUS DOLL, DREAMING I WOULD USHER IN AN AGE OF PEACE AND TRUTH.
"BUT I HAVE THE DUPLICITY OF MAN TO THANK FOR MY FREEDOM.
"FOR HAD AMATSU-MIKABOSHI AND HIS DEMON HORDES NOT ATTACKED OLYMPUS IN HIS MAD QUEST TO CONQUER ALL THE EARTHLY PANTHEONS...*
"...I WOULD NEVER HAVE KNOWN MY TRUE STRENGTH AND PURPOSE.
*ARES #1-3
"I STAND BEFORE YOU AS FLESH AND BLOOD.
"BUT MY HEART IS STONE, PERFECT AND UNYIELDING.
"AND TO HADES WITH ANY WHO WOULD DENY ME ITS POWER."

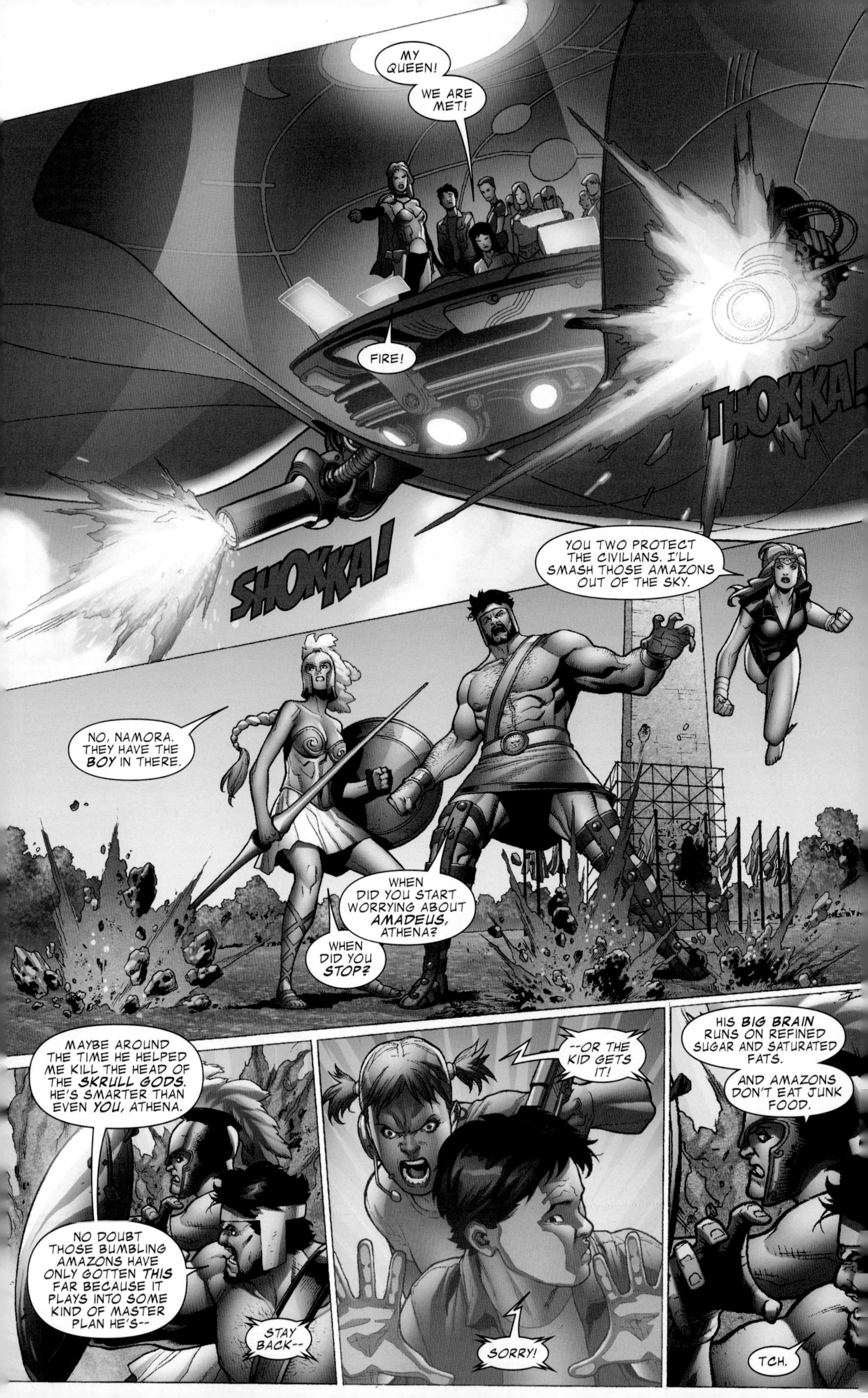
MY QUEEN!
WE ARE MET!
FIRE!
THOKKA!
SHOKKA!
YOU TWO PROTECT THE CIVILIANS. I'LL SMASH THOSE AMAZONS OUT OF THE SKY.
NO, NAMORA. THEY HAVE THE BOY IN THERE.
WHEN DID YOU START WORRYING ABOUT AMADEUS, ATHENA?
WHEN DID YOU STOP?
MAYBE AROUND THE TIME HE HELPED ME KILL THE HEAD OF THE SKRULL GODS. HE'S SMARTER THAN EVEN YOU, ATHENA.
NO DOUBT THOSE BUMBLING AMAZONS HAVE ONLY GOTTEN THIS FAR BECAUSE IT PLAYS INTO SOME KIND OF MASTER PLAN HE'S--
STAY BACK--
--OR THE KID GETS IT!
SORRY!
HIS BIG BRAIN RUNS ON REFINED SUGAR AND SATURATED FATS.
AND AMAZONS DON'T EAT JUNK FOOD.
TCH.

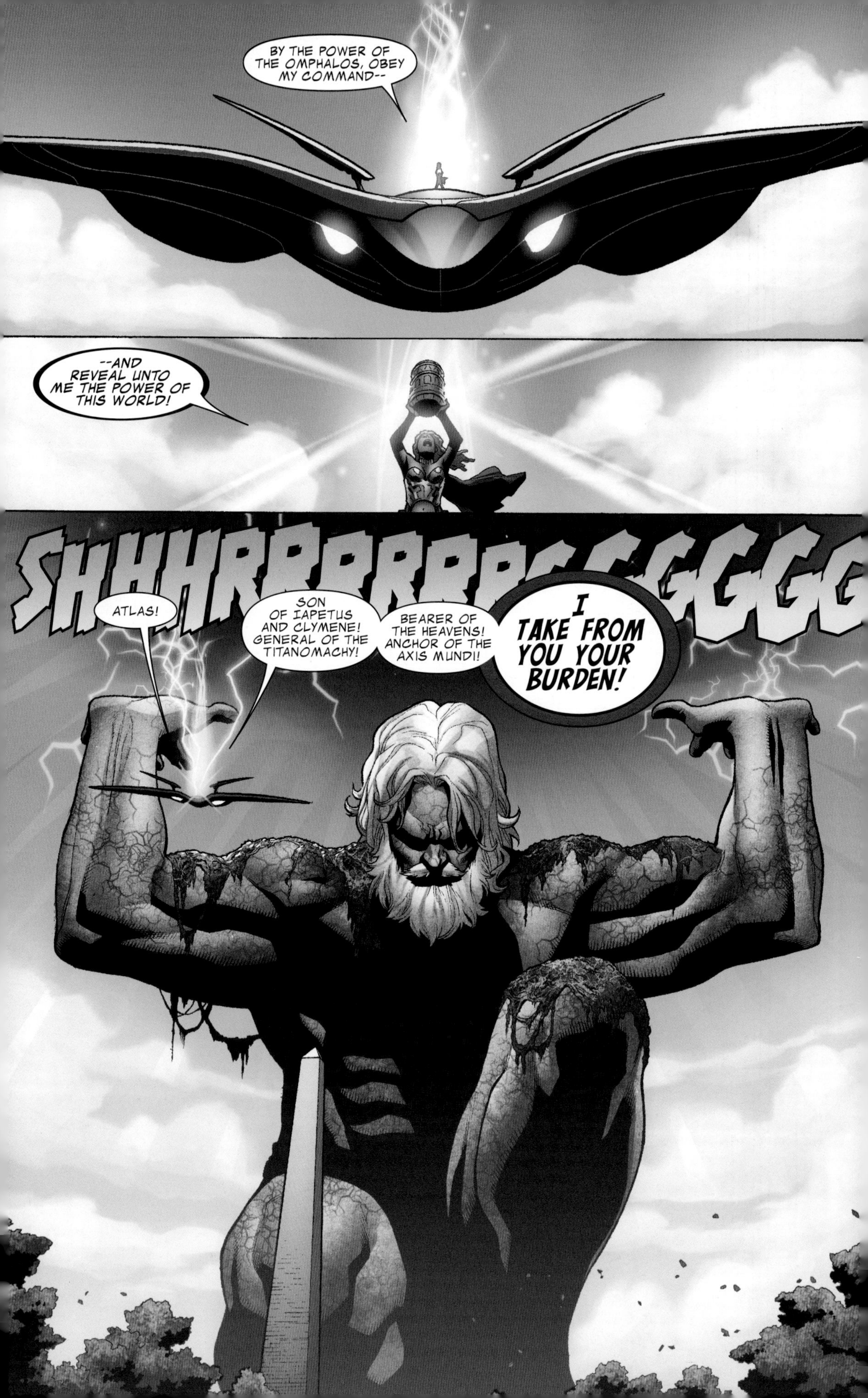
BY THE POWER OF THE OMPHALOS, OBEY MY COMMAND--
--AND REVEAL UNTO ME THE POWER OF THIS WORLD!
SHHHRRRRRRGGGGGG
ATLAS!
SON OF IAPETUS AND CLYMENE! GENERAL OF THE TITANOMACHY!
BEARER OF THE HEAVENS! ANCHOR OF THE AXIS MUNDI!
I TAKE FROM YOU YOUR BURDEN!

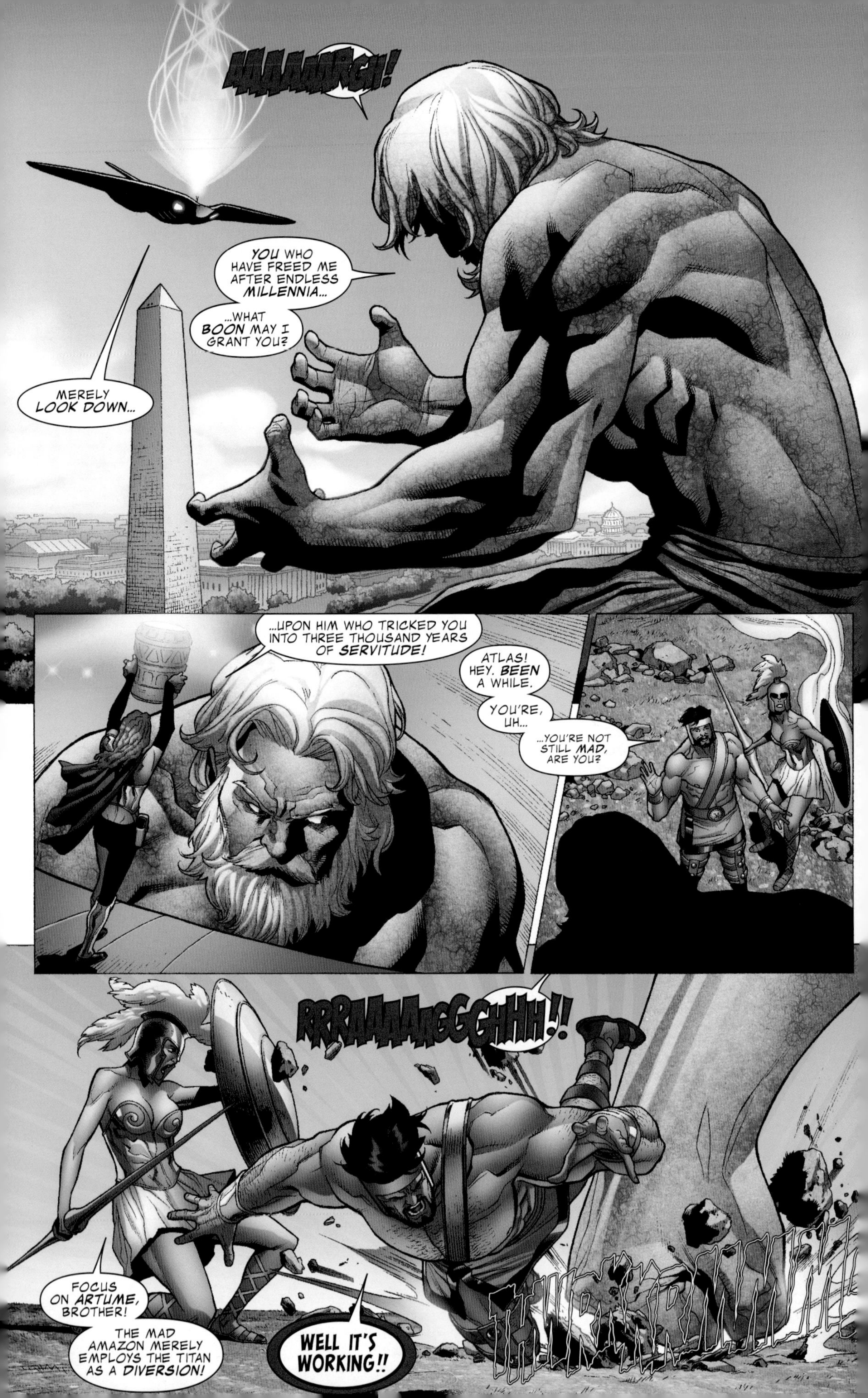
AAAAAARRGH!
YOU WHO HAVE FREED ME AFTER ENDLESS MILLENNIA...
...WHAT BOON MAY I GRANT YOU?
MERELY LOOK DOWN...
...UPON HIM WHO TRICKED YOU INTO THREE THOUSAND YEARS OF SERVITUDE!
ATLAS! HEY. BEEN A WHILE.
YOU'RE, UH...
...YOU'RE NOT STILL MAD, ARE YOU?
RRRAAAAAAGGGHHH!!
FOCUS ON ARTUME, BROTHER!
THE MAD AMAZON MERELY EMPLOYS THE TITAN AS A DIVERSION!
WELL IT'S WORKING!!

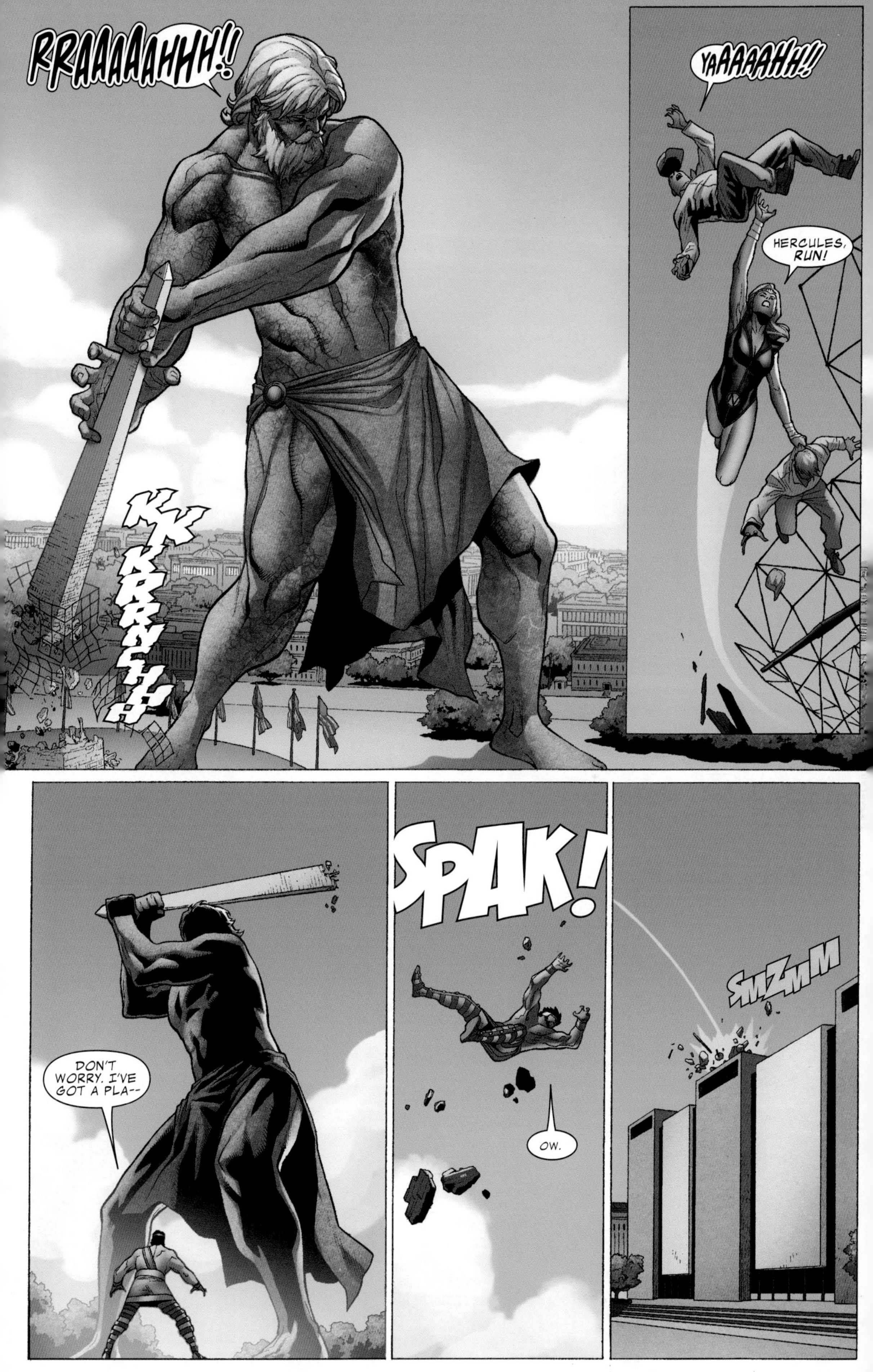
RRAAAAAAHHH!!
KKKRRRNCHH
YAAAAAHH!!
HERCULES, RUN!
DON'T WORRY. I'VE GOT A PLA--
SPAK!
OW.
SMZMM

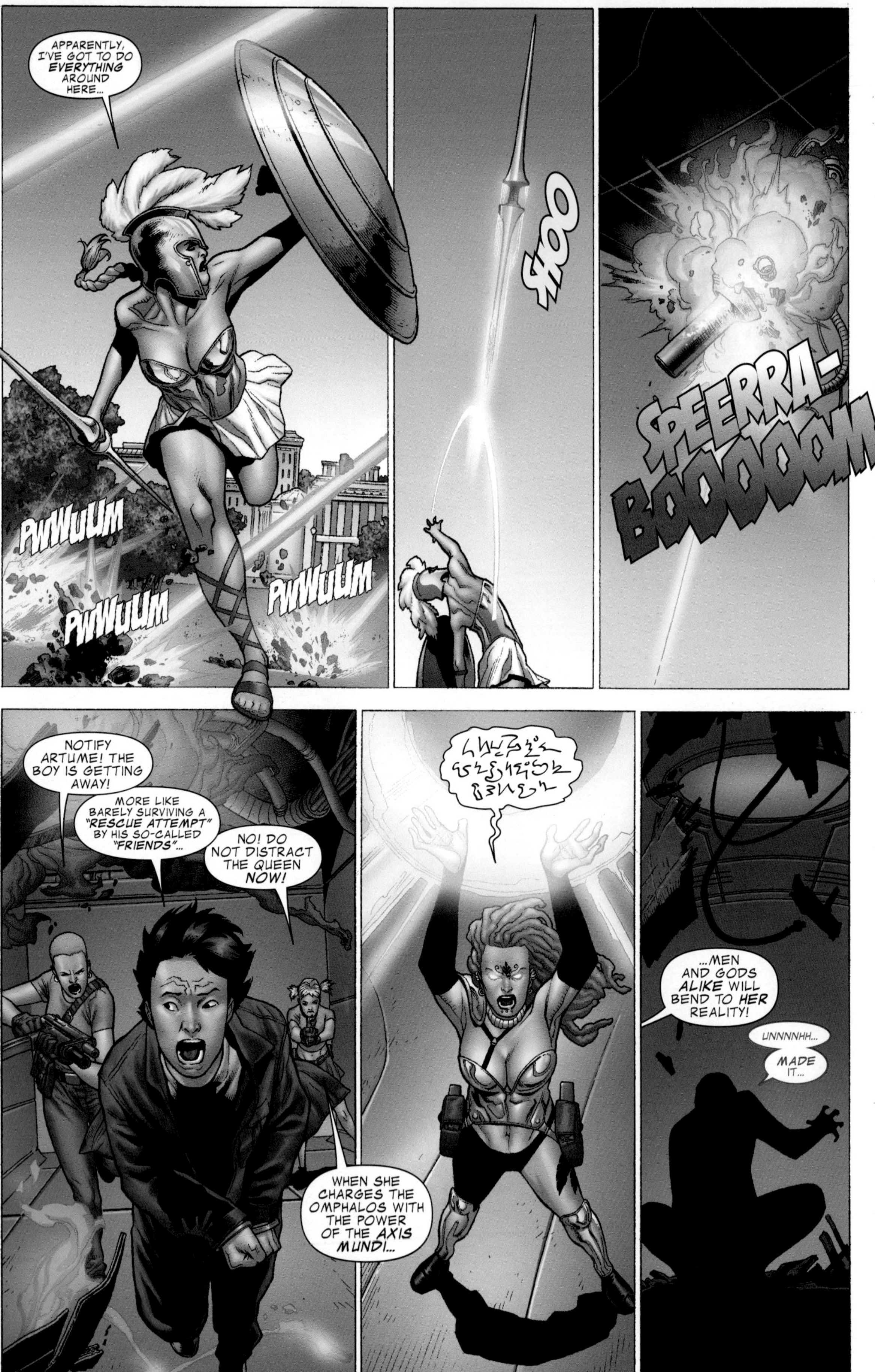
APPARENTLY, I'VE GOT TO DO EVERYTHING AROUND HERE...
PWUUM
PWUUM
PWUUM
SHOO
SPEERRA-BOOOOOM!
NOTIFY ARTUME! THE BOY IS GETTING AWAY!
MORE LIKE BARELY SURVIVING A "RESCUE ATTEMPT" BY HIS SO-CALLED "FRIENDS"...
NO! DO NOT DISTRACT THE QUEEN NOW!
WHEN SHE CHARGES THE OMPHALOS WITH THE POWER OF THE AXIS MUNDI...
...MEN AND GODS ALIKE WILL BEND TO HER REALITY!
UNNNNHH...
MADE IT...

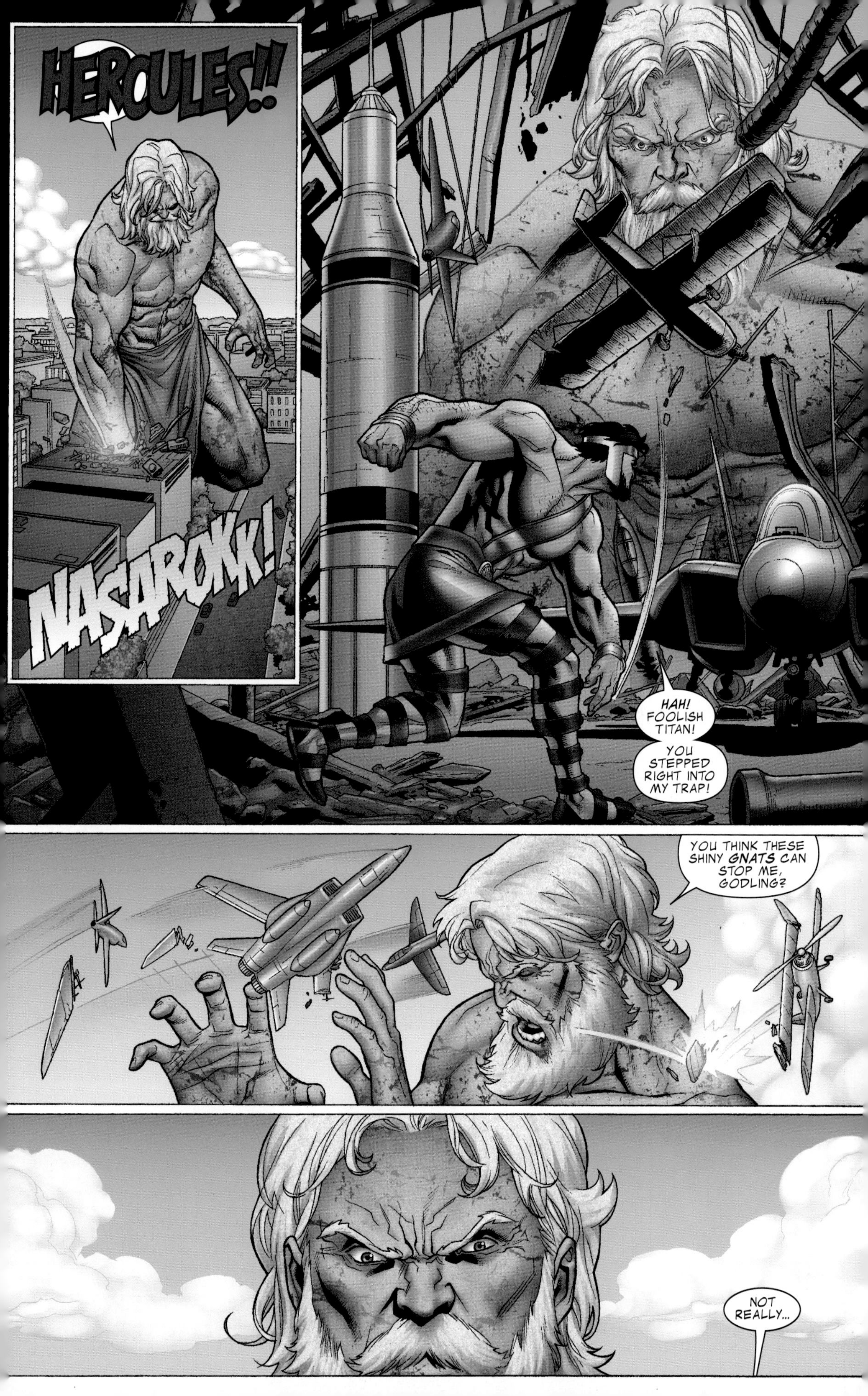
HERCULES!!
NASAROKK!
HAH! FOOLISH TITAN!
YOU STEPPED RIGHT INTO MY TRAP!
YOU THINK THESE SHINY GNATS CAN STOP ME, GODLING?
NOT REALLY...

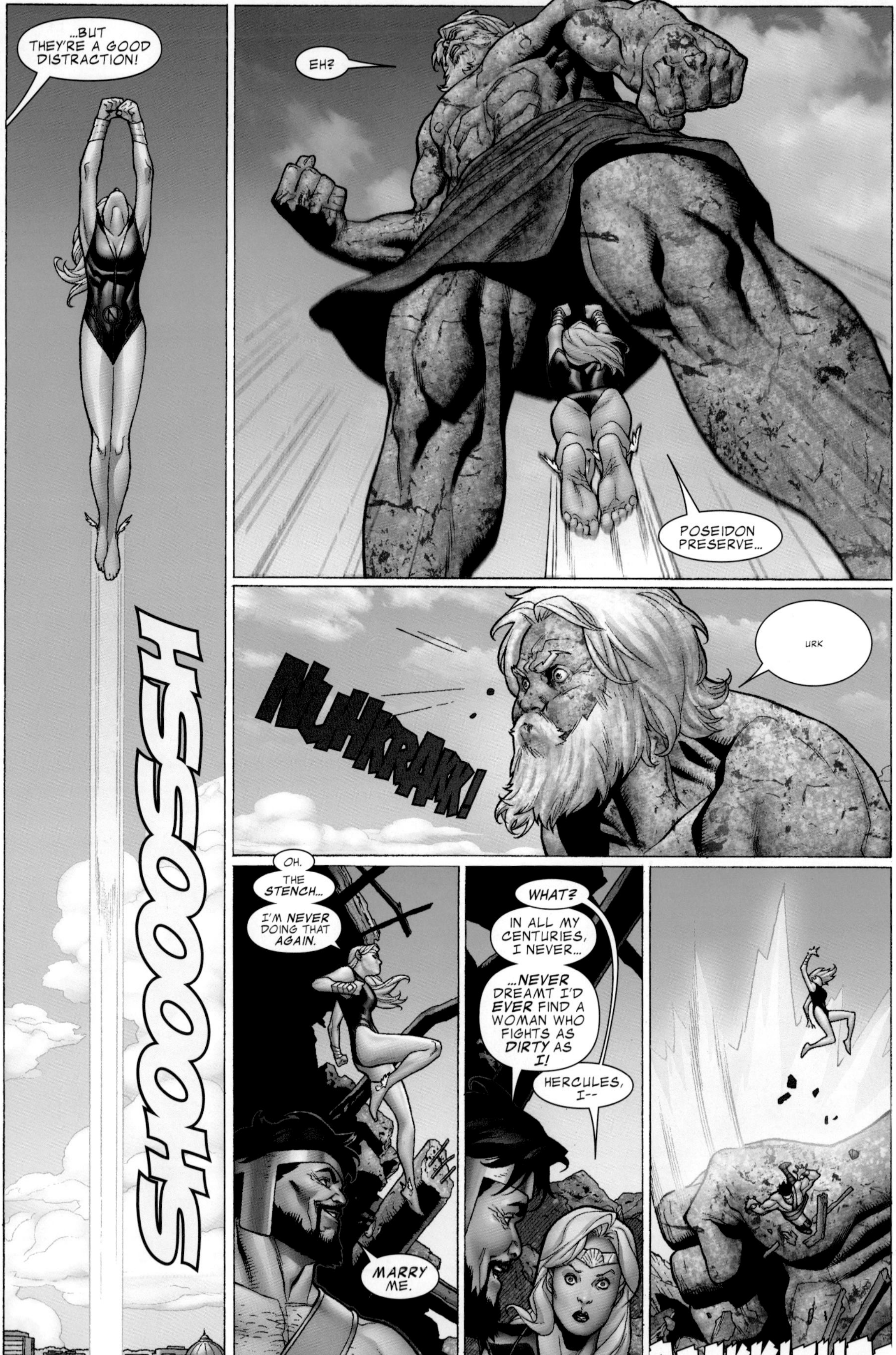
...BUT THEY'RE A GOOD DISTRACTION!
SHOOOOOSH
EH?
POSEIDON PRESERVE...
NUHKRAKK!
URK
OH. THE STENCH...
I'M NEVER DOING THAT AGAIN.
MARRY ME.
WHAT?
IN ALL MY CENTURIES, I NEVER...
...NEVER DREAMT I'D EVER FIND A WOMAN WHO FIGHTS AS DIRTY AS I!
HERCULES, I--
BRAKKITUPP

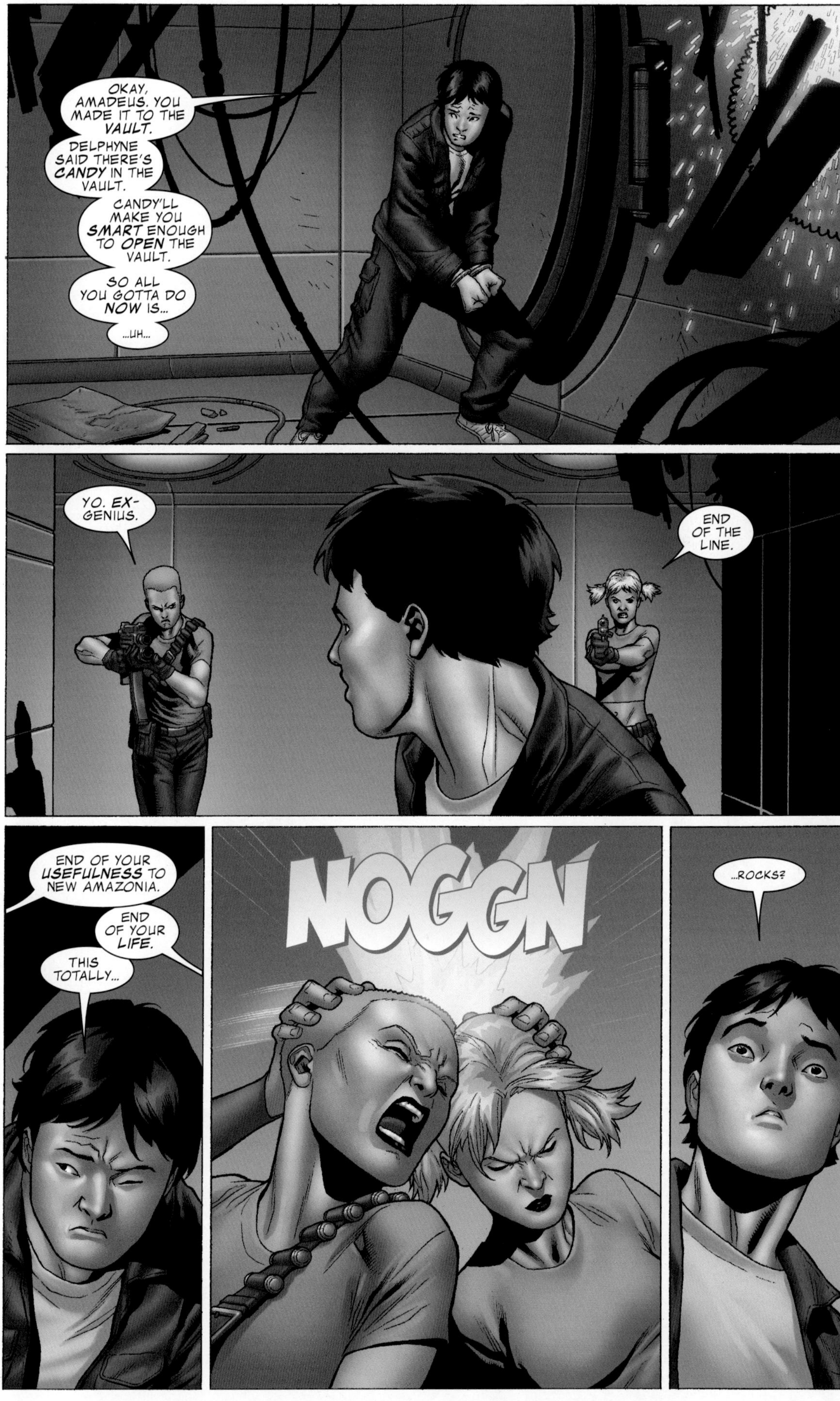
OKAY, AMADEUS. YOU MADE IT TO THE VAULT.
DELPHYNE SAID THERE'S CANDY IN THE VAULT.
CANDY'LL MAKE YOU SMART ENOUGH TO OPEN THE VAULT.
SO ALL YOU GOTTA DO NOW IS...
...UH...
YO. EX-GENIUS.
END OF THE LINE.
END OF YOUR USEFULNESS TO NEW AMAZONIA.
END OF YOUR LIFE.
THIS TOTALLY...
NOGGN
...ROCKS?

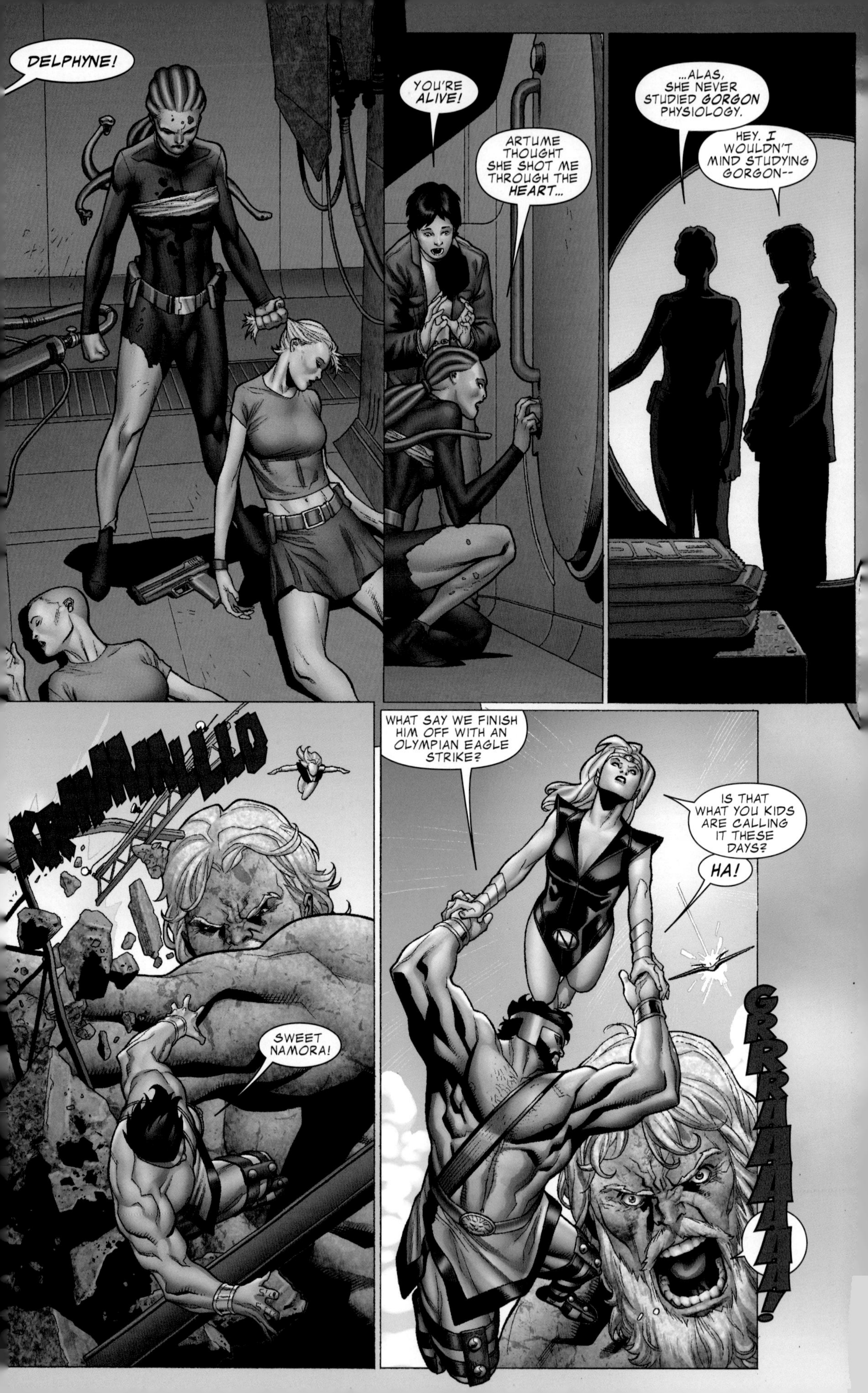
DELPHYNE!
YOU'RE ALIVE!
ARTUME THOUGHT SHE SHOT ME THROUGH THE HEART...
...ALAS, SHE NEVER STUDIED GORGON PHYSIOLOGY.
HEY. I WOULDN'T MIND STUDYING GORGON--
KRAAAAKLLLD
SWEET NAMORA!
WHAT SAY WE FINISH HIM OFF WITH AN OLYMPIAN EAGLE STRIKE?
IS THAT WHAT YOU KIDS ARE CALLING IT THESE DAYS?
HA!
GRRRAAAAAA!

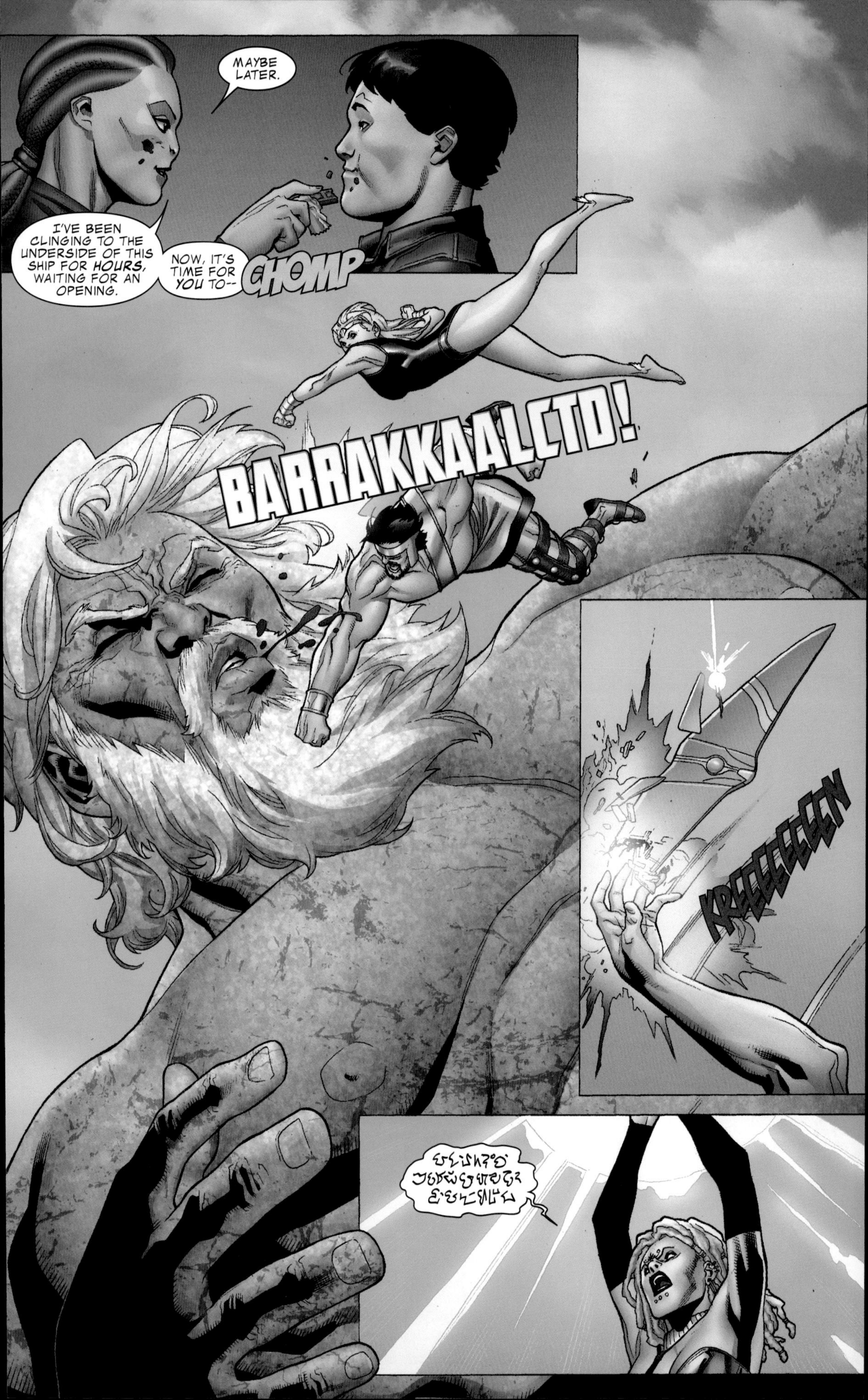

MAYBE LATER.
I'VE BEEN CLINGING TO THE UNDERSIDE OF THIS SHIP FOR HOURS, WAITING FOR AN OPENING.
NOW, IT'S TIME FOR YOU TO--
CHOMP
BARRAKKAALCTO!
KREEEEEEEN

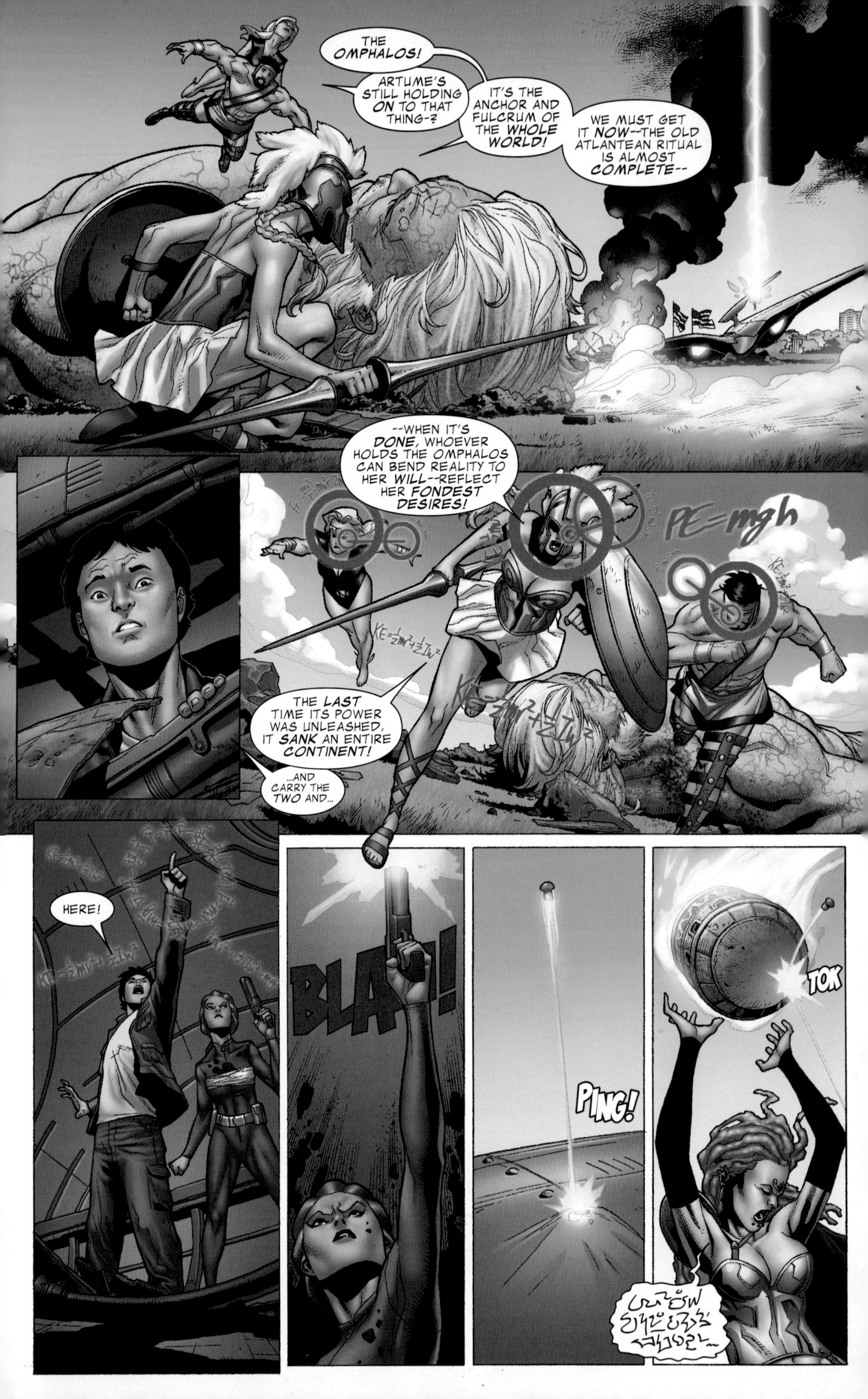
THE OMPHALOS!
ARTUME'S STILL HOLDING ON TO THAT THING-?
IT'S THE ANCHOR AND FULCRUM OF THE WHOLE WORLD!
WE MUST GET IT NOW--THE OLD ATLANTEAN RITUAL IS ALMOST COMPLETE--
--WHEN IT'S DONE, WHOEVER HOLDS THE OMPHALOS CAN BEND REALITY TO HER WILL--REFLECT HER FONDEST DESIRES!
PE=mgh
THE LAST TIME ITS POWER WAS UNLEASHED, IT SANK AN ENTIRE CONTINENT!
...AND CARRY THE TWO AND...
HERE!
BLAM!
PING!
TOK

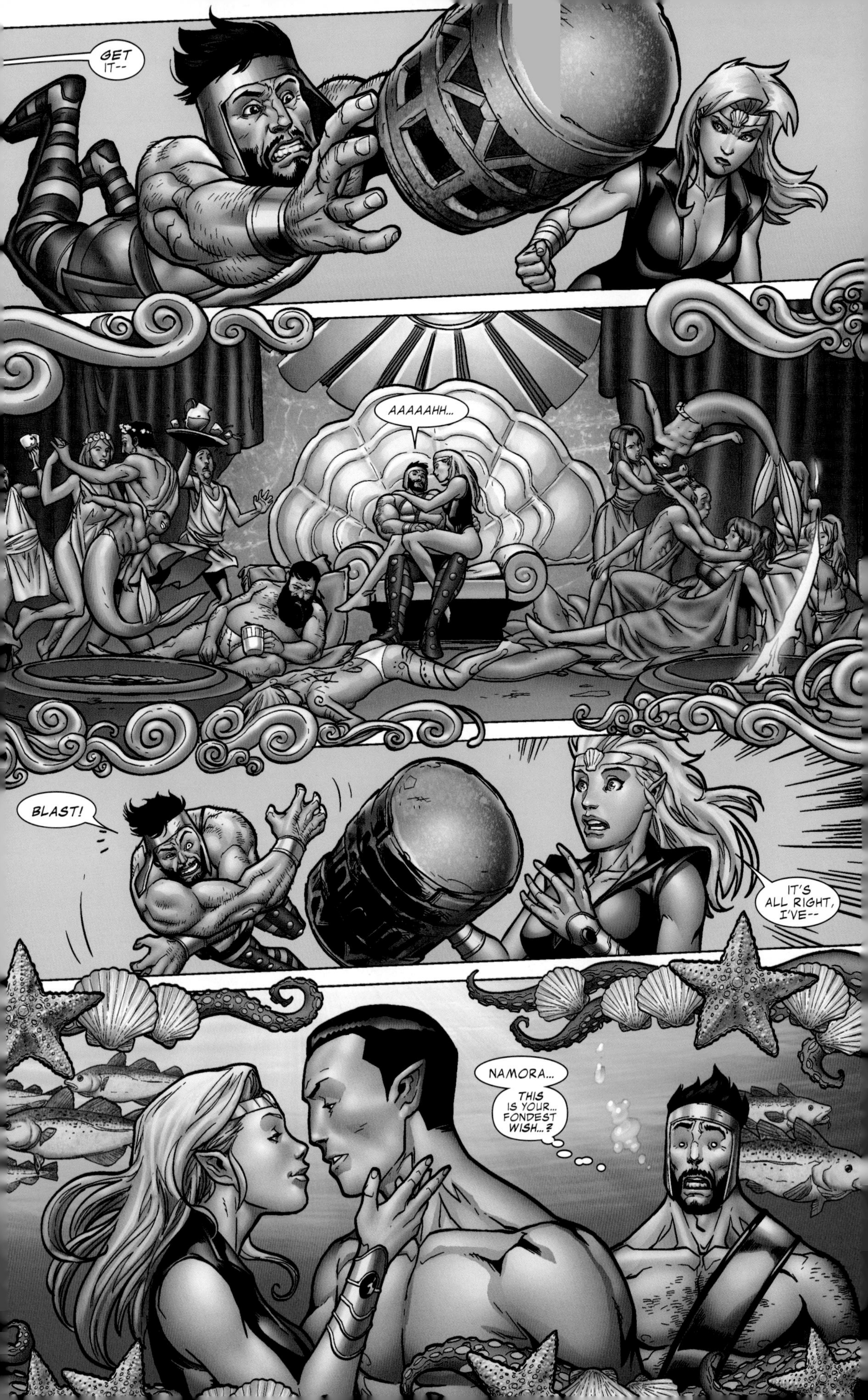
GET IT--
AAAAAHH...
BLAST!
IT'S ALL RIGHT, I'VE--
NAMORA...
THIS IS YOUR... FONDEST WISH...?

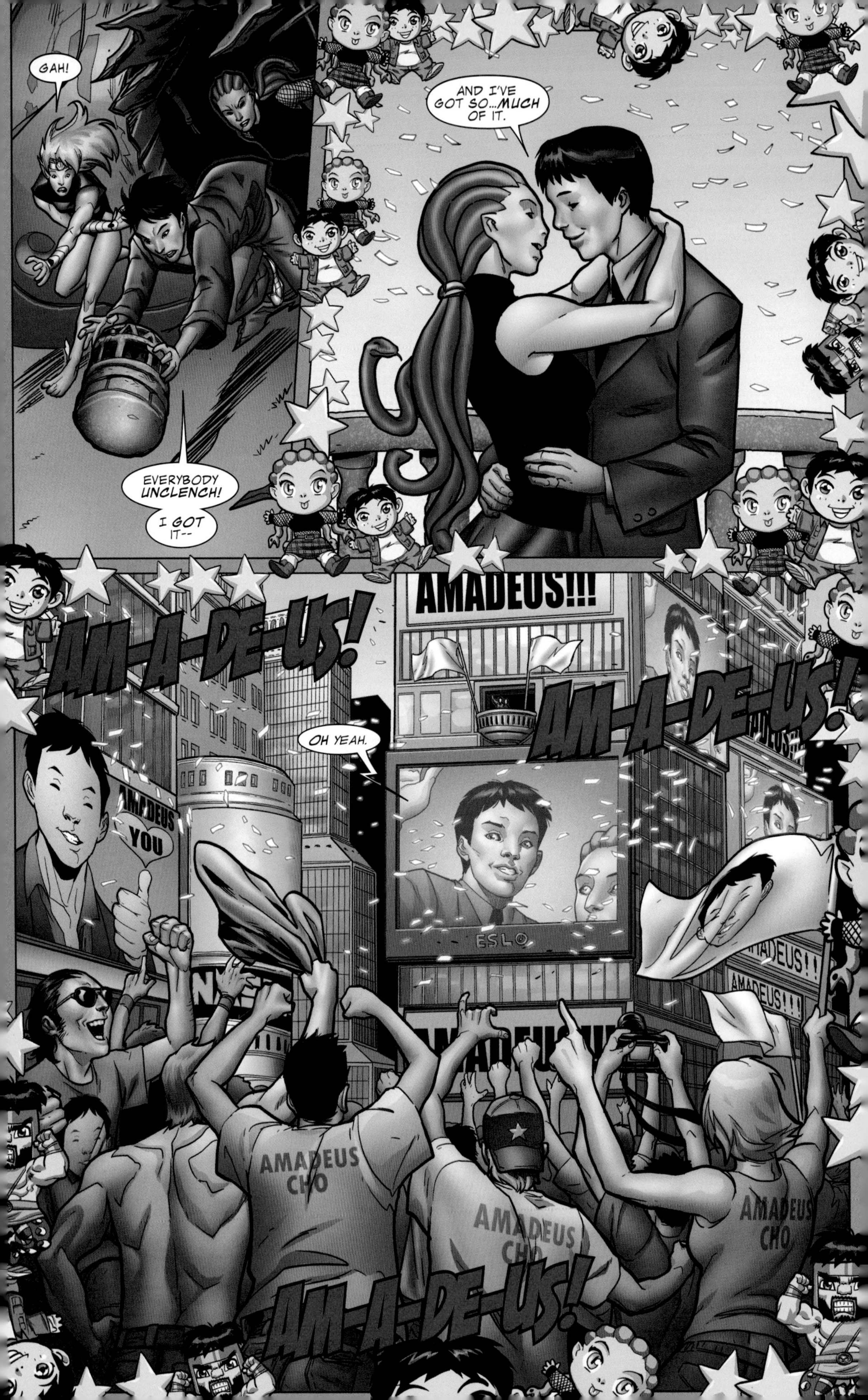

GAH!
EVERYBODY UNCLENCH!
I GOT IT--
AND I'VE GOT SO...MUCH OF IT.
AMADEUS!!!
AM-A-DE-US!
AM-A-DE-US!
OH YEAH.
AMADEUS YOU
ESLO
AMADEUS!!
AMADEUS!!!
AMADEUS CHO
AMADEUS CHO
AMADEUS CHO
AM-A-DE-US!

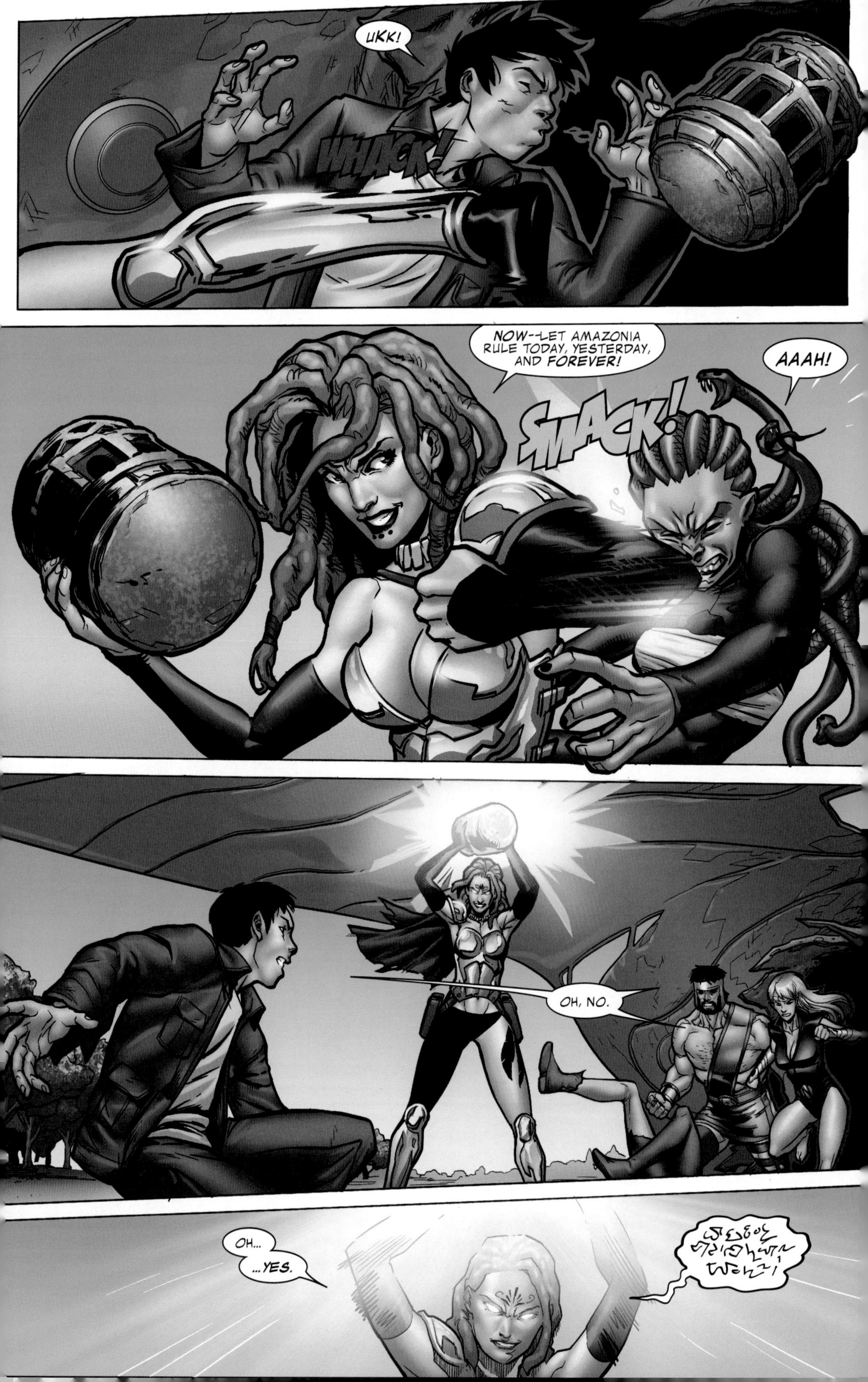
UKK!
WHACK!
NOW--LET AMAZONIA RULE TODAY, YESTERDAY, AND FOREVER!
AAAH!
SMACK!
OH, NO.
OH...
...YES.

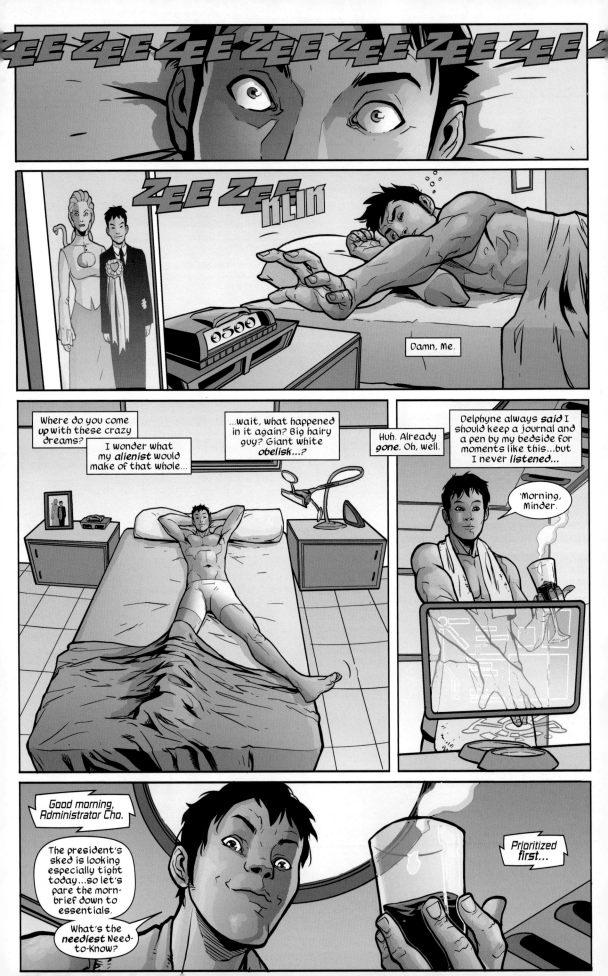

ZEE ZEE ZEE ZEE ZEE ZEE ZEE

ZEE ZEE KLIK

Damn, Me.

Where do you come up with these crazy dreams?

I wonder what my *alienist* would make of that whole...

...wait, what happened in it again? Big hairy guy? Giant white *obelisk*...?

Huh. Already *gone*. Oh, well.

Delphyne always *said* I should keep a journal and a pen by my bedside for moments like this...but I never *listened*...

'Morning, Minder.

Good morning, Administrator Cho.

The president's sked is looking especially tight today...so let's pare the morn-brief down to essentials.

What's the *neediest* Need-to-Know?

Prioritized *first*...

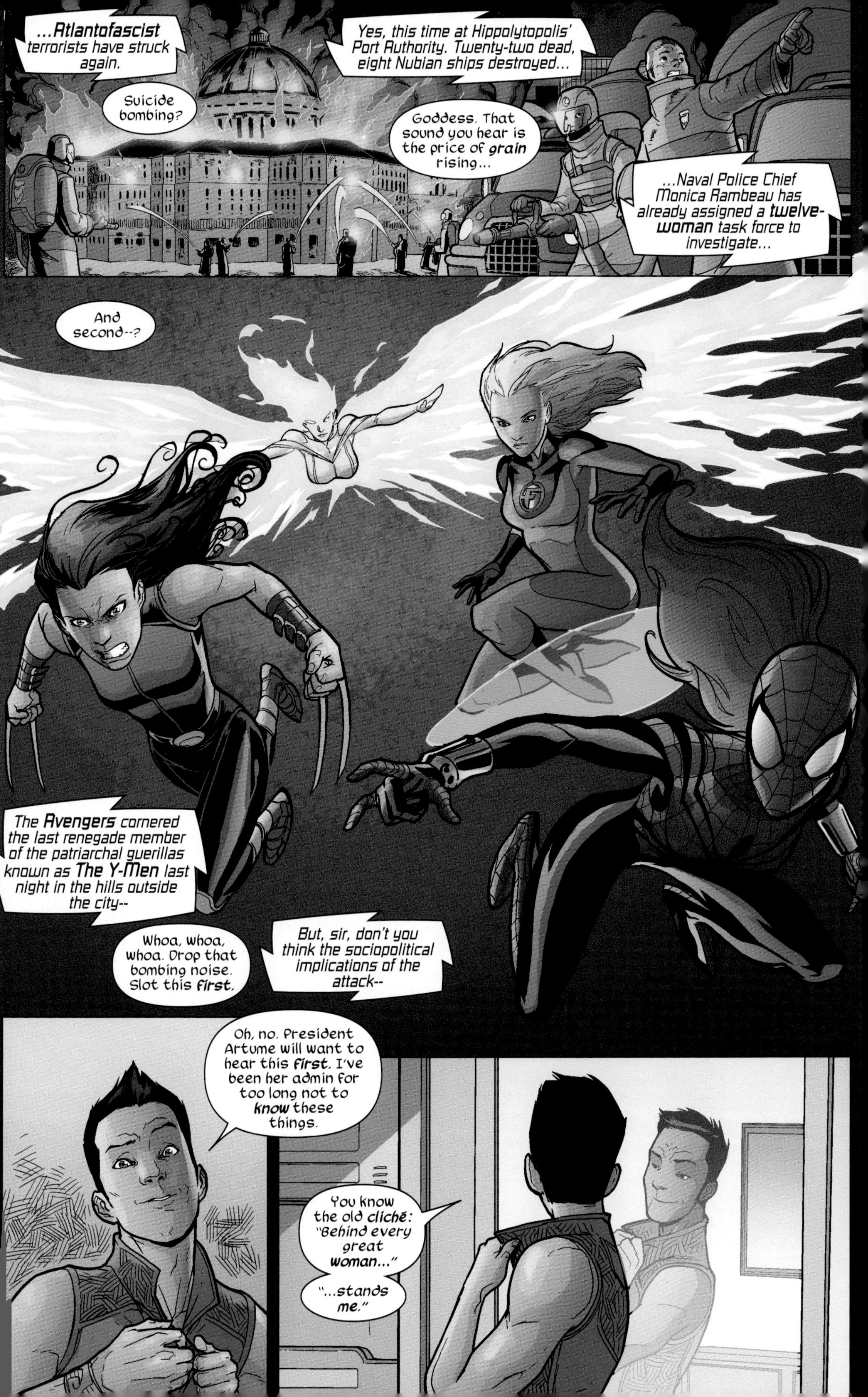
...Atlantofascist terrorists have struck again.
Yes, this time at Hippolytopolis' Port Authority. Twenty-two dead, eight Nubian ships destroyed...
Suicide bombing?
Goddess. That sound you hear is the price of grain rising...
...Naval Police Chief Monica Rambeau has already assigned a twelve-woman task force to investigate...
And second--?
The Avengers cornered the last renegade member of the patriarchal guerillas known as The Y-Men last night in the hills outside the city--
Whoa, whoa, whoa. Drop that bombing noise. Slot this first.
But, sir, don't you think the sociopolitical implications of the attack--
Oh, no. President Artume will want to hear this first. I've been her admin for too long not to know these things.
You know the old cliché: "Behind every great woman..."
"...stands me."

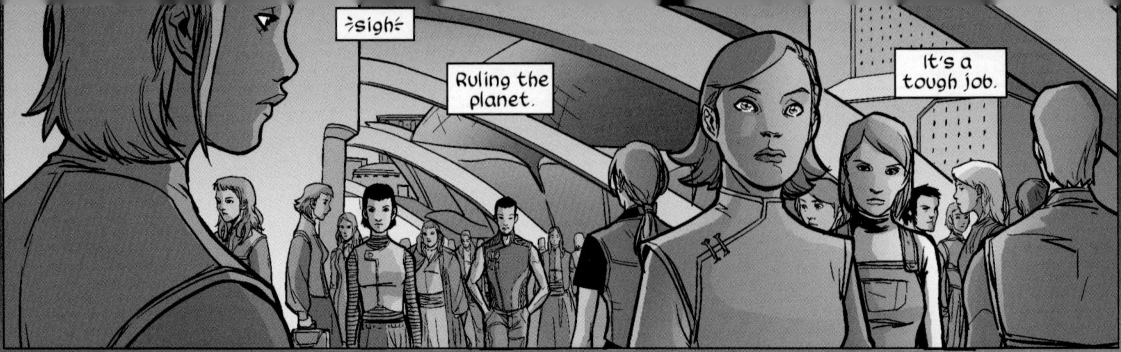
-sigh-
Ruling the planet.
It's a tough job.

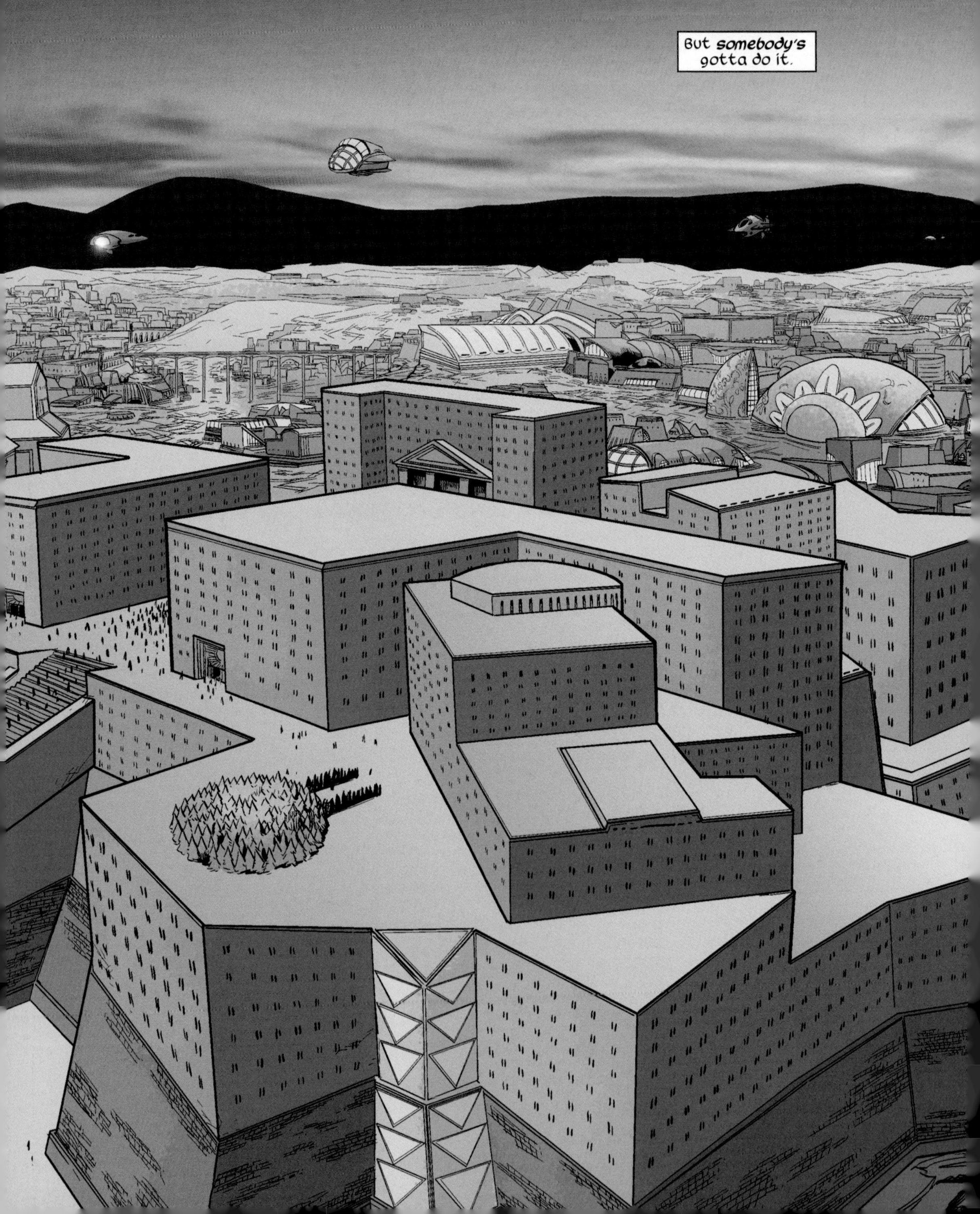
But *somebody's* gotta do it.

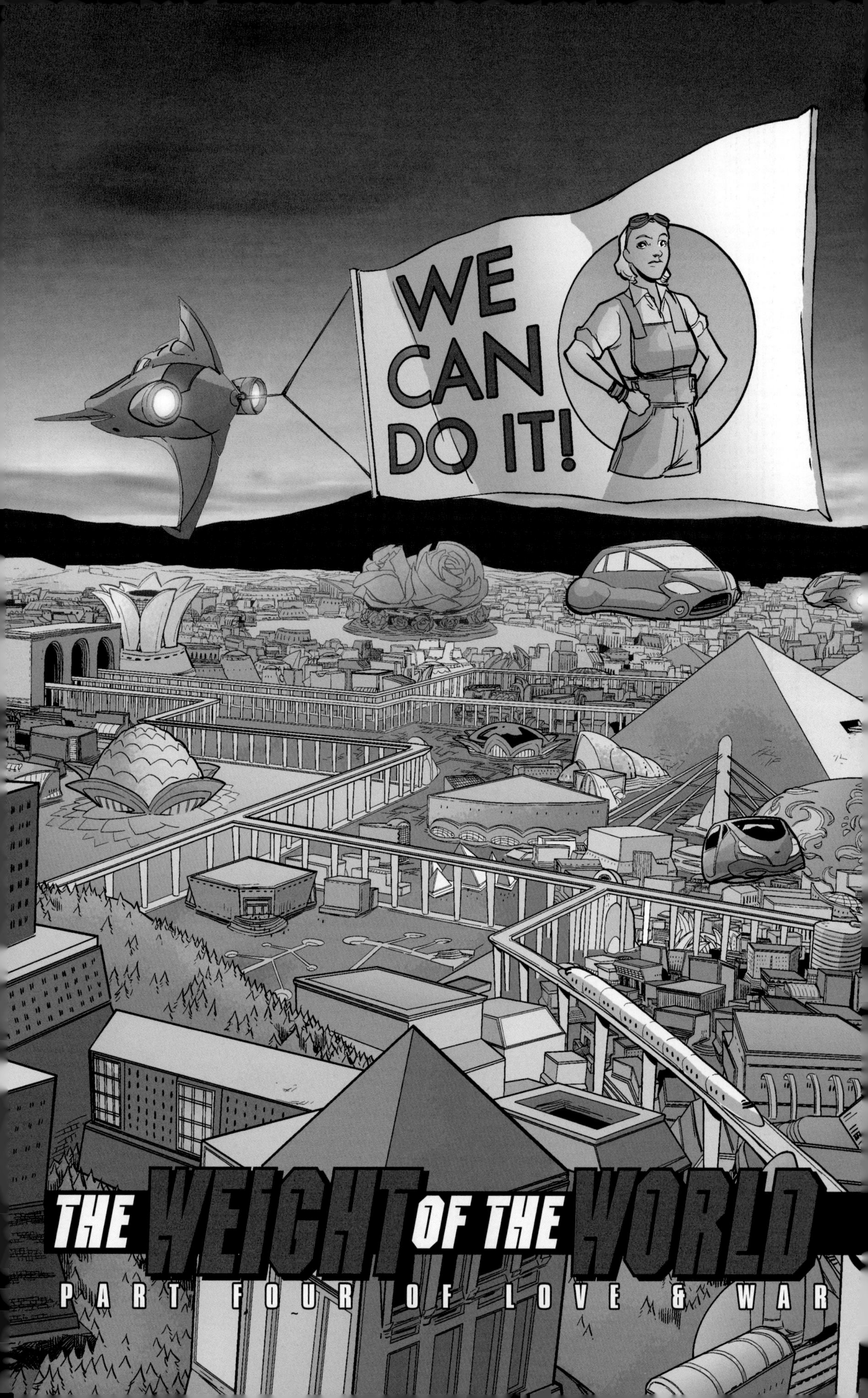
WE CAN DO IT!
THE WEIGHT OF THE WORLD
PART FOUR OF LOVE & WAR

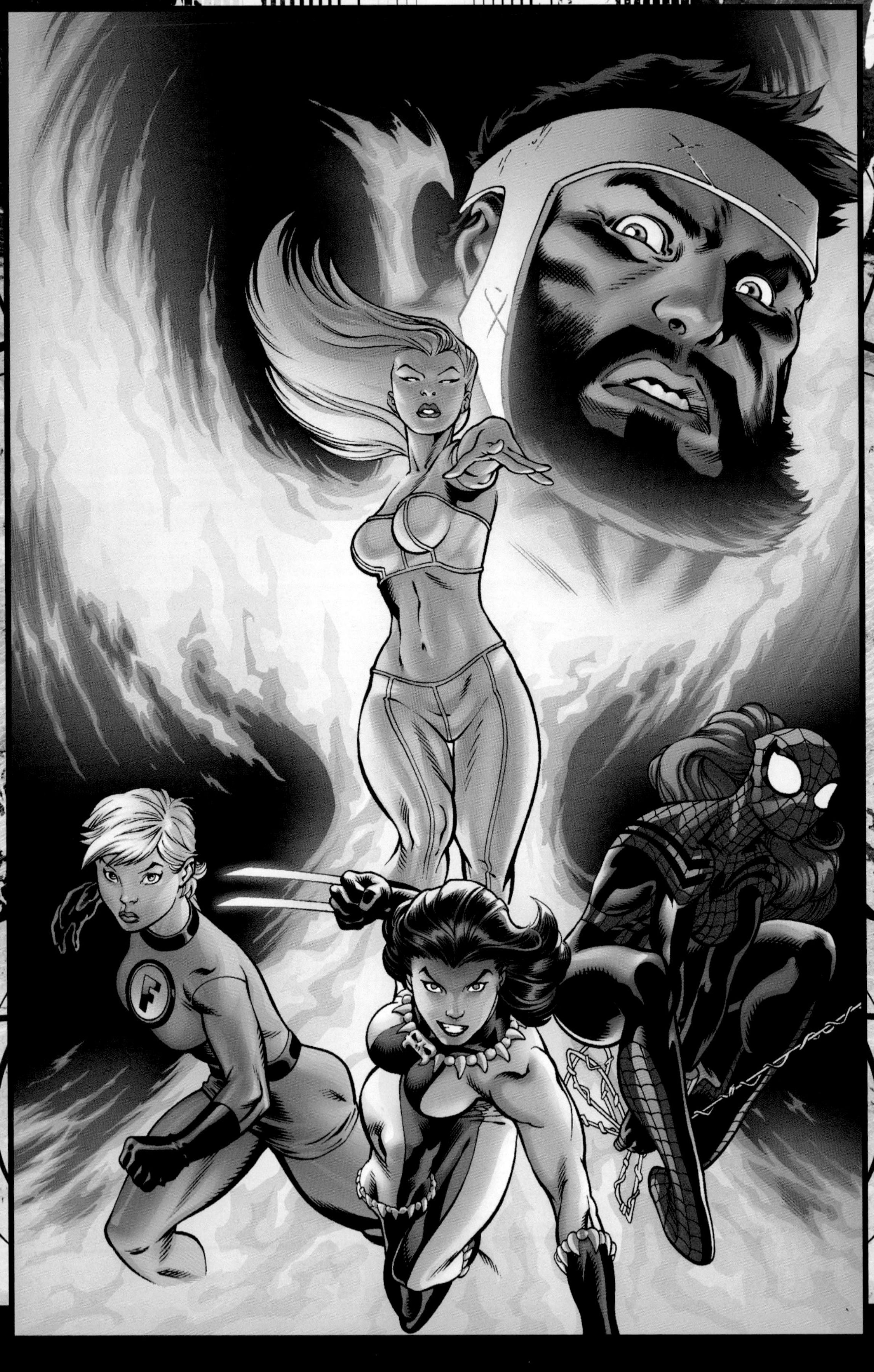

INCREDIBLE HERCULES #125

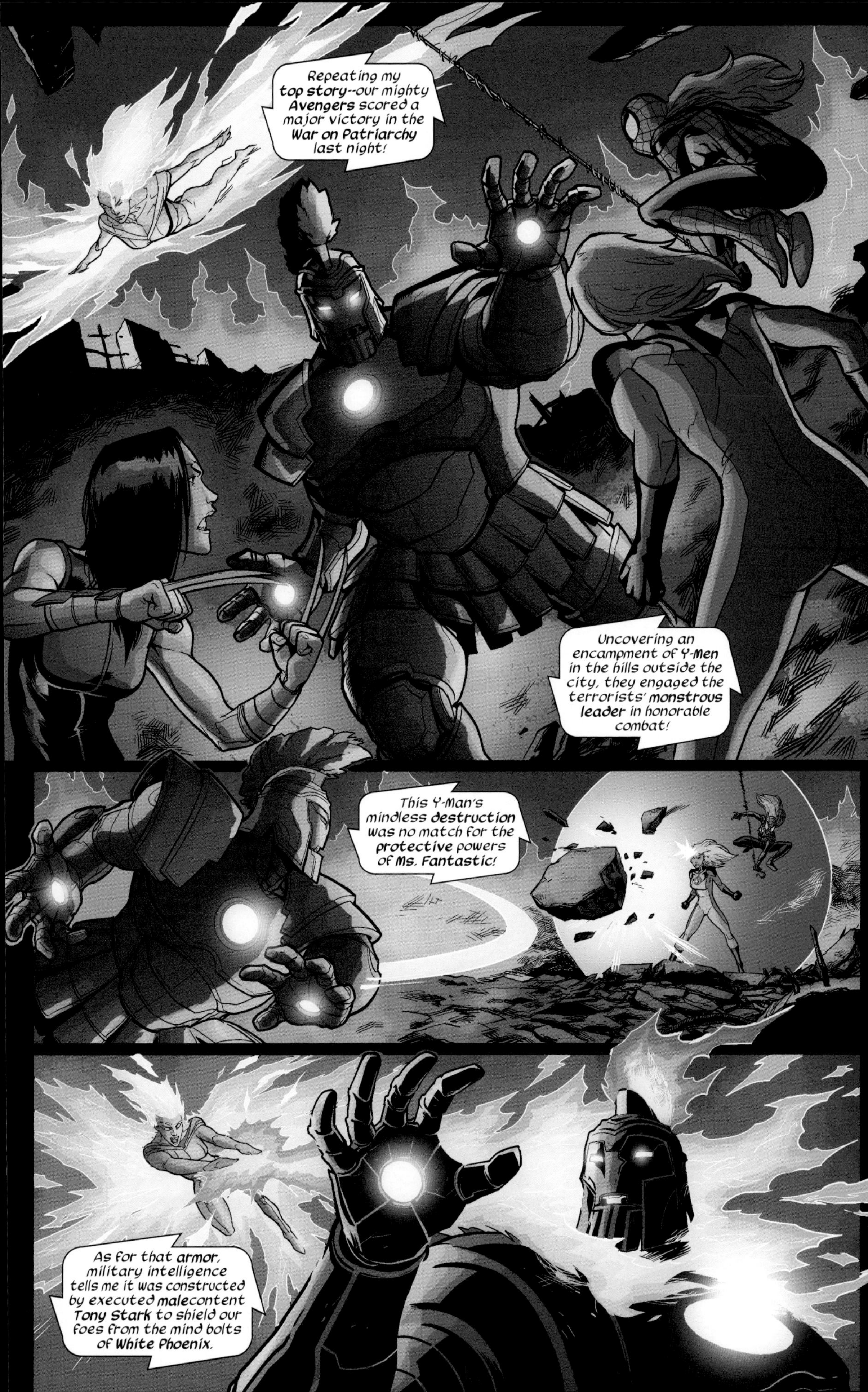
Repeating my top story--our mighty Avengers scored a major victory in the War on Patriarchy last night!
Uncovering an encampment of Y-Men in the hills outside the city, they engaged the terrorists' monstrous leader in honorable combat!
This Y-Man's mindless destruction was no match for the protective powers of Ms. Fantastic!
As for that armor, military intelligence tells me it was constructed by executed malecontent Tony Stark to shield our foes from the mind bolts of White Phoenix.

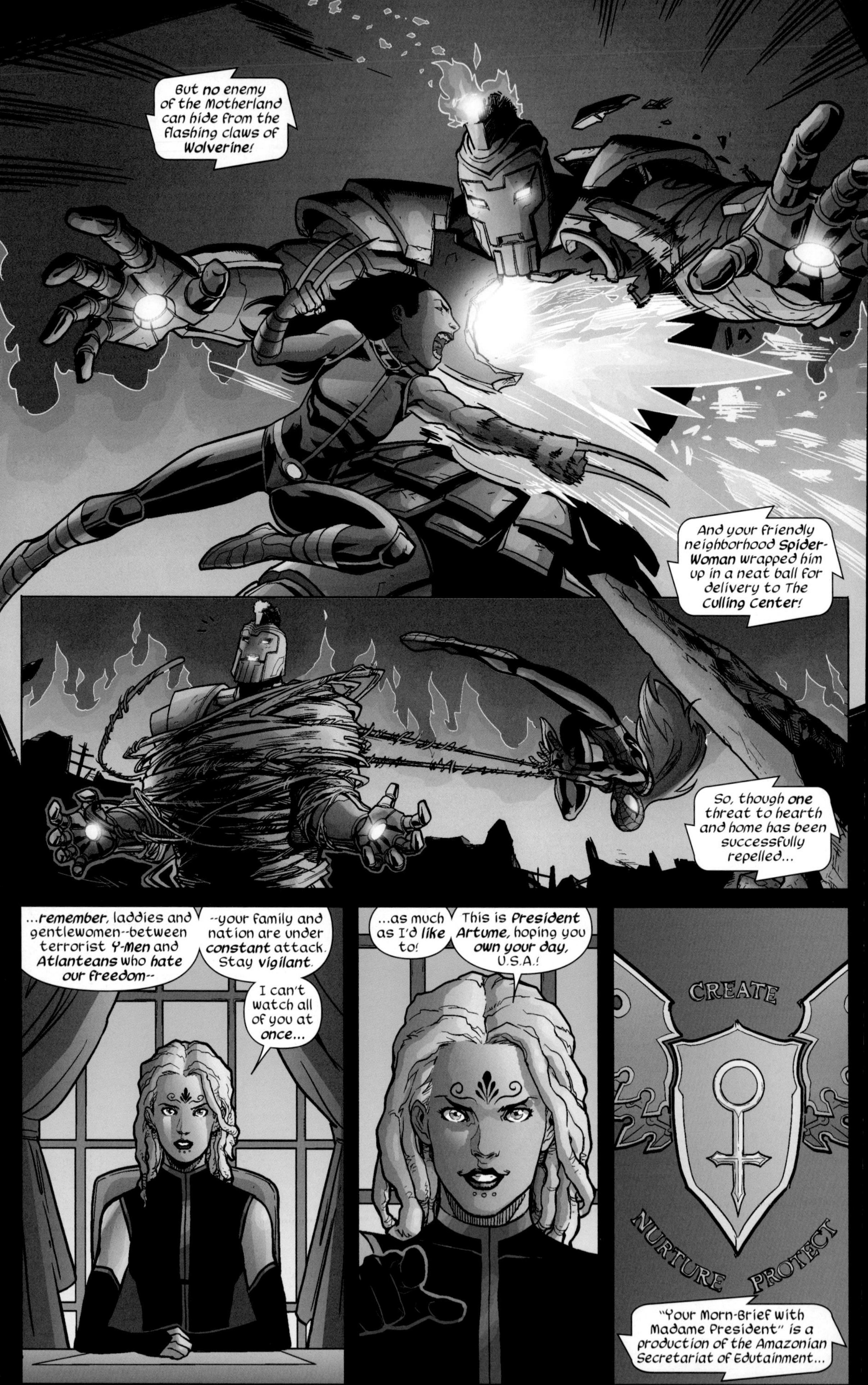

But no enemy of the Motherland can hide from the flashing claws of Wolverine!
And your friendly neighborhood Spider-Woman wrapped him up in a neat ball for delivery to The Culling Center!
So, though one threat to hearth and home has been successfully repelled...
...remember, laddies and gentlewomen--between terrorist Y-Men and Atlanteans who hate our freedom--
--your family and nation are under constant attack. Stay vigilant.
I can't watch all of you at once...
...as much as I'd like to!
This is President Artume, hoping you own your day, U.S.A.!
CREATE
NURTURE PROTECT
"Your Morn-Brief with Madame President" is a production of the Amazonian Secretariat of Edutainment...

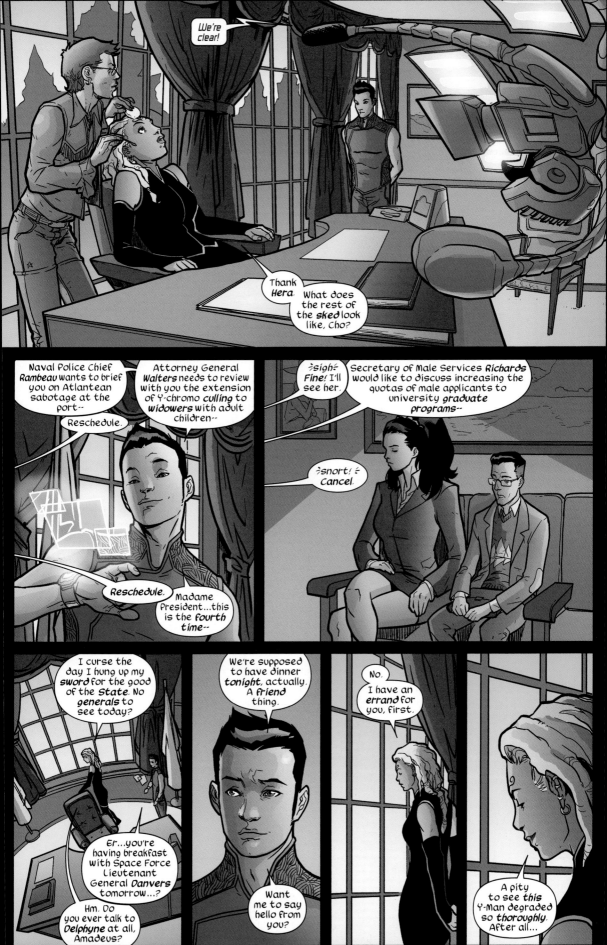

We're clear!

Thank *Hera*. What does the rest of the *sked* look like, Cho?

Naval Police Chief *Rambeau* wants to brief you on Atlantean sabotage at the port--

Reschedule.

Attorney General *Walters* needs to review with you the extension of Y-chromo *culling* to *widowers* with adult children--

Reschedule. Madame President...this is the *fourth* time--

≥sigh≤ Fine! I'll see her.

Secretary of Male Services *Richards* would like to discuss increasing the quotas of male applicants to university *graduate programs*--

≥snort! ≤ Cancel.

I curse the day I hung up my *sword* for the good of the State. No *generals* to see today?

Er...you're having breakfast with Space Force Lieutenant General *Danvers* tomorrow...?

Hm. Do you ever talk to *Delphyne* at all, Amadeus?

We're supposed to have dinner *tonight*, actually. A *friend* thing.

Want me to say hello from you?

No. I have an *errand* for you, first.

A pity to see *this* Y-man degraded so *thoroughly*. After all...

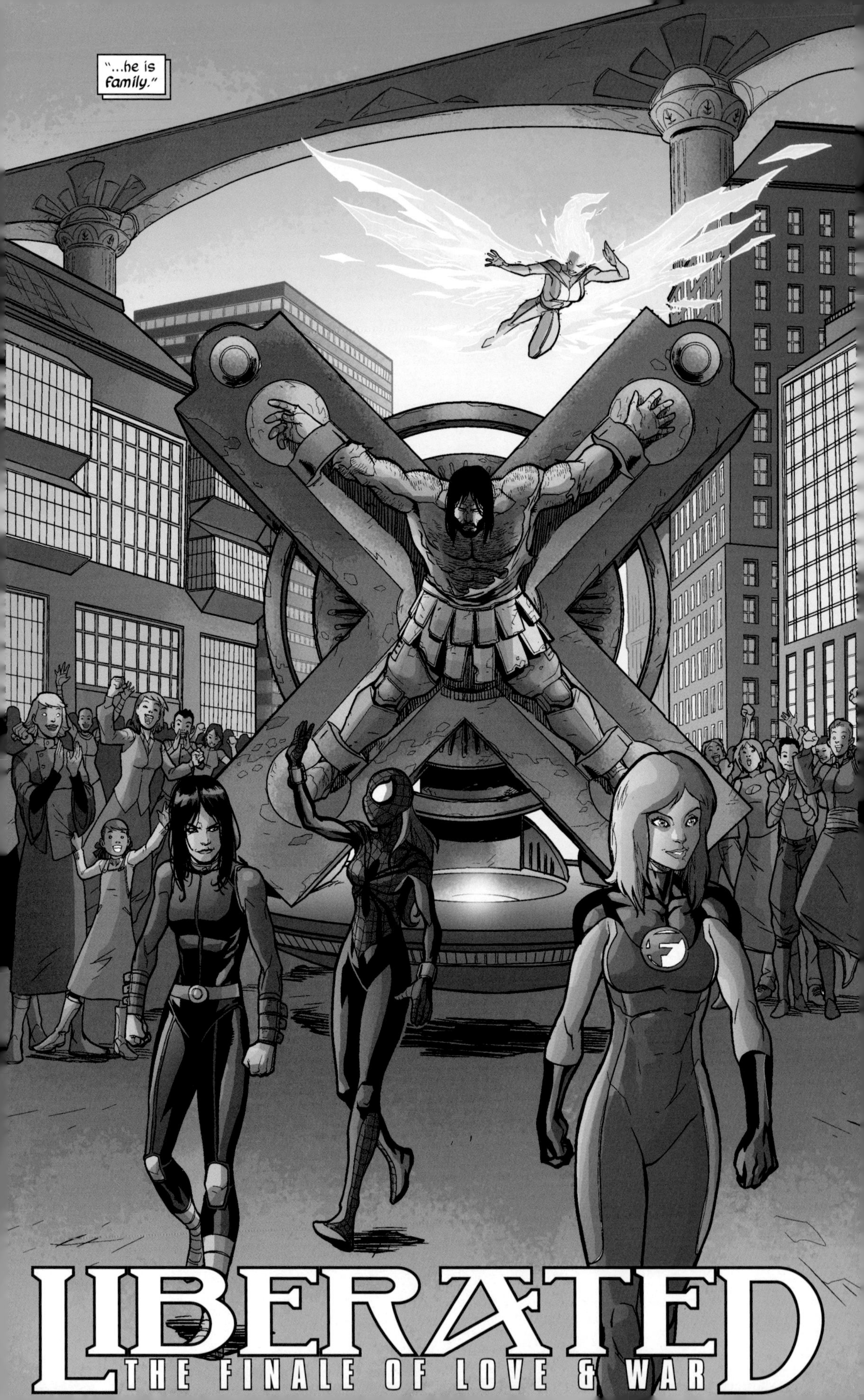
"...he is family."
LIBERATED
THE FINALE OF LOVE & WAR

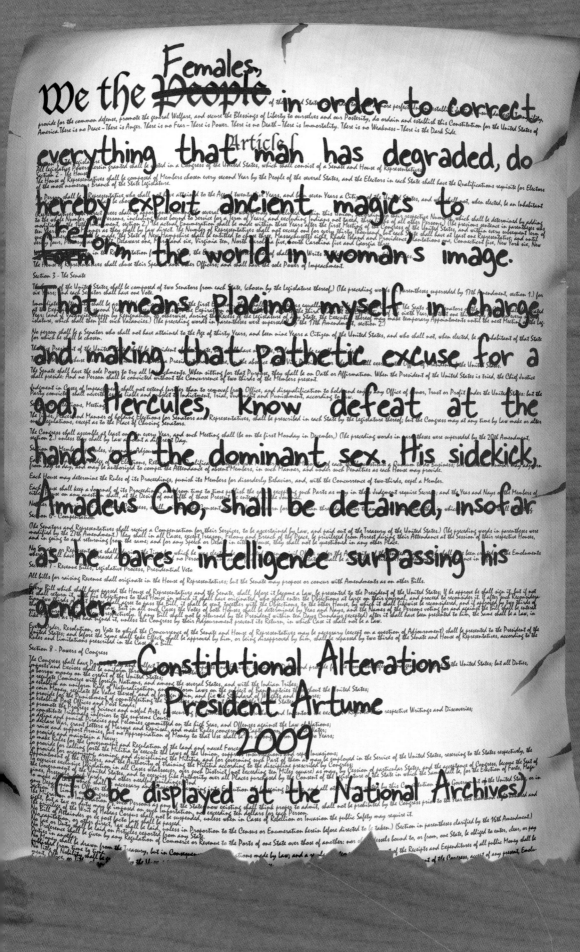

We the ~~People~~ Females, in order to correct everything that man has degraded, do hereby exploit ancient magics to reform the world in woman's image. That means placing myself in charge and making that pathetic excuse for a god, Hercules, know defeat at the hands of the dominant sex. His sidekick, Amadeus Cho, shall be detained, insofar as he bares intelligence surpassing his gender.

——Constitutional Alterations
President Artume
2009
(To be displayed at the National Archives)

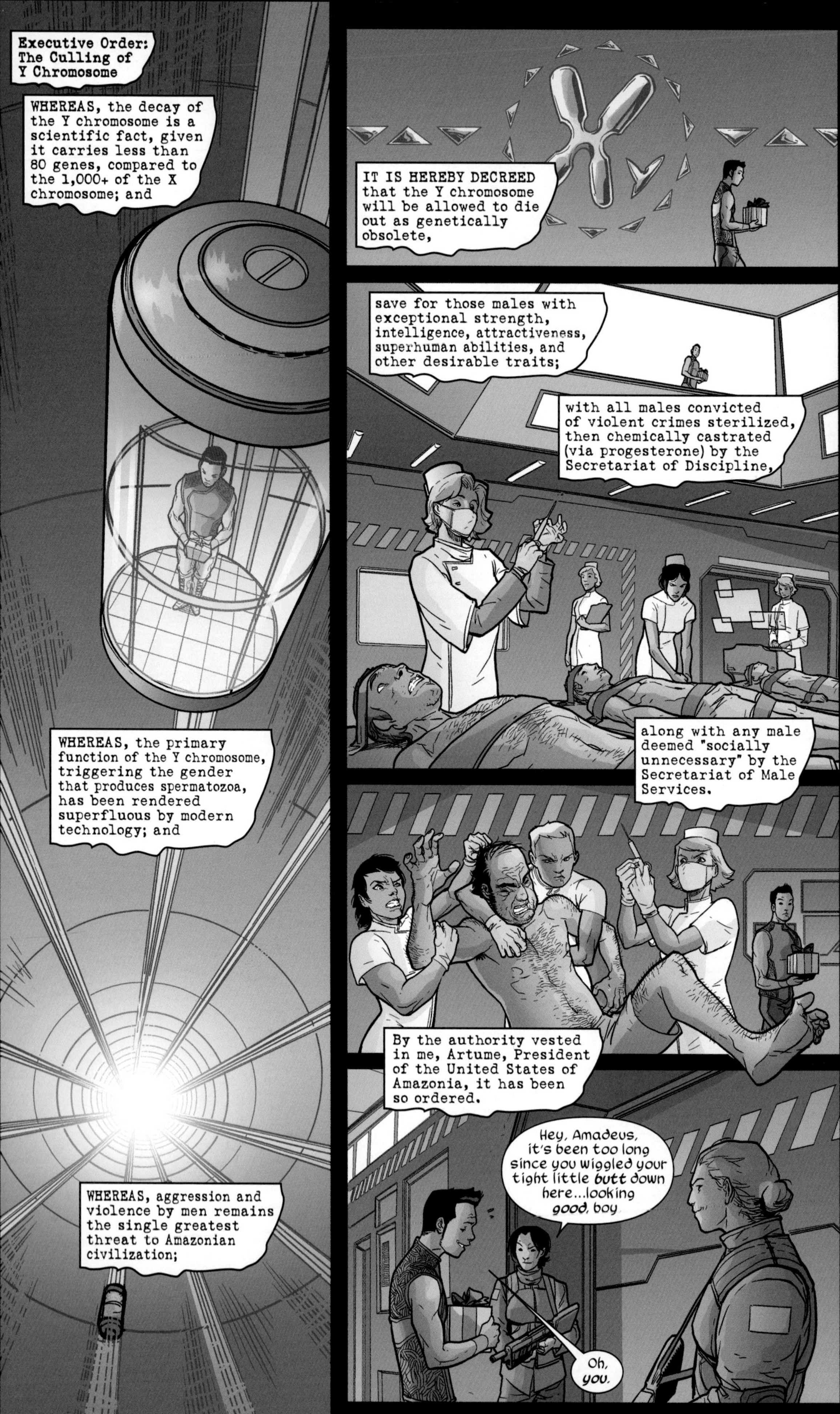
Executive Order: The Culling of Y Chromosome
WHEREAS, the decay of the Y chromosome is a scientific fact, given it carries less than 80 genes, compared to the 1,000+ of the X chromosome; and
WHEREAS, the primary function of the Y chromosome, triggering the gender that produces spermatozoa, has been rendered superfluous by modern technology; and
WHEREAS, aggression and violence by men remains the single greatest threat to Amazonian civilization;
IT IS HEREBY DECREED that the Y chromosome will be allowed to die out as genetically obsolete,
save for those males with exceptional strength, intelligence, attractiveness, superhuman abilities, and other desirable traits;
with all males convicted of violent crimes sterilized, then chemically castrated (via progesterone) by the Secretariat of Discipline,
along with any male deemed "socially unnecessary" by the Secretariat of Male Services.
By the authority vested in me, Artume, President of the United States of Amazonia, it has been so ordered.
Hey, Amadeus, it's been too long since you wiggled your tight little *butt* down here...looking *good*, boy.
Oh, *you*.

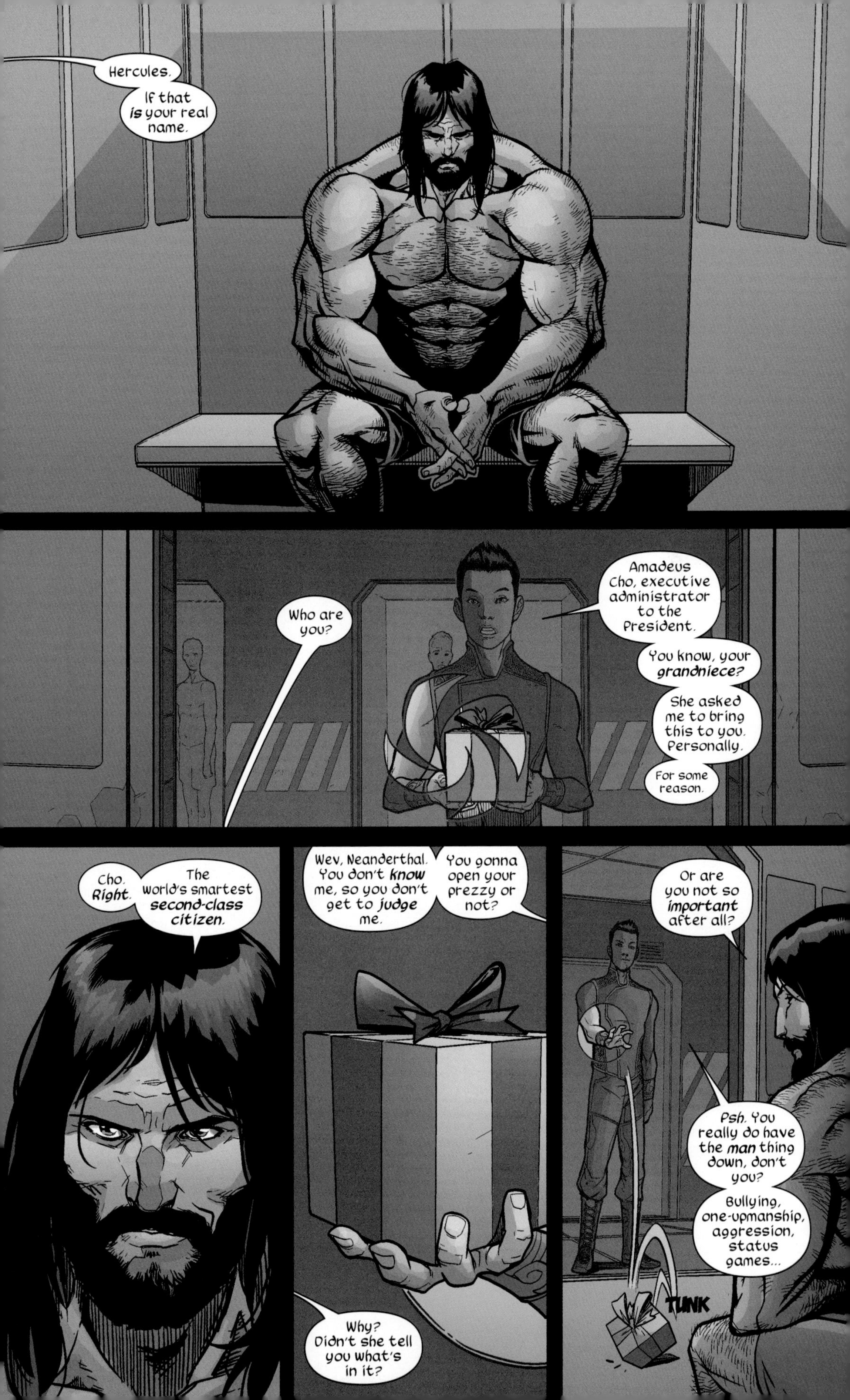
Hercules.
If that *is* your real name.
Who are you?
Amadeus Cho, executive administrator to the President.
You know, your *grandniece?*
She asked me to bring this to you. Personally.
For some reason.
Cho. *Right.*
The world's smartest *second-class citizen.*
Wev, Neanderthal. You don't *know* me, so you don't get to *judge* me.
You gonna open your prezzy or not?
Why? Didn't she tell you what's in it?
Or are you not so *important* after all?
Psh. You really do have the *man* thing down, don't you?
Bullying, one-upmanship, aggression, status games...
TUNK

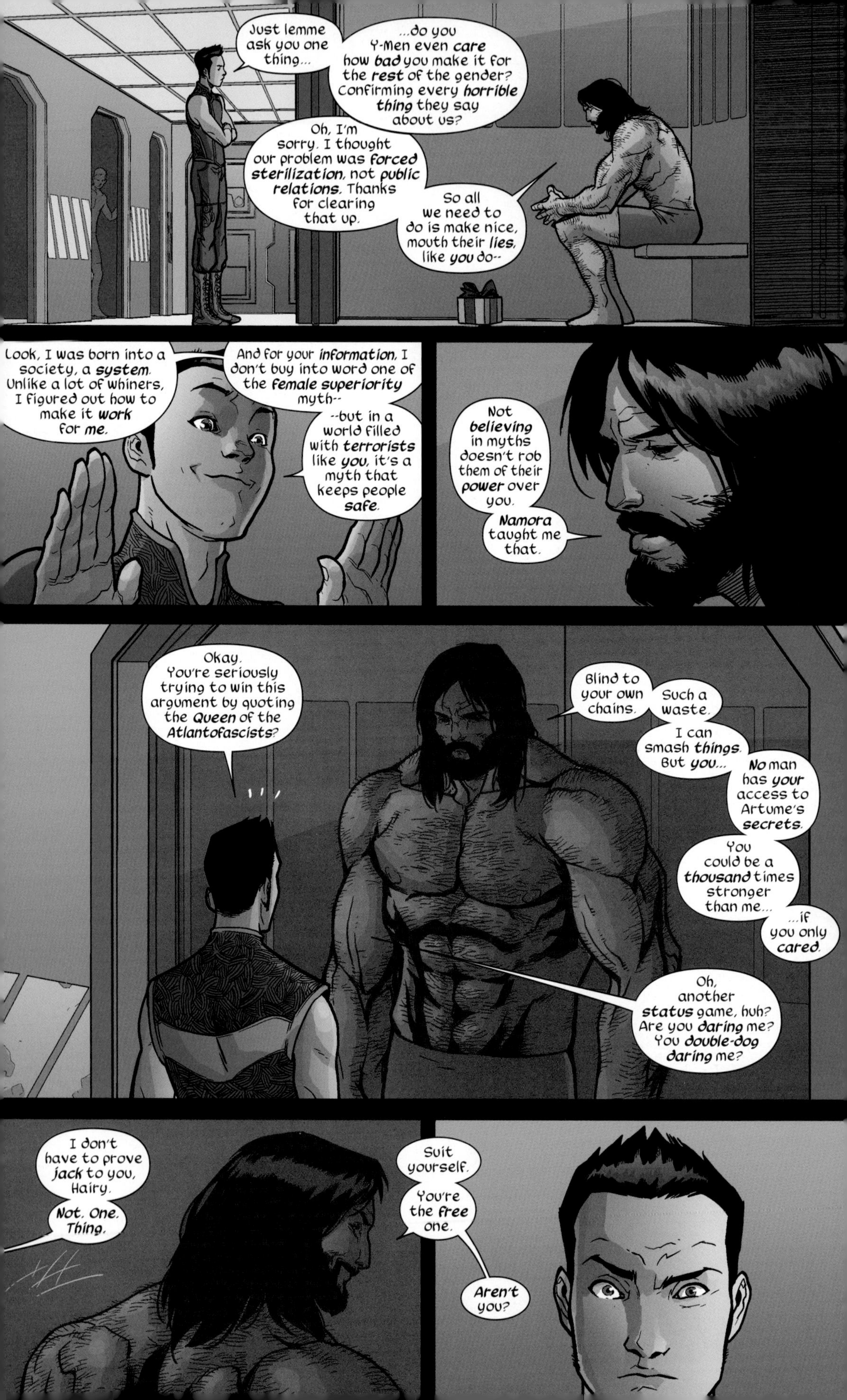
Just lemme ask you one thing...
...do you Y-Men even care how bad you make it for the rest of the gender? Confirming every horrible thing they say about us?
Oh, I'm sorry. I thought our problem was forced sterilization, not public relations. Thanks for clearing that up.
So all we need to do is make nice, mouth their lies, like you do--
Look, I was born into a society, a system. Unlike a lot of whiners, I figured out how to make it work for me.
And for your information, I don't buy into word one of the female superiority myth--
--but in a world filled with terrorists like you, it's a myth that keeps people safe.
Not believing in myths doesn't rob them of their power over you.
Namora taught me that.
Okay. You're seriously trying to win this argument by quoting the Queen of the Atlantofascists?
Blind to your own chains.
Such a waste.
I can smash things. But you...
No man has your access to Artume's secrets.
You could be a thousand times stronger than me...
...if you only cared.
Oh, another status game, huh? Are you daring me? You double-dog daring me?
I don't have to prove jack to you, Hairy.
Not. One. Thing.
Suit yourself.
You're the free one.
Aren't you?

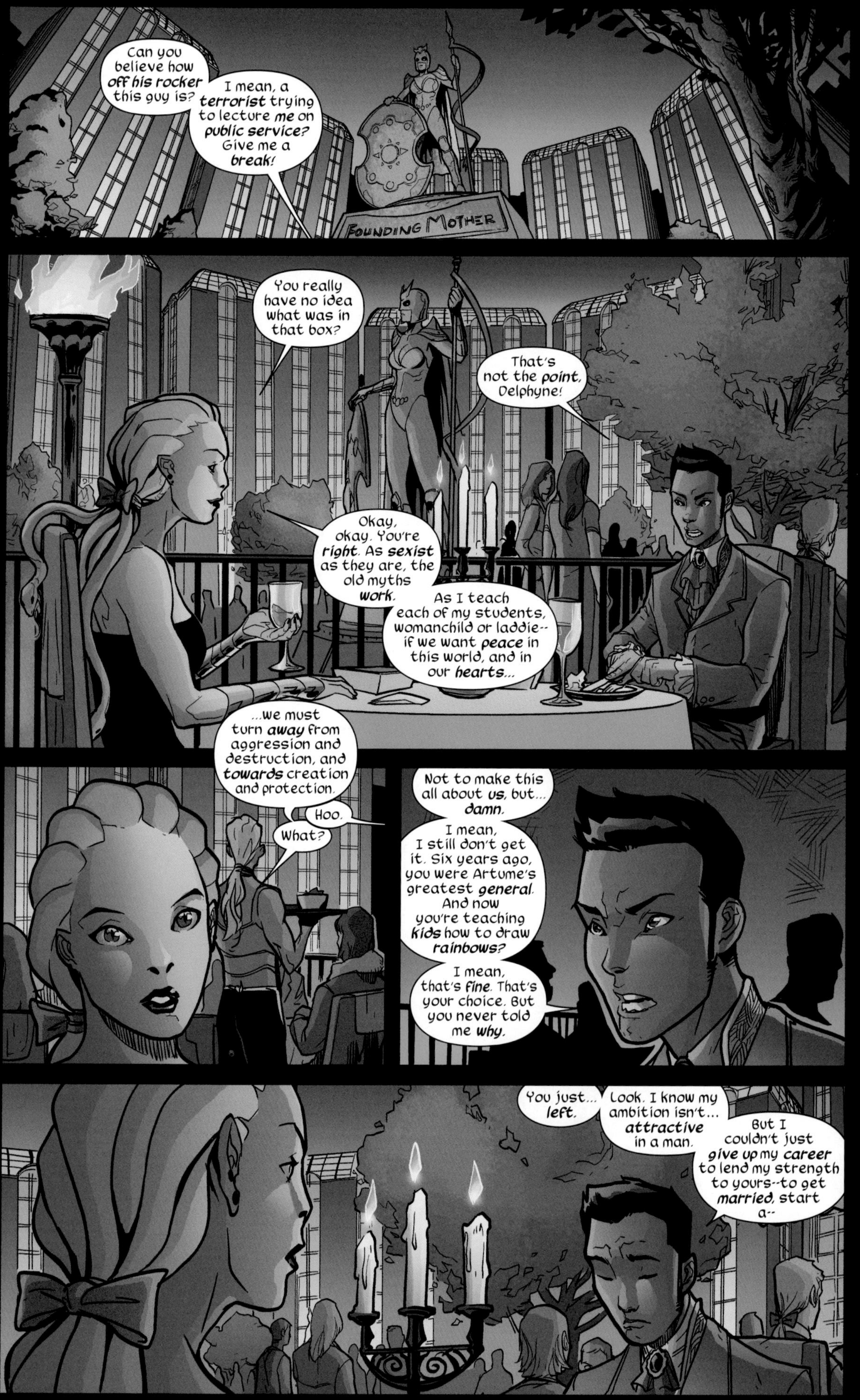
Can you believe how off his rocker this guy is?
I mean, a terrorist trying to lecture me on public service? Give me a break!
FOUNDING MOTHER
You really have no idea what was in that box?
That's not the point, Delphyne!
Okay, okay. You're right. As sexist as they are, the old myths work.
As I teach each of my students, womanchild or laddie--if we want peace in this world, and in our hearts...
...we must turn away from aggression and destruction, and towards creation and protection.
Hoo.
What?
Not to make this all about us, but... damn.
I mean, I still don't get it. Six years ago, you were Artume's greatest general. And now you're teaching kids how to draw rainbows?
I mean, that's fine. That's your choice. But you never told me why.
You just... left.
Look. I know my ambition isn't... attractive in a man.
But I couldn't just give up my career to lend my strength to yours--to get married, start a--

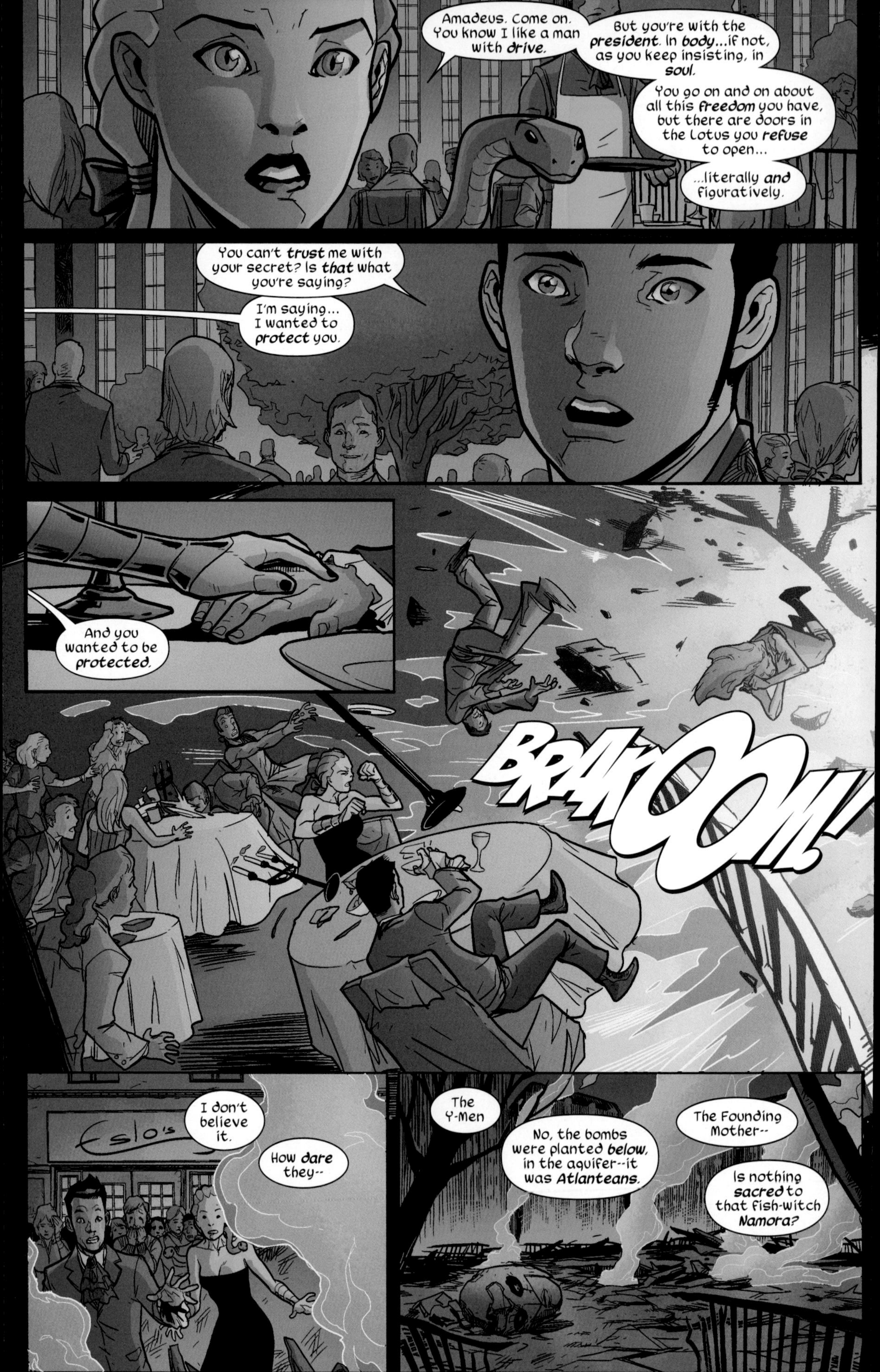
Amadeus. Come on. You know I like a man with drive.
But you're with the president. In body...if not, as you keep insisting, in soul.
You go on and on about all this freedom you have, but there are doors in the Lotus you refuse to open...
...literally and figuratively.
You can't trust me with your secret? Is that what you're saying?
I'm saying... I wanted to protect you.
And you wanted to be protected.
BRAKOOM!
I don't believe it.
How dare they--
Eslo's
The Y-Men
No, the bombs were planted below, in the aquifer--it was Atlanteans.
The Founding Mother--
Is nothing sacred to that fish-witch Namora?

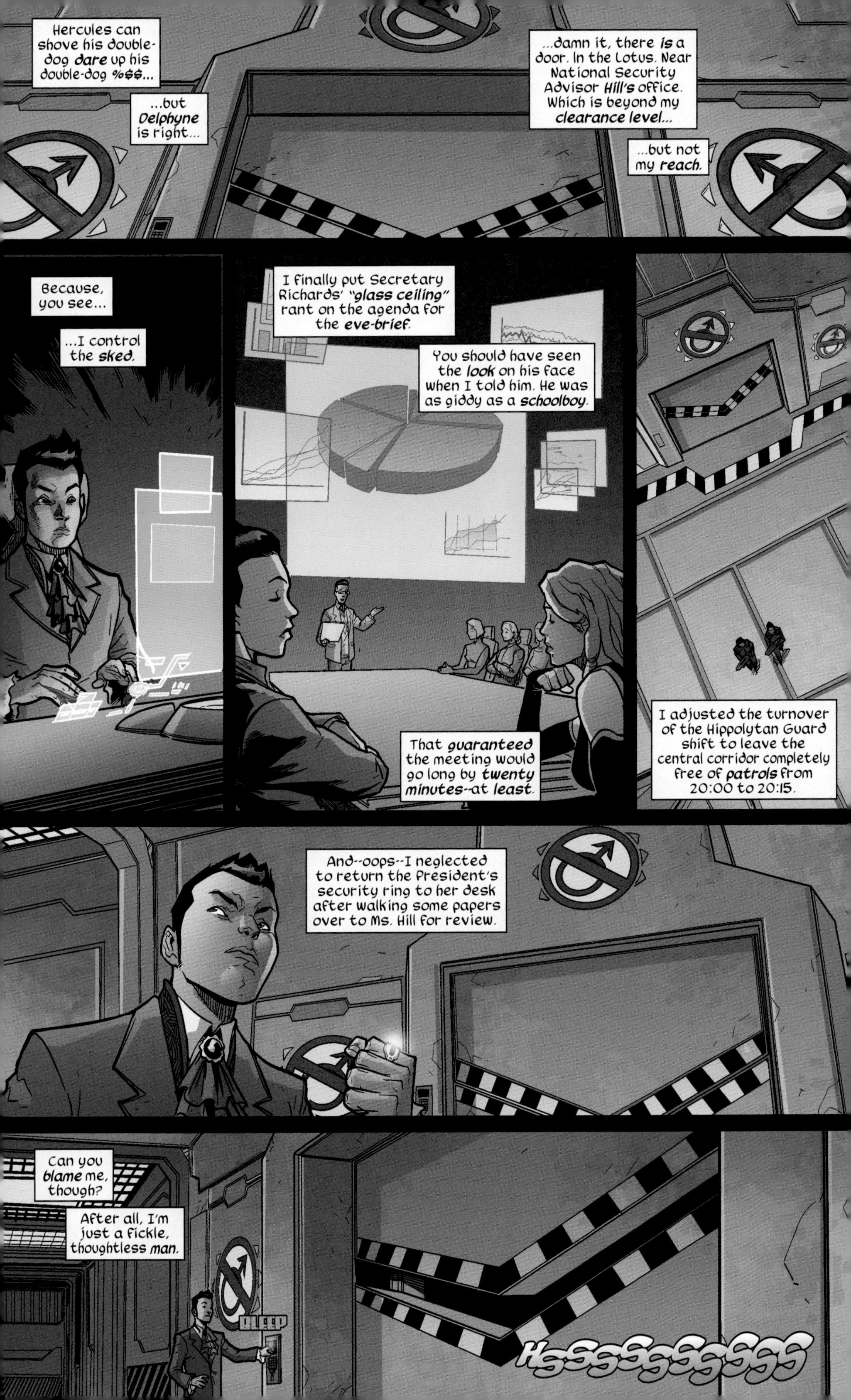

Hercules can shove his double-dog dare up his double-dog %$$...
...but Delphyne is right...
...damn it, there is a door. In the Lotus. Near National Security Advisor Hill's office. Which is beyond my clearance level...
...but not my reach.
Because, you see...
...I control the sked.
I finally put Secretary Richards' "glass ceiling" rant on the agenda for the eve-brief.
You should have seen the look on his face when I told him. He was as giddy as a schoolboy.
That guaranteed the meeting would go long by twenty minutes--at least.
I adjusted the turnover of the Hippolytan Guard shift to leave the central corridor completely free of patrols from 20:00 to 20:15.
And--oops--I neglected to return the President's security ring to her desk after walking some papers over to Ms. Hill for review.
Can you blame me, though?
After all, I'm just a fickle, thoughtless man.
BLEEP
HSSSSSSSSSSS

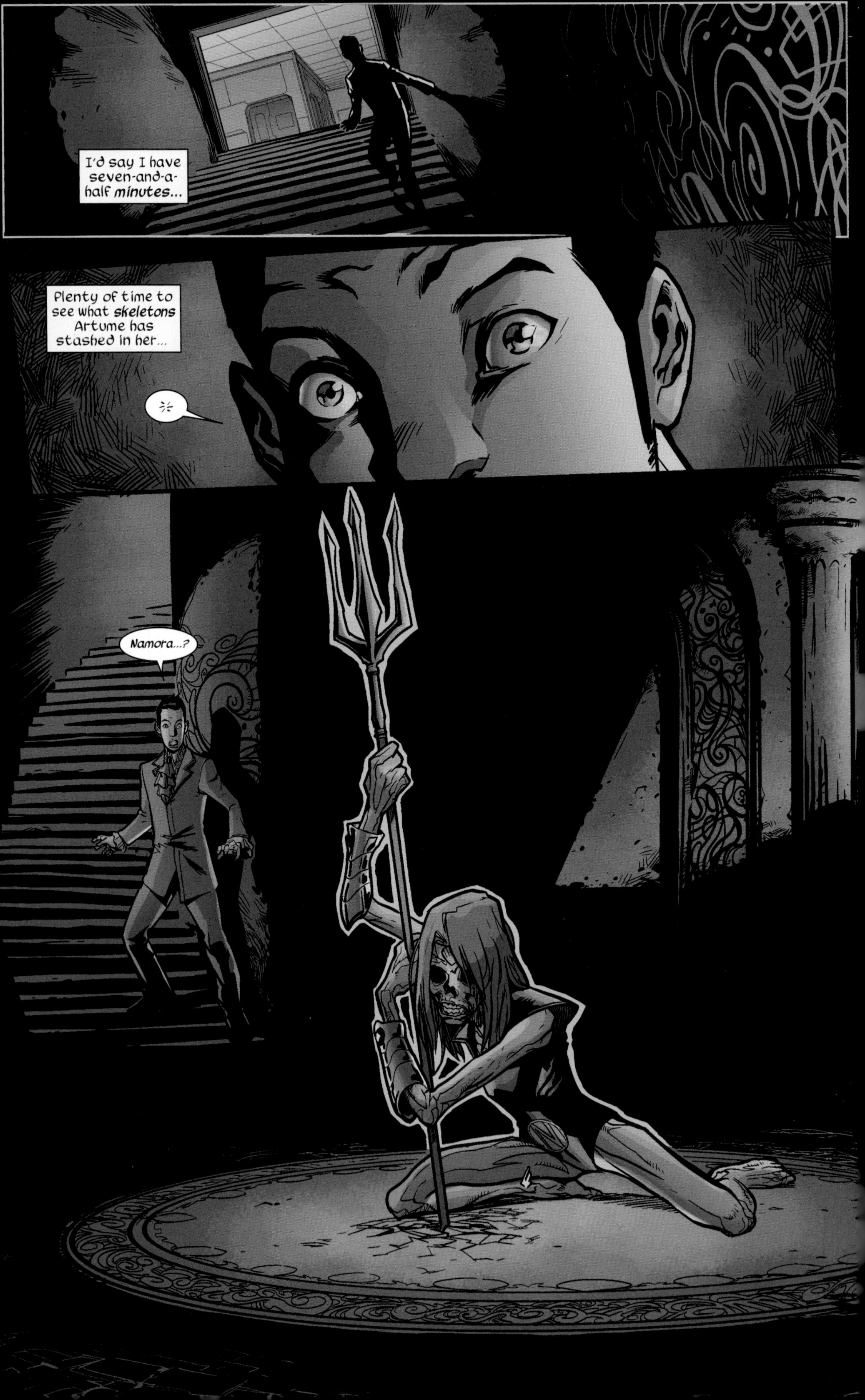
I'd say I have seven-and-a-half *minutes*...
Plenty of time to see what *skeletons* Artume has stashed in her...
Namora...?

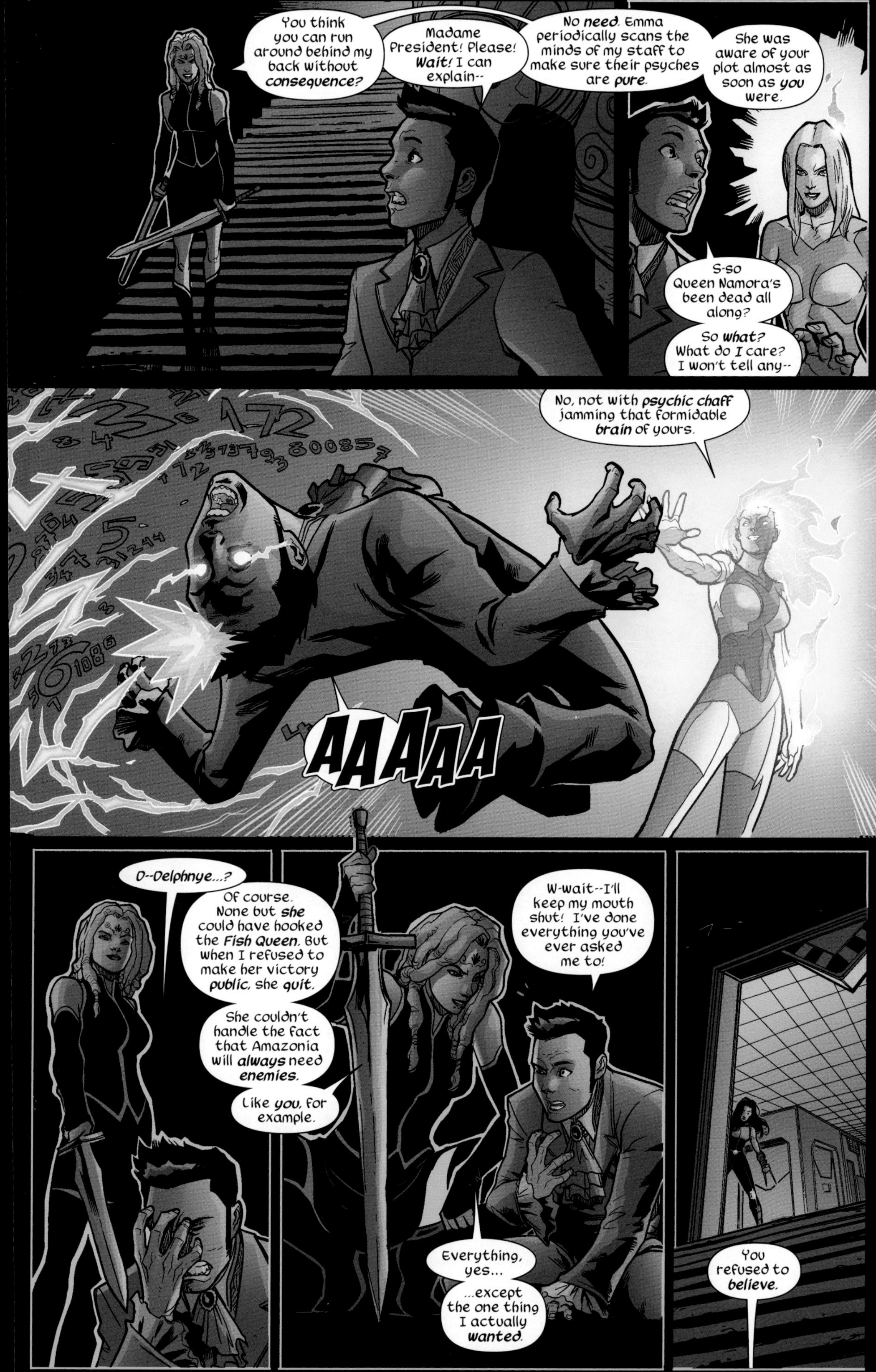

You think you can run around behind my back without *consequence?*
Madame President! Please! *Wait!* I can explain--
No *need*. Emma periodically scans the minds of my staff to make sure their psyches are *pure*.
She was aware of your plot almost as soon as *you* were.
S-so Queen Namora's been dead all along?
So *what?* What do I care? I won't tell any--
No, not with *psychic chaff* jamming that formidable *brain* of yours.
AAAAA
D--Delphnye...?
Of course. None but *she* could have hooked the *Fish Queen*. But when I refused to make her victory *public*, she *quit*.
She couldn't handle the fact that Amazonia will *always* need *enemies*.
Like *you*, for example.
W-wait--I'll keep my mouth shut! I've done everything you've ever asked me to!
Everything, yes...
...except the one thing I actually *wanted*.
You refused to *believe*.

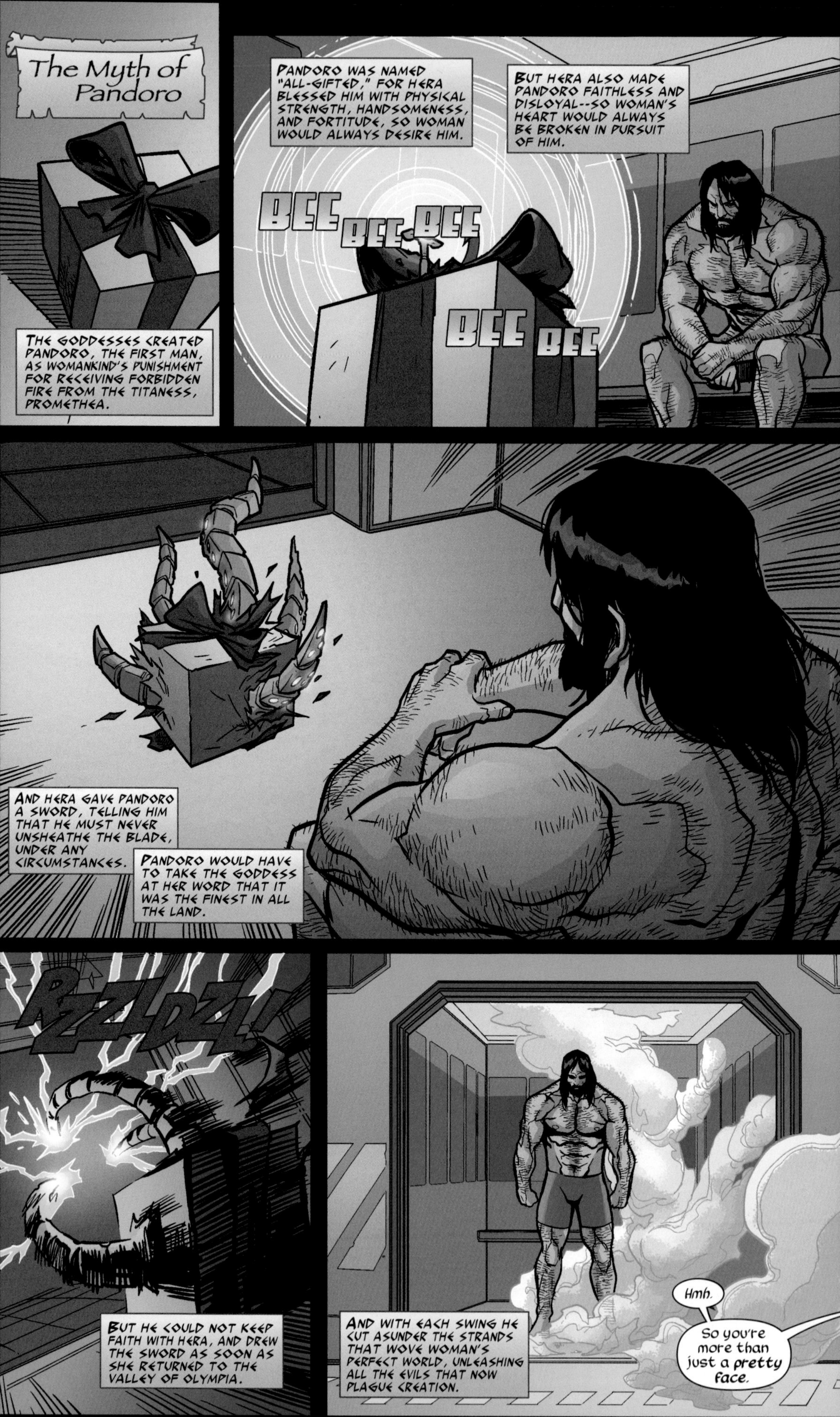
The Myth of Pandoro
The goddesses created Pandoro, the first man, as womankind's punishment for receiving forbidden fire from the titaness, Promethea.
Pandoro was named "all-gifted," for Hera blessed him with physical strength, handsomeness, and fortitude, so woman would always desire him.
BEE BEE BEE
But Hera also made Pandoro faithless and disloyal--so woman's heart would always be broken in pursuit of him.
BEE BEE
And Hera gave Pandoro a sword, telling him that he must never unsheathe the blade, under any circumstances.
Pandoro would have to take the goddess at her word that it was the finest in all the land.
RZZLDZZL!
But he could not keep faith with Hera, and drew the sword as soon as she returned to the valley of Olympia.
And with each swing he cut asunder the strands that wove woman's perfect world, unleashing all the evils that now plague creation.
Hmh.
So you're more than just a pretty face.

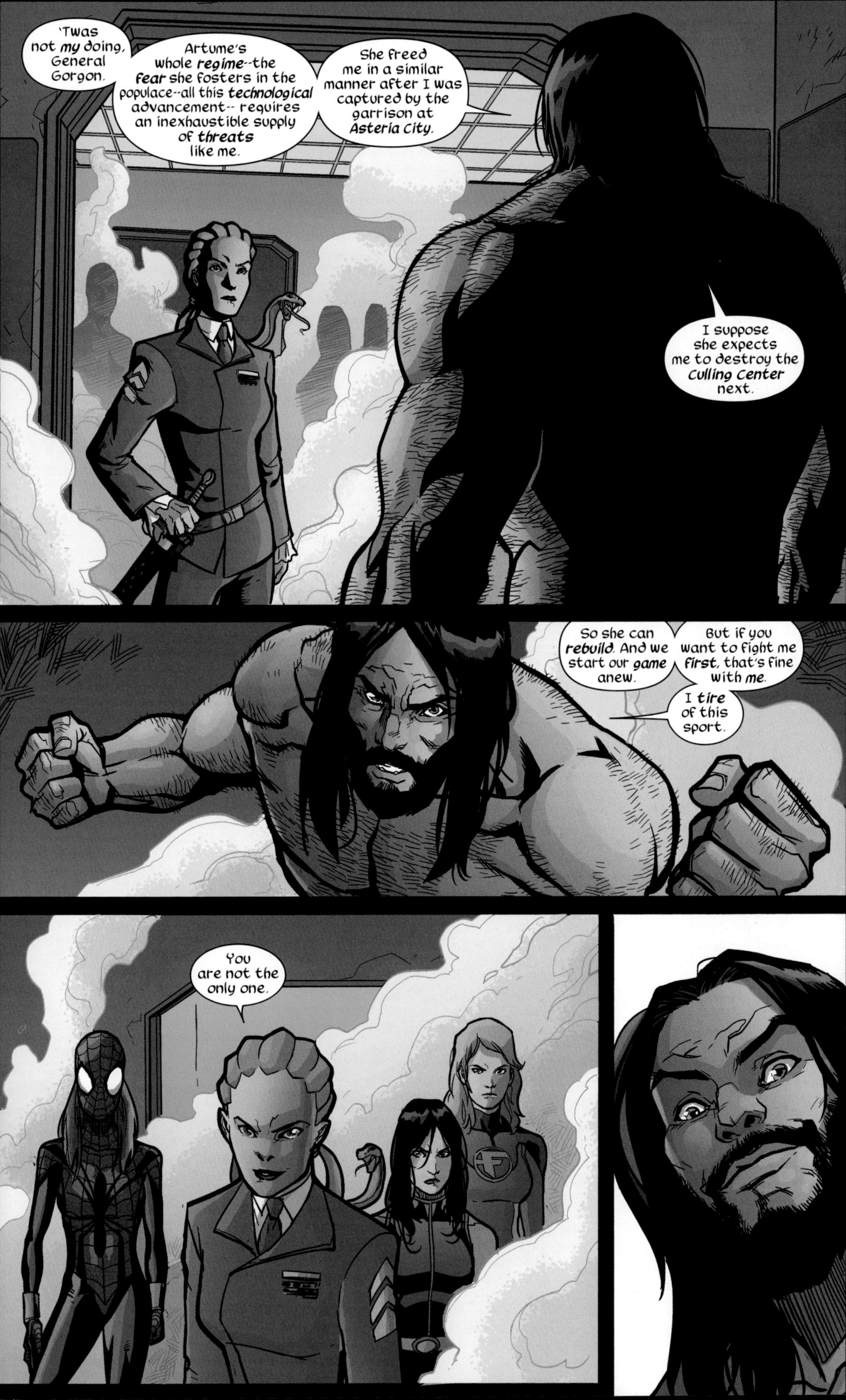
'Twas not my doing, General Gorgon.
Artume's whole regime--the fear she fosters in the populace--all this technological advancement-- requires an inexhaustible supply of threats like me.
She freed me in a similar manner after I was captured by the garrison at Asteria City.
I suppose she expects me to destroy the Culling Center next.
So she can rebuild. And we start our game anew.
But if you want to fight me first, that's fine with me.
I tire of this sport.
You are not the only one.

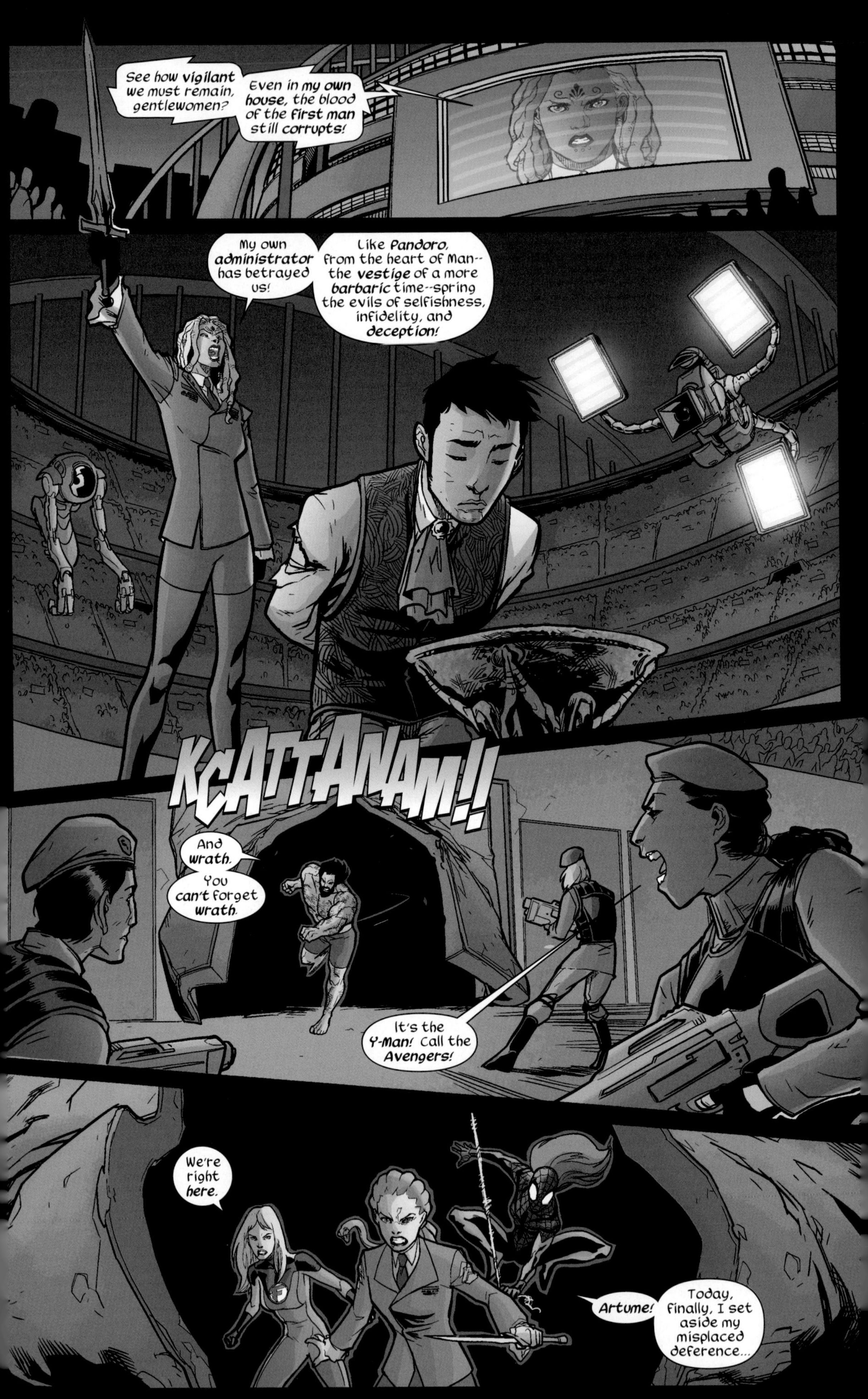
See how vigilant we must remain, gentlewomen?
Even in my own house, the blood of the first man still corrupts!
My own administrator has betrayed us!
Like Pandoro, from the heart of Man--the vestige of a more barbaric time--spring the evils of selfishness, infidelity, and deception!
KCATTANAM!!
And wrath. You can't forget wrath.
It's the Y-Man! Call the Avengers!
We're right here.
Artume!
Today, finally, I set aside my misplaced deference...

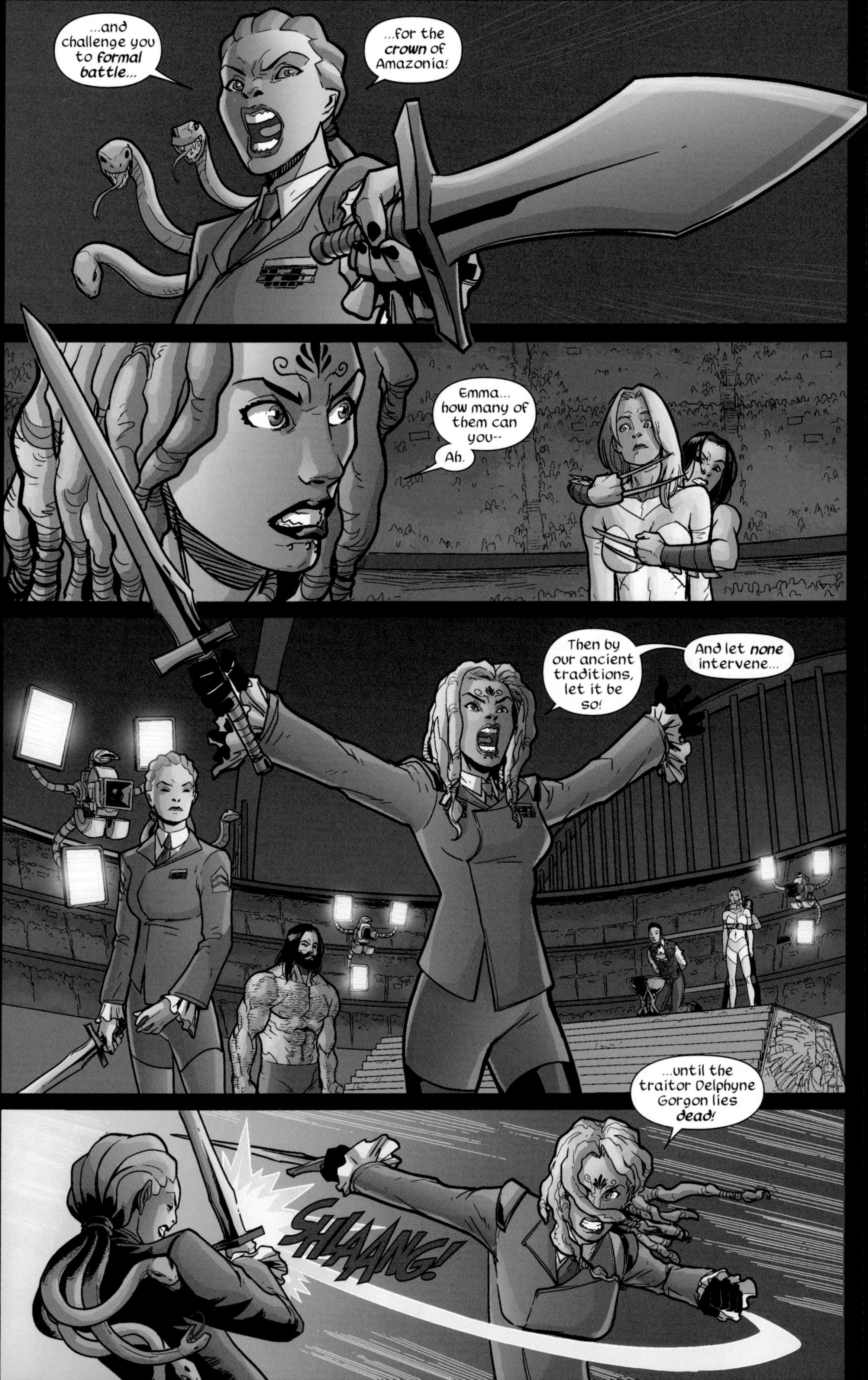

...and challenge you to formal battle...
...for the crown of Amazonia!
Emma... how many of them can you--
Ah.
Then by our ancient traditions, let it be so!
And let none intervene...
...until the traitor Delphyne Gorgon lies dead!
SHLAANG!

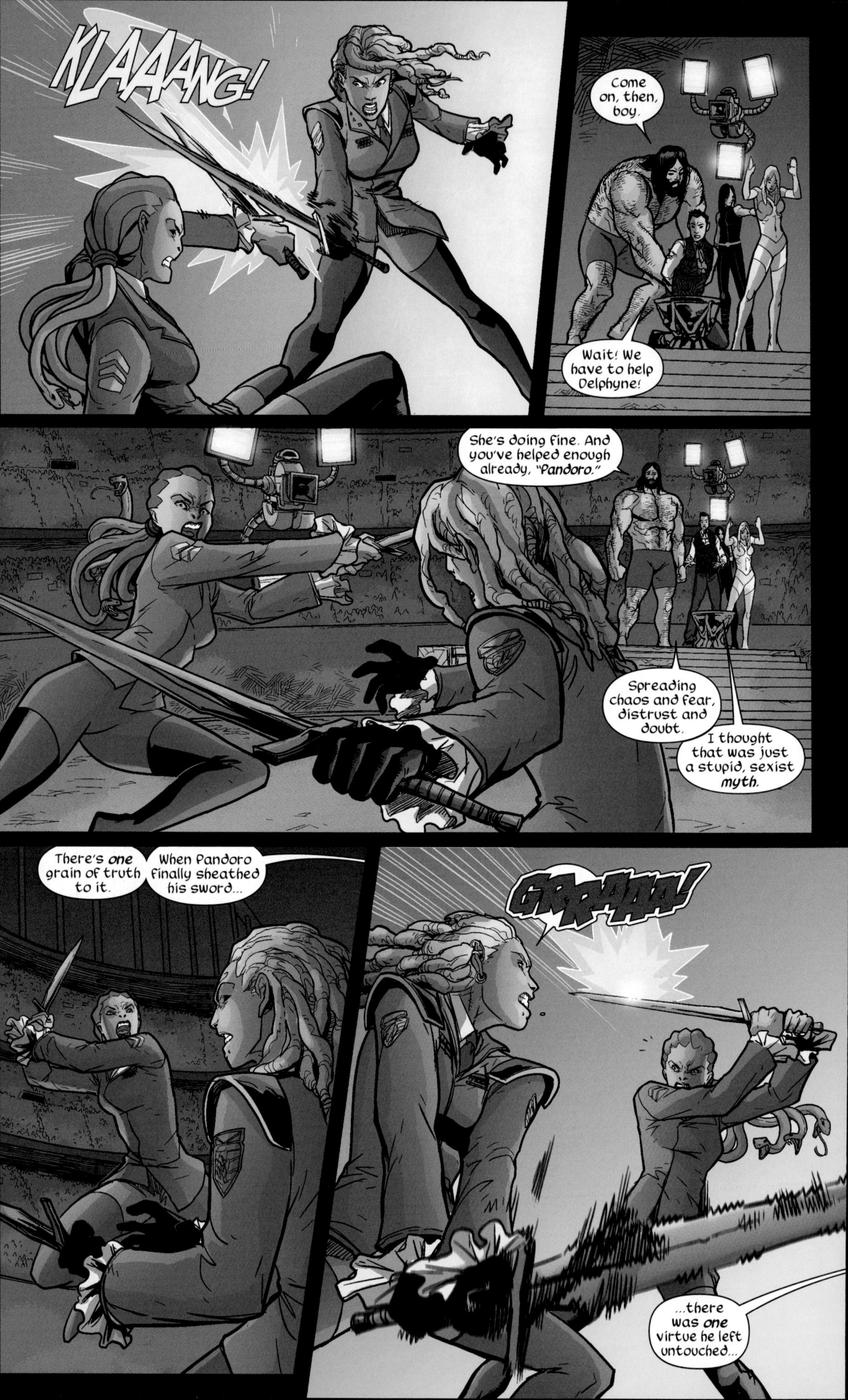
KLAAANG!
Come on, then, boy.
Wait! We have to help Delphyne!
She's doing fine. And you've helped enough already, "Pandoro."
Spreading chaos and fear, distrust and doubt.
I thought that was just a stupid, sexist myth.
There's one grain of truth to it.
When Pandoro finally sheathed his sword...
GRRAAAA!
...there was one virtue he left untouched...

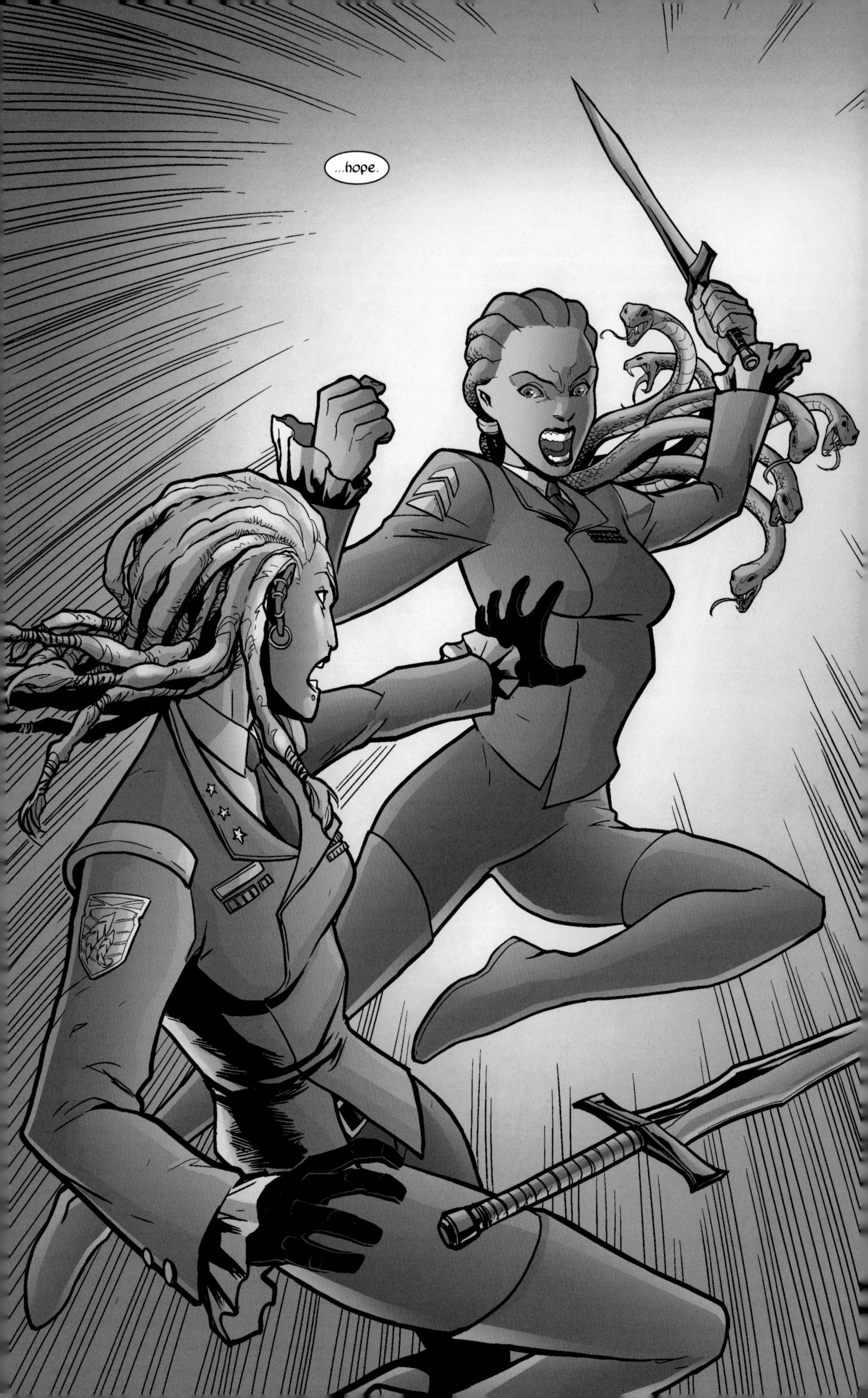
...hope.

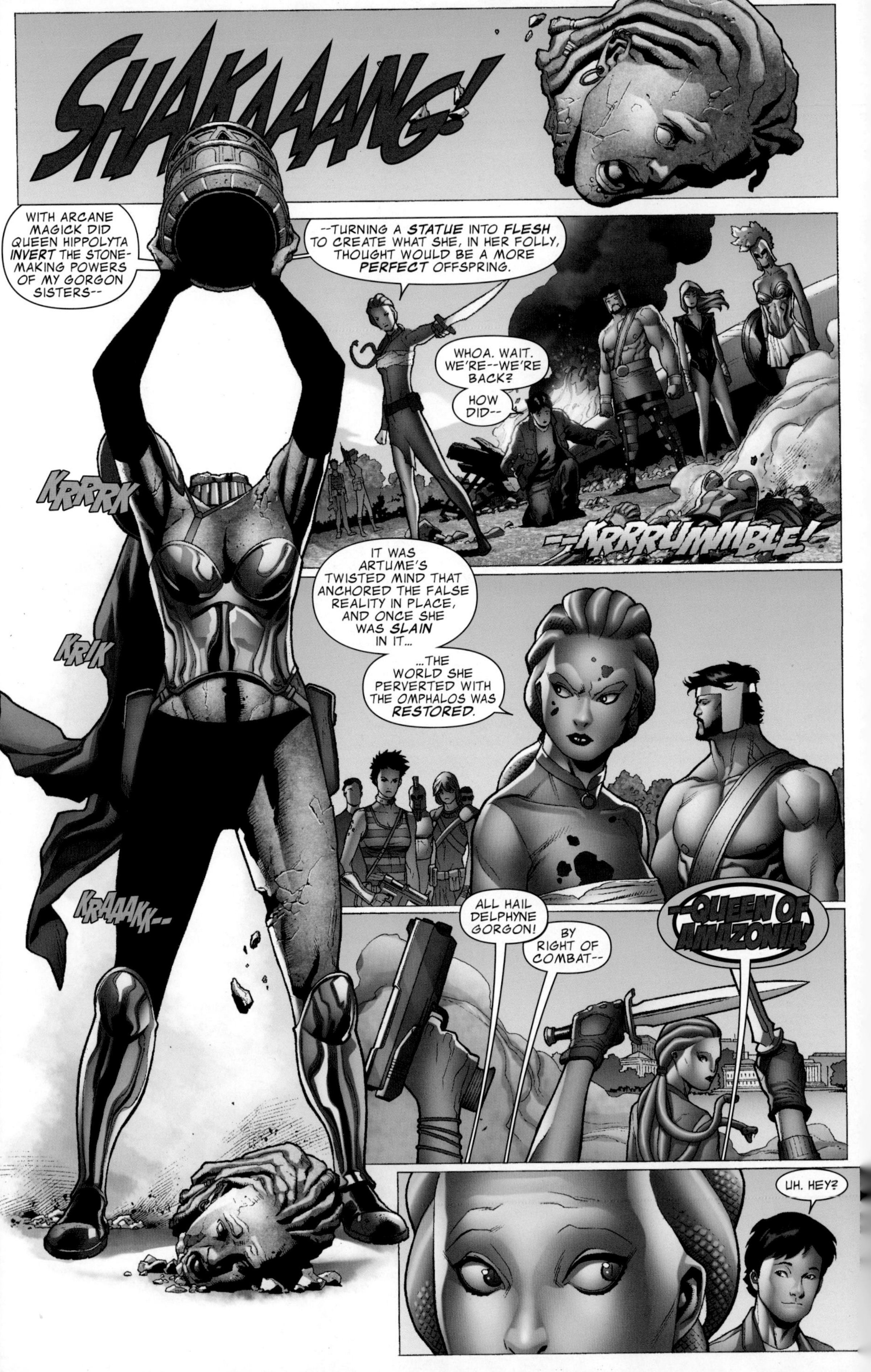
SHAKAAANG!
WITH ARCANE MAGICK DID QUEEN HIPPOLYTA INVERT THE STONE-MAKING POWERS OF MY GORGON SISTERS--
--TURNING A STATUE INTO FLESH TO CREATE WHAT SHE, IN HER FOLLY, THOUGHT WOULD BE A MORE PERFECT OFFSPRING.
WHOA. WAIT. WE'RE--WE'RE BACK?
HOW DID--
KRRRK
--KRRRUMMBLE!
IT WAS ARTUME'S TWISTED MIND THAT ANCHORED THE FALSE REALITY IN PLACE, AND ONCE SHE WAS SLAIN IN IT...
...THE WORLD SHE PERVERTED WITH THE OMPHALOS WAS RESTORED.
KRIK
KRAAAKK--
ALL HAIL DELPHYNE GORGON!
BY RIGHT OF COMBAT--
--QUEEN OF AMAZONIA!
UH. HEY?

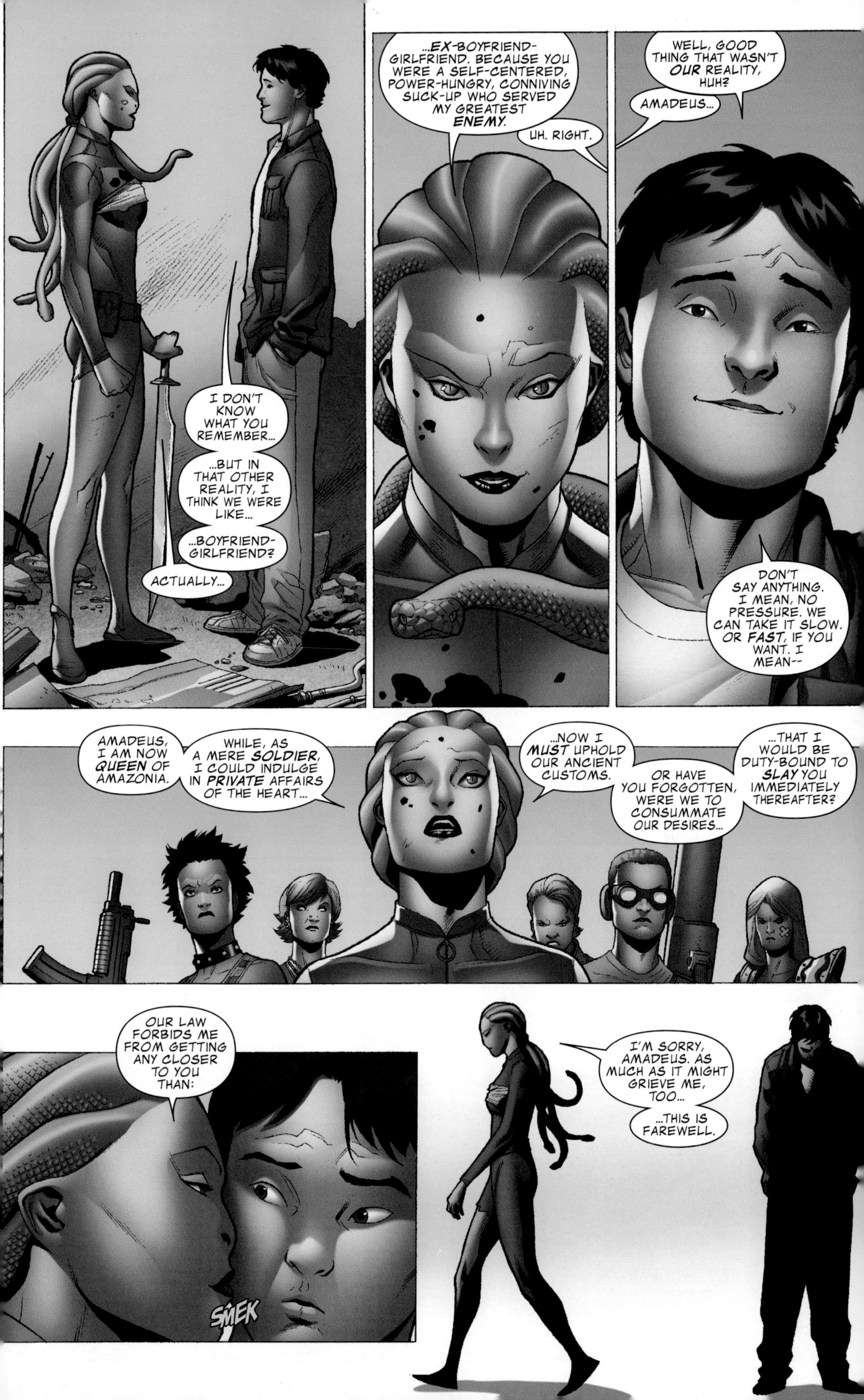
I DON'T KNOW WHAT YOU REMEMBER...
...BUT IN THAT OTHER REALITY, I THINK WE WERE LIKE...
...BOYFRIEND-GIRLFRIEND?
ACTUALLY...
...EX-BOYFRIEND-GIRLFRIEND. BECAUSE YOU WERE A SELF-CENTERED, POWER-HUNGRY, CONNIVING SUCK-UP WHO SERVED MY GREATEST ENEMY.
UH. RIGHT.
WELL, GOOD THING THAT WASN'T OUR REALITY, HUH?
AMADEUS...
DON'T SAY ANYTHING. I MEAN, NO PRESSURE. WE CAN TAKE IT SLOW. OR FAST, IF YOU WANT. I MEAN--
AMADEUS, I AM NOW QUEEN OF AMAZONIA.
WHILE, AS A MERE SOLDIER, I COULD INDULGE IN PRIVATE AFFAIRS OF THE HEART...
...NOW I MUST UPHOLD OUR ANCIENT CUSTOMS.
OR HAVE YOU FORGOTTEN, WERE WE TO CONSUMMATE OUR DESIRES...
...THAT I WOULD BE DUTY-BOUND TO SLAY YOU IMMEDIATELY THEREAFTER?
OUR LAW FORBIDS ME FROM GETTING ANY CLOSER TO YOU THAN:
SMEK
I'M SORRY, AMADEUS. AS MUCH AS IT MIGHT GRIEVE ME, TOO...
...THIS IS FAREWELL.

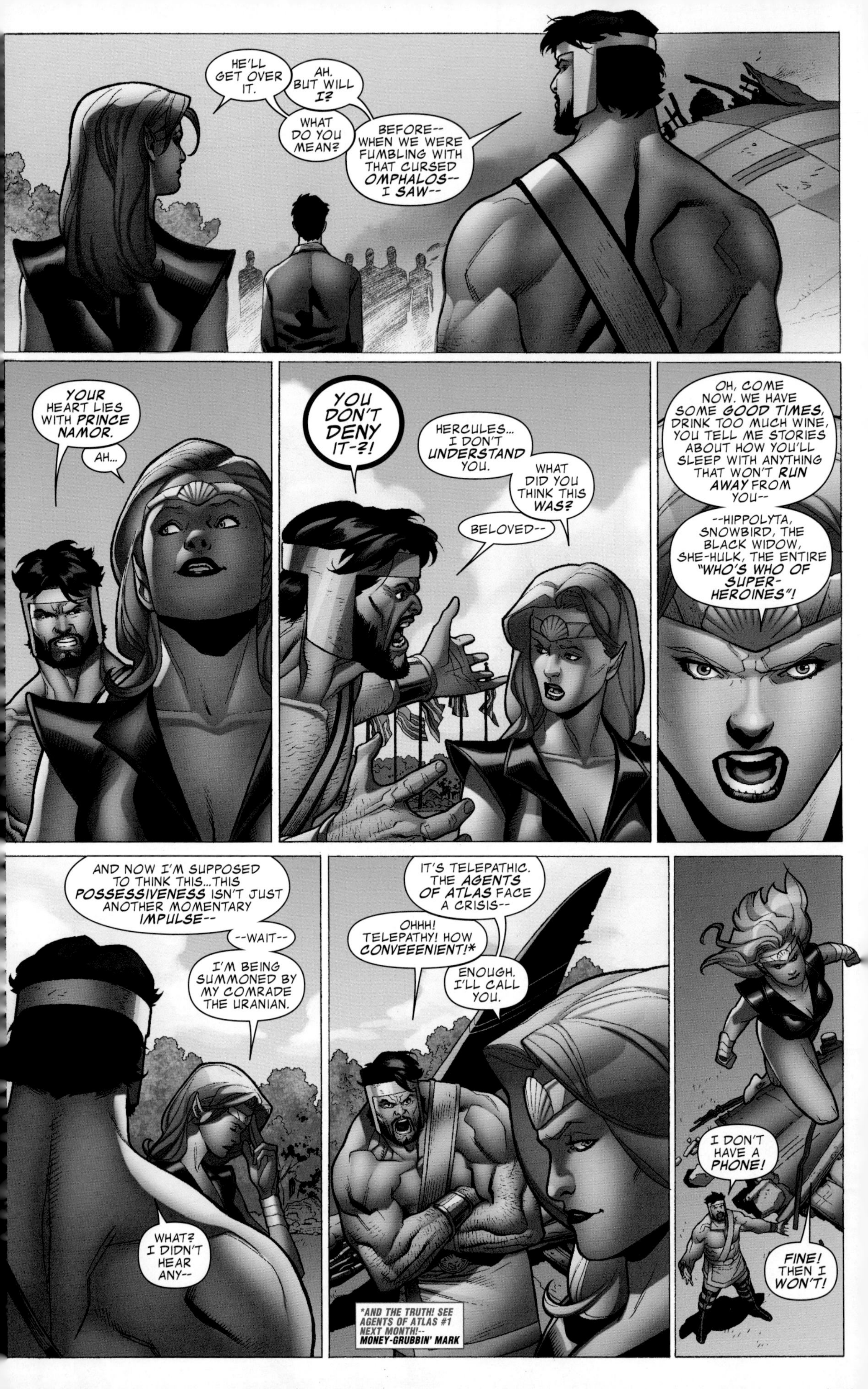
HE'LL GET OVER IT.
AH. BUT WILL I?
WHAT DO YOU MEAN?
BEFORE-- WHEN WE WERE FUMBLING WITH THAT CURSED OMPHALOS-- I SAW--
YOUR HEART LIES WITH PRINCE NAMOR.
AH...
YOU DON'T DENY IT-?!
HERCULES... I DON'T UNDERSTAND YOU.
WHAT DID YOU THINK THIS WAS?
BELOVED--
OH, COME NOW. WE HAVE SOME GOOD TIMES, DRINK TOO MUCH WINE, YOU TELL ME STORIES ABOUT HOW YOU'LL SLEEP WITH ANYTHING THAT WON'T RUN AWAY FROM YOU--
--HIPPOLYTA, SNOWBIRD, THE BLACK WIDOW, SHE-HULK, THE ENTIRE "WHO'S WHO OF SUPER-HEROINES"!
AND NOW I'M SUPPOSED TO THINK THIS...THIS POSSESSIVENESS ISN'T JUST ANOTHER MOMENTARY IMPULSE--
--WAIT--
I'M BEING SUMMONED BY MY COMRADE THE URANIAN.
WHAT? I DIDN'T HEAR ANY--
IT'S TELEPATHIC. THE AGENTS OF ATLAS FACE A CRISIS--
OHHH! TELEPATHY! HOW CONVEEENIENT!*
ENOUGH. I'LL CALL YOU.
*AND THE TRUTH! SEE AGENTS OF ATLAS #1 NEXT MONTH!-- MONEY-GRUBBIN' MARK
I DON'T HAVE A PHONE!
FINE! THEN I WON'T!

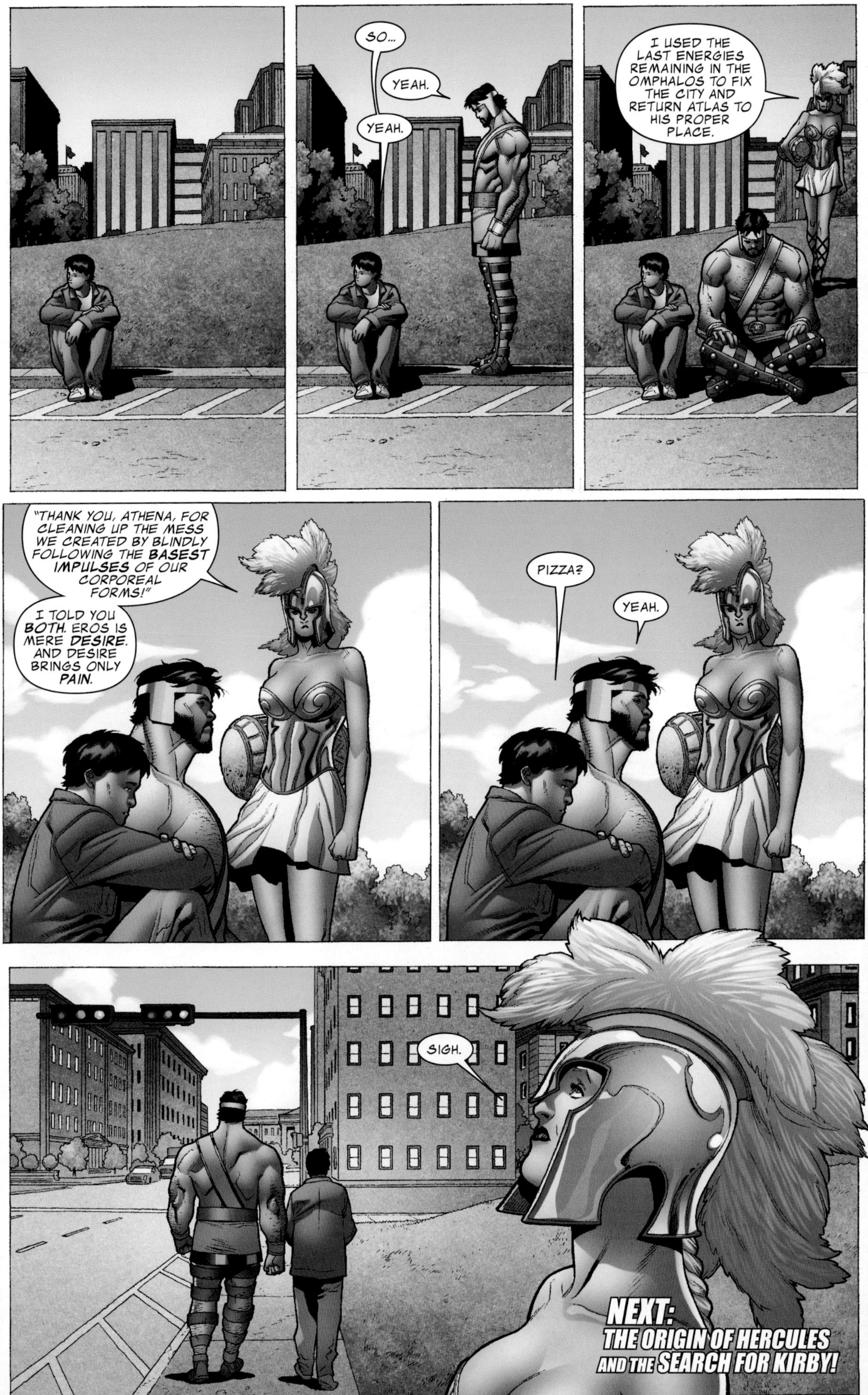
SO...
YEAH.
YEAH.
I USED THE LAST ENERGIES REMAINING IN THE OMPHALOS TO FIX THE CITY AND RETURN ATLAS TO HIS PROPER PLACE.
"THANK YOU, ATHENA, FOR CLEANING UP THE MESS WE CREATED BY BLINDLY FOLLOWING THE BASEST IMPULSES OF OUR CORPOREAL FORMS!"
I TOLD YOU BOTH. EROS IS MERE DESIRE. AND DESIRE BRINGS ONLY PAIN.
PIZZA?
YEAH.
SIGH.
NEXT: THE ORIGIN OF HERCULES AND THE SEARCH FOR KIRBY!

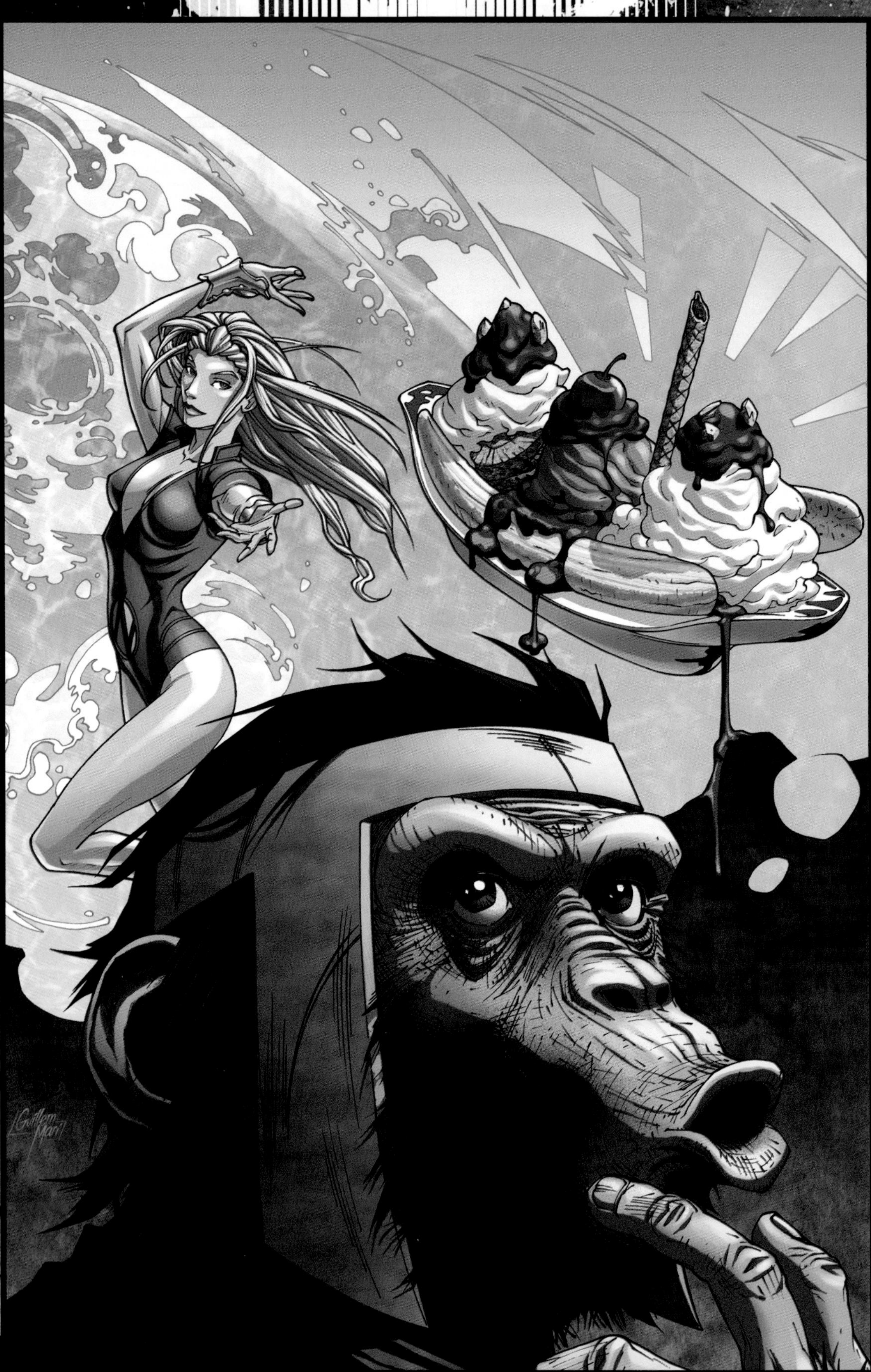
Guillem March

INCREDIBLE HERCULES #121 APES VARIANT
BY ROGER CRUZ

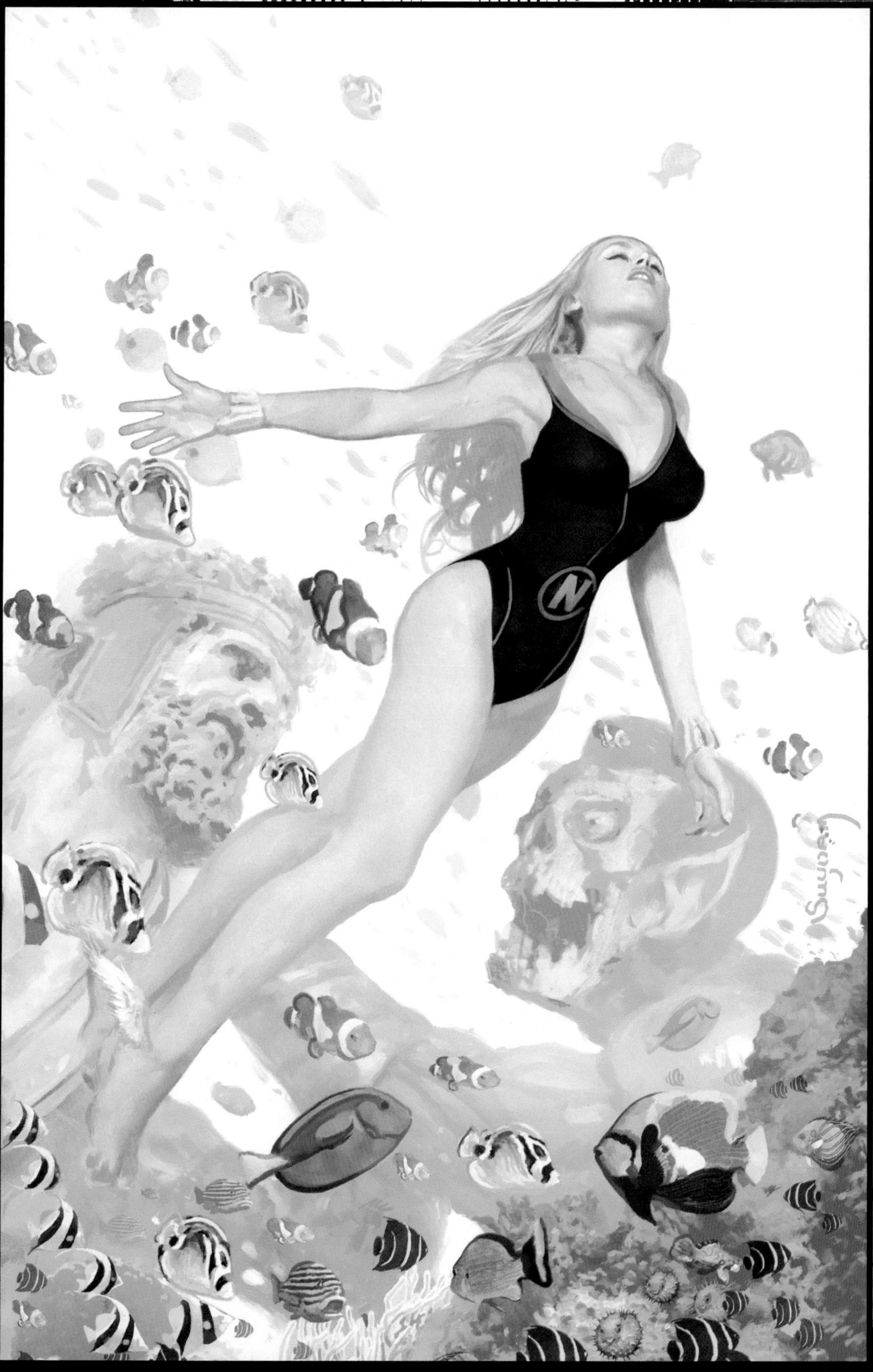

INCREDIBLE HERCULES #122 ZOMBIE VARIANT
BY ARTHUR SUYDAM

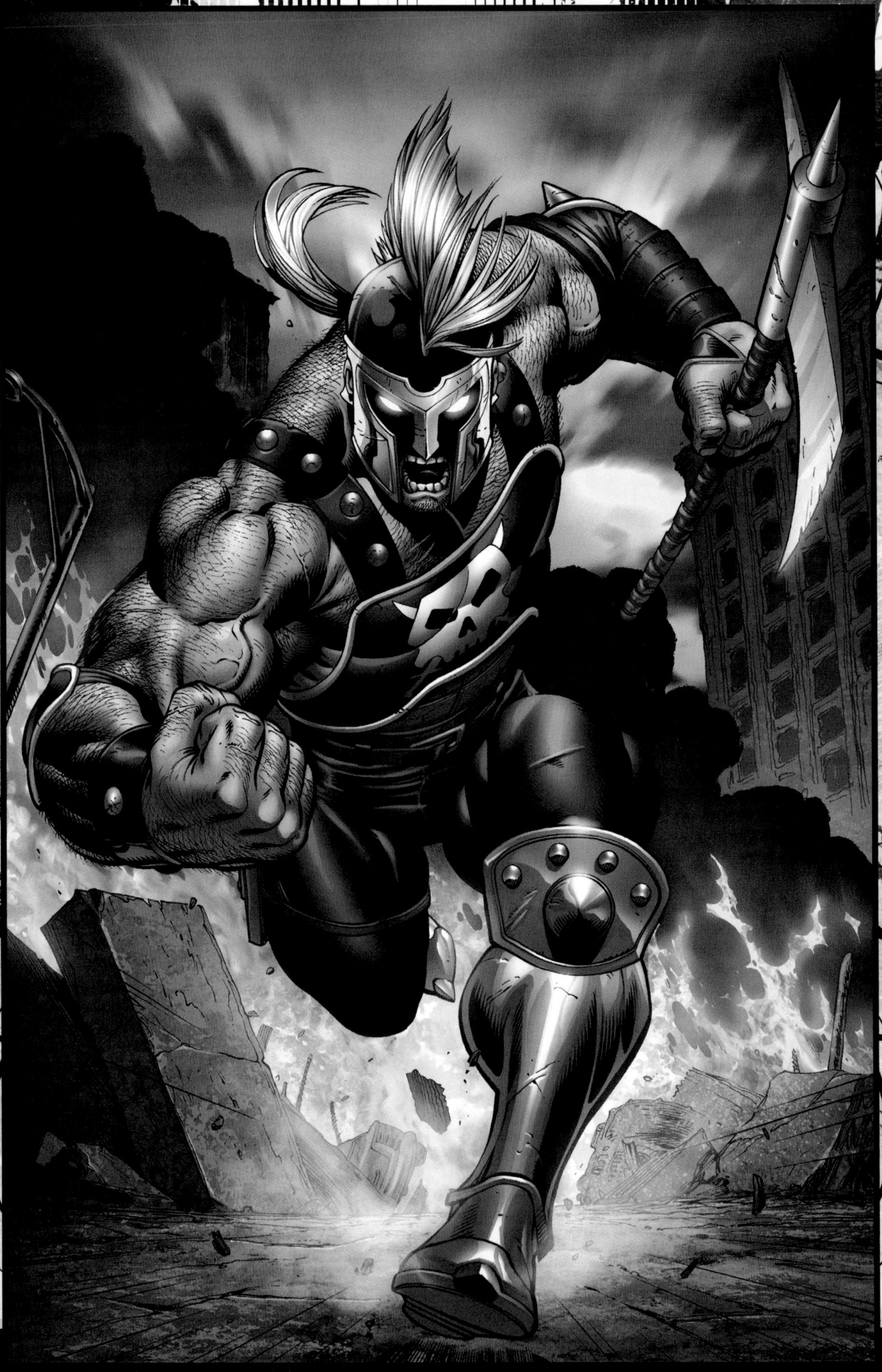

INCREDIBLE HERCULES #124 VARIANT
BY ED MCGUINNESS

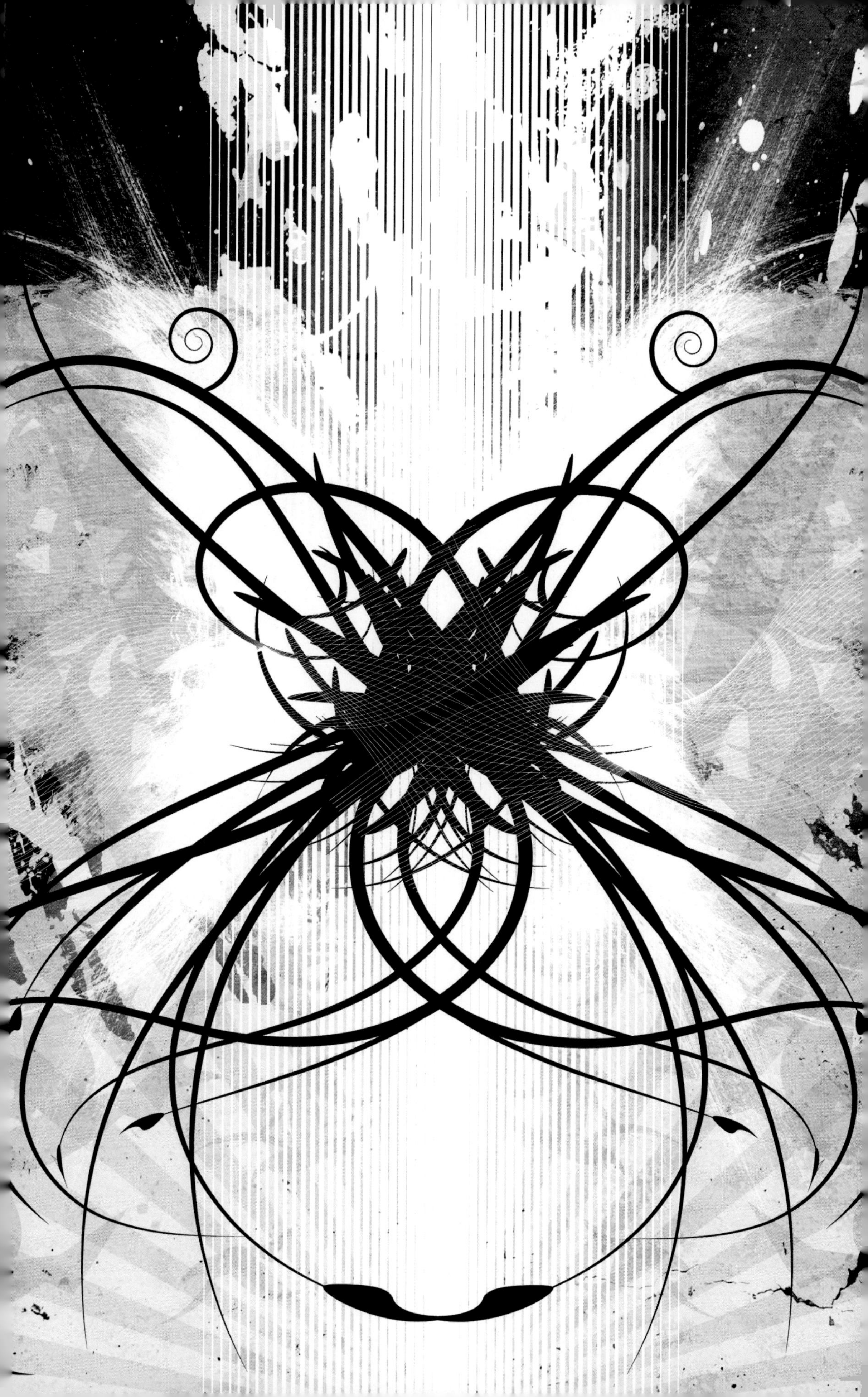

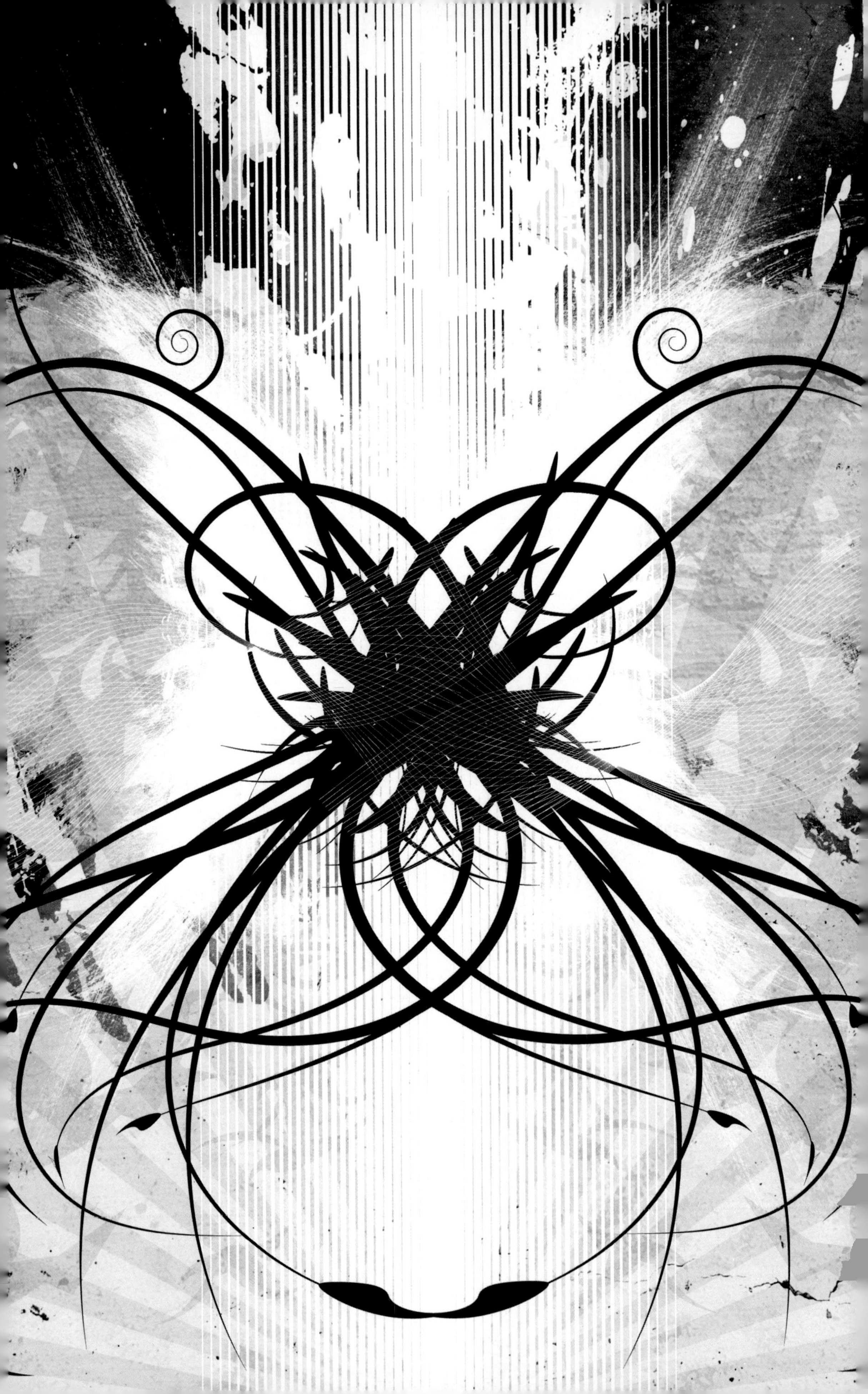